GW01018189

ICT Systems
Support Pathway

for the iPRO Certificate for IT Practitioners

Level 2

Jenny Lawson • Andrew Smith

ELECTRONICS DEPARTMENT
ST. LOYE'S COLLEGE
FAIRFIELD HOUSE
TOPSHAM ROAD
EXETER EX2 6EP

www.heinemann.co.uk
✓ Free online support
✓ Useful weblinks
✓ 24 hour online ordering

01865 888058

Heinemann Educational Publishers
Halley Court, Jordan Hill, Oxford OX2 8EJ
Part of Harcourt Education

Heinemann is a registered trademark of
Harcourt Education Limited

Text © Jenny Lawson, Andrew Smith 2006

First published 2006

09 08 07 06
10 9 8 7 6 5 4 3 2 1

British Library Cataloguing in Publication Data is available
from the British Library on request.

10-digit ISBN 0 435 45062 X

13-digit ISBN 978 0 435 450 62 8

Typset by Macmillan India Ltd
Original illustrations © Harcourt Education Limited, 2006
Cover design by Alamy Images
Printed by CPI Bath Press Ltd

Cover photo: Getty Images

Acknowledgements
The publishers and author Jenny Lawson are grateful to Sweet & Maxwell for permission to use their logo and for assistance in the creation of case studies in this book.

The publishers also wish to thank the following for their kind permission to reproduce the photos in this book:
Alamy 181, 189; Canon 101, 304; Corbis 97, 125, 151, 163; Epson 104, 147 (right); Getty Images/Photodisc 105,144, 300; Harcourt Ltd/Gareth Boden 95 (top and bottom), 103, 111, 112, 113, 118, 119, 122, 125, 133, 135, 138, 140, 144, 176, 179 (top and bottom), 180, 182, 185, 187, 189, 191, 193; Harcourt Ltd/Trevor Clifford 106, 139, 141, 147, 296; iStockPhoto.com 96, 109, 126, 142, 173, 182, 183, 296, 298, 299; Logitech 301; Micro Displays GMBH 132

Every effort has been made to contact copyright holders of material reproduced in this book. Any omissions will be rectified in subsequent printings if notice is given to the publishers.

The publishers also wish to thank the following for their kind permission to use their screenshots in this book:
Adobe 45, 263; AVG 256, 257, 265; Fresh Diagnose 309–10; Google 56; PC Magazine 30; VNC 255–8, 261; WinZip 14, 51.
Microsoft product screen shot(s) reprinted with permission from Microsoft Corporation.

Websites
Please note that the examples of websites suggested in this book were up to date at the time of writing. It is essential for tutors to preview each site before using it to ensure that the URL is still accurate and the content is appropriate. We suggest that tutors bookmark useful sites and consider enabling students to access them through the school or college intranet.

Contents

Introduction   v

Unit 1 Providing customer support   1

1.1 Providing technical information and support   3
1.2 Identifying potential improvements   33
1.3 Creating routine and complex automated procedures   64

Unit 2 Maintaining equipment and IT systems   87

2.1 Carry out routine preventative and remedial maintenance
    procedures for equipment components and sub-assemblies   88
2.2 Identify and locate common types of faults on communications systems
    to system or equipment level   115
2.3 Identify repair options and select the most appropriate option   153
2.4 Take actions to rectify faults, including referral, and confirm that faults
    have been rectified   161
2.5 Bring repaired equipment back into service   162
2.6 Check the effectiveness of preventative and remedial maintenance procedures 165

Unit 3 Installing hardware/equipment and systems   169

3.1 Install hardware and ancillary components such as PC system,
    network components, printers   170
3.2 Load and configure the system software   199
3.3 Carry out post-installation functional testing   217
3.4 Address routine problems   221
3.5 Remove different types of equipment and follow procedures for transporting
    and storing equipment   229
3.6 Conform with regulations affecting the disposal of ICT packaging   232

Unit 4 Installing and maintaining applications and systems testing   235

4.1 Install applications   236
4.2 Uninstalling software   274
4.3 Apply common types of test procedures and analyse results   293

Index   322

Introduction

The iPRO qualifications are available at levels 2 and 3, and students can choose either the generic route or complete the ICT Systems Support or Software Development specialist pathways. This book covers the units for level 2 ICT Systems Support Pathway.

This qualification, the iPRO Certificate for IT Practitioners – ICT Systems Support, has been designed by OCR to provide accreditation for the full breadth of essential knowledge, understanding and skills that would be needed by a competent employee whose job involves supporting ICT systems in the workplace.

The aims of the qualification are:

- to develop understanding of the ICT industry and its environment
- to develop practical skills in installation, maintenance and testing of ICT systems
- to develop practical skills in supporting customers
- to develop generic non-technical skills that will support personal effectiveness in the workplace
- to encourage progression by assisting in the development of skills and knowledge that learners will need to undertake further study.

The qualification contains 17 units, eight specifically related to the Systems Support Pathway. Certification is available at unit level. 240 guided learning hours are required to achieve the Certificate, 360 to achieve the Diploma.

No	Unit	Mandatory/ Optional	Hours
1	**Providing customer support**	**Mandatory**	**60**
2	**Maintaining equipment and IT systems**	**Optional**	**120**
3	**Installing hardware/equipment and systems**	**Optional**	**60**
4	**Installing and maintaining applications and systems testing**	**Optional**	**60**
5	Supporting system operation	Optional	60
6	Contributing to repair centre procedure and decommissioning ICT equipment	Optional	60
7	IT Essentials 1 (Cisco)	Optional	120
8	A+ Certificate in Computer Maintenance and Installation (CompTIA)	Optional	120

For a full award Certificate with the IT Practitioners – ICT Systems Support, a candidate must achieve three units from the ICT Systems Support Pathway including:

- Unit 1
- one of Units 2, 7, 8
- one of Units 3–6 or 9–11.

For a full generic Certificate, a candidate must achieve four units from either the Software Development or ICT Systems Support Pathways, including:

- Unit 1
- any three other Units.

For a full award Diploma with the IT Practitioners – ICT Systems Support Pathway, a candidate must achieve five units from the Systems Support Pathway, including:

- Unit 1
- one of Units 2, 7 or 8
- any three other Units.

For a full generic Diploma, a candidate must achieve six units from either the Software Development or ICT Systems Support Pathways, including:

- Unit 1
- Any five other Units.

Unit 1 (Providing customer support) is externally assessed through an externally set and marked on demand assignment. Other units (2, 3–6) are locally set practical activities that are externally assessed. Unit 7 is assessed through a Cisco set electronic online test. Unit 8 is assessed through a CompTIA set electronic online test.

The table on page v shows the hours you might expect to spend on each unit. The units shown in bold are covered in this book.

This book provides sufficient mateial to complete the ICT Systems Support Pathway Certificate. It can also be used together with our *Level 2 iPRO Certificate for IT Practitioners Software Development Pathway* or our *A+ Certificate in Computer Maintenance and Installation* books to complete the generic Certificate, the ICT Systems Support Pathway Diploma or the generic Diploma.

1 Providing Customer Support

This unit focuses on customer support: how best to provide it to the end-user. It introduces the support which may be required by the end-users of ICT, such as users of standalone and networked ICT systems, and these may be either external or internal to an organisation. As a practical unit, it will encourage you to develop and refine your practical problem-solving skills.

Learning outcomes

In completing this unit, you will achieve these learning outcomes:

- You will be able to identify and provide the basic types of technical information and support required by end-users, using appropriate communication methods to collect information.
- You will assist in reviews to identify potential improvements in the use of resources and automated procedures.
- You will create routine automated procedures and assist others to create more complex automated procedures.

How this unit will be assessed

This unit is externally assessed by OCR. The assessment will take the form of an externally set and marked-on-demand assignment, which must not be locally assessed. Your work for this unit will be dispatched by your college to the examiner-moderator in either a single unit or full assessment record folder (ARF), depending on whether you are claiming the full award.

A **single unit ARF** is a generic card folder which must be used by candidates for the submission of work for any one unit within a qualification. A **full ARF** is a card folder used by a centre to submit a candidate's work for more than one unit or where the candidate has entered for a full award.

Practical tasks

1 Obtain a copy of the specification for this unit.
 Compare the specification with the material provided in this unit.
 Notice which topics will be completely new to you. With others in your group, discuss how you could share your knowledge so that you make the best use of your combined experiences.
2 Find the sample assignment material on OCR's website.
 The assignment is split into several tasks. Check that you understand what is expected of you for each task.

 Discuss the sample material with others in your group. Identify any aspects that you think might prove tricky, and discuss how you might help each other to gain any extra skills that you will need.

This unit is split into three elements which are organised into three sections:

- Providing technical information and support
- Identifying potential improvements in the use of resources
- Creating routine and complex automated procedures

In this unit, a single case study is used to illustrate the variety of user needs within a single organisation: Sweet & Maxwell.

THOMSON
™
SWEET & MAXWELL

The Sweet & Maxwell logo

CASE STUDY – Sweet & Maxwell

Sweet & Maxwell is part of the Thomson Corporation. With over 200 years of history in legal publishing, Sweet & Maxwell produces publications across a wide range of subjects in a variety of formats to meet customers' needs – books, journals, periodicals, loose-leafs, CD-ROMs and online services.

Sweet & Maxwell employs over 600 people, housed on four floors in their London office.

1 Follow the links from www.heinemann.co.uk/hotlinks to the Sweet & Maxwell website. Read their mission statements and recent press releases.
2 Refer to the OCR sample case study material. Identify the text that tells you some background information about the company.

1.1 Providing technical information and support

In this first element of the unit, you need to be able to identify and provide basic types of technical information and support required by end-users, and you will need to use appropriate communication methods to collect information. Let's break this down!

- *What are the needs of end-users?*
  This depends on the type of user, but will probably include training (page 7) and locating sources of technical information (page 11) for the user.
- *How will you record the requirements of your end-user?*
  The various recording options available to you are explained on pages 15–22.
- *What information will you record?*
  The level of detail necessary is covered on pages 22–24.
- *Where will you find this information?*
  A variety of sources available to you are discussed on pages 25–32.

Determining end-user requirements

Technical support is geared to meet the needs of users. To do this, you need to communicate with the users, and find out as much as possible about what their computer system currently does, and what they would like it to do.

This will also involve your researching and identifying the differing types of end-user requirements:

- What are the end-user's training requirements?
- Where can users locate technical information?
- Where can users find FAQs and what information do they provide?
- What hints and tips are available to the user?

In this section, these four questions are asked – and answered.

Requirements of different types of end-user

You need to be able to determine end-user requirements, for differing types of end-user:

- End-users may be single users (such as a manager) or a group of users (such as the staff).
- End-users may have a variety of technical expertise: data operators, managers, and technical staff.

1 Study the OCR sample case study, and identify the users.

2 Categorise the users according to any factors that you consider to be important.

Data operators

Data operators spend most of their working day at a keyboard.

- They may be involved with data entry, working from batches of hard copy documents.
- They may work in a call centre, handling telephone enquiries and making onscreen changes to client account information.
- Their work may arrive by email and require onscreen action, and hence much keyboard use.

Data operators tend to be fast typists and need to be able to interface with the computer in the most efficient way using these keyboarding skills. Excessive use of the mouse can result in problems like RSI (repetitive strain injury).

For a data operator, **shortcuts** (page 69) as used by **power users** will speed up their work and reduce the risk of injury due to prolonged use of a mouse.

See also page 62, for details of how **menus** can be designed with the power user in mind.

Managers

Managers spend most of their working day managing people. Much time will be spent in meetings, and not so much at the keyboard. However, the manager will rely on the computer system to provide information, from which decisions can be made, and for email communication with colleagues.

> ## GLOSSARY
>
> A **power user** will prefer to use hotkeys on the keyboard rather than the mouse-driven menu selections.

CASE STUDY – Penny at Sweet & Maxwell

Penny is a manager at Sweet & Maxwell. On average, Penny receives 50 emails a day. These emails may be from her immediate line manager, managers on the same level as her, or members of her own team, or others within Sweet & Maxwell. Some emails are addressed to Penny; for some emails, she is just copied in for information.

Like other employees at Sweet & Maxwell, Penny may receive more emails in a single day than she can process; so she has to prioritise her time. It is important to read and respond to urgent emails, but also not to overlook others completely.

(Continued)

1 Penny aims to process emails from her line manager within 30 minutes of receiving the email. So, processing these emails is her highest priority.

How might Penny organise her inbox so that these emails come to her notice as soon as they arrive?

2 Some emails are marked urgent, either by a flag, or by the word 'URGENT' appearing in the subject line.

How could Penny customise her communications software so that these emails are separated from others that arrive?

3 Consider your own emails.

Discuss with others in your group how you might segregate emails so that you can process them more efficiently.

For managers and others who rely on IT to support communication, the software can be customised. Users need not feel overwhelmed by the volume of emails arriving in their inboxes. Instead, emails can be automatically directed into sub-inboxes, according to rules decided by the user. Helping users to make the best use of their email software is discussed in section 1.2 (page 50).

To help managers, and other users too, the user interface needs to be intuitive. To achieve this, **visualisation** techniques are used so that the user recognises activities instantly. For example, icons are used to represent tasks that are used every day (see Figure 1.1).

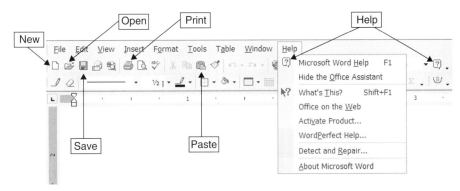

▲ FIGURE 1.1 *Icons*

Technicians

Technicians should have the most experience of using a computer.

● They will be involved in keeping the computer system working for the other users: the data operators and the managers.

● They will be responsible for keeping the data secure, and this would involve taking backups, and restoring data in the event of a problem.

The desktop support team at Sweet & Maxwell comprises six people, five of whom are permanently employed; one is a contractor. This team provides desk support for more than 600 employees who work at the Sweet & Maxwell offices in London, and the 600-plus computers provided for their use. One of the support team concentrates on supporting the 100-plus employees who also use laptops, allowing them to work from more than one office, or from home.

▲ FIGURE 1.2 *A member of an IT support team in action*

Another team of four specialists look after the communications within the organisation, i.e. the Intranet, the servers and email communications with outside organisations.

1 Find out what IT support is provided at your college.

   How big is the IT support team?

   How many computers do they look after?

   How many people might call on them for support?

2 What procedures are in place to keep your data secure?

   How would you restore a data file that had become corrupted?

Technicians need to use tools provided with the operating system, and may use special language commands to instruct the computer:

- DOS commands are used to write batch files (page 78).
- Visual Basic is used to code macros (page 74).

Training requirements

The training requirements of end-users depend on a number of factors:

- What type of work do they need to do on the computer?
- How do they need to interface with the computer?
- What software applications do they need to be able to use?
- What languages do they need to understand?

Also, staff training needs depend on the type of person – how they learn best, and their level of IT expertise – as well as how they need to use IT in their day-to-day work. There are a number of recognised theories about learning styles (Figure 1.3), but no right or wrong ways to learn.

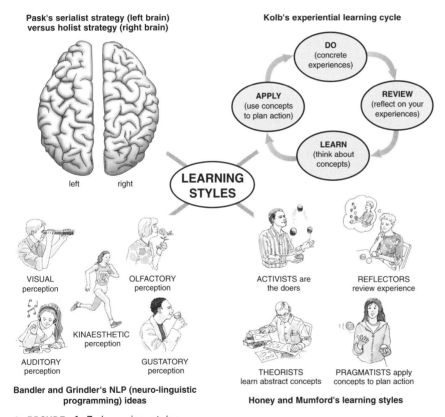

▲ FIGURE 1.3 *Learning styles*

Instead, it is important for the trainer to identify which learning style most suits the learner, and to make sure that groups of learners have a sufficient variety of material that the teaching matches all their preferred learning styles.

Go out and try!

1 Think about how best you learn. Then answer the questions in Table 1.1.

	Learning styles		
1	When learning new skills do you like a step-by-step approach?	YES	NO
2	Do you like rules and structure?	YES	NO
3	Do you prefer to rely on facts rather than your own experience?	YES	NO
4	Do you enjoy illustrations and explanations given as stories?	YES	NO
5	Do you like to see the 'big picture' before finding out the details?	YES	NO
6	Do you enjoy games and simulations as a way of learning?	YES	NO
7	Can you learn from reading a book?	YES	NO
8	Do you enjoy completing structured worksheets?	YES	NO
9	Do you learn from doing questions from past exam papers?	YES	NO
10	Can you learn more from charts and diagrams than from written text?	YES	NO
11	Can you learn from listening to lectures or discussions?	YES	NO
12	Can you learn from taking part in work experience?	YES	NO

TABLE 1.1 *Styles of learning*

2 Research the Internet for information about the learning styles theories described in Figure 1.3 to help you to identify your preferred learning style. Compare your findings with others in your group. Discuss how your teachers can meet the needs of all of your group within one lesson.

Some users may learn best away from their normal work environment. They may need to be sent on a **training course** to learn how to make the best use of their computer.

- The course might be for beginners: how to use the mouse and starting to use Windows-based software.
- The course might concentrate on a particular application, like word processing using Microsoft *Word*®.
- The course may be for those with good skills but concentrates on a particular feature, such as mail merge using Microsoft *Word*® and *Access*®.

For some users, **on-the-job training** may be more suitable.

- For them, reading some **training notes** and following the **step-by-step instructions** may be the best way forward.
- For others, a simple **demonstration** may be needed. This provides the opportunity for the user to ask questions. It also means that an explanation can be given to meet the specific needs of that user.

The demonstrator needs to be clear about what exactly the user wants to be shown, how much they already know and how much time is available for the demonstration. With this information, the demonstrator can plan what to cover, use the appropriate terminology and show just enough to meet the needs of the user.

It is important that you use the correct terminology, and that it is understood by your user.

It is also important to put the user at ease during a demonstration. Someone who is good at their job may seem quite confident, normally. However, they can feel vulnerable when faced with a computer application they cannot master. This makes it difficult for them to relax and take in what you are telling them. So, good relationships between the support technicians and end-users can help to make the support team more accessible. This is especially true for those users who need the most help (Figure 1.4).

▲ FIGURE 1.4 *Communication is important*

You may really enjoy giving demonstrations, but need to learn to limit the amount of information you try to pass to others. Your enthusiasm for the neat tricks available on a PC may well carry you away, but leave the end-user completely lost! So, decide what they need to know to solve their problem. Supply that information in a friendly and informative way, and then stop. Before you leave, offer to give them more help next time they need it.

One essential ingredient for successful training is that a budget is set aside. Plans also need to be drawn up to schedule training, so that those most in need of training receive it, ahead of others who are not so urgently in need of help.

Training needs to be fitted into the normal working day and this can have an adverse impact on the normal flow of work. So, care needs to be taken to provide training at times when staff are most able to make the best use of it.

- For some staff, on-site training provides a convenient option. It may be given at the worker's desk or in a nearby meeting room.
- For other staff, concentration levels may be low, and the temptation may be to return to their desks in the lunch break to deal with any backlog of messages rather than taking a much-needed break so that learning can be maximised after the break. For these staff, off-site training might provide them with sufficient distance from their everyday work.

CASE STUDY - Training

Sweet & Maxwell offer one-to-one training sessions for staff who need to be brought up to speed on any particular software application that is installed on their workstation. These sessions last for 30 to 45 minutes and take place at the employee's desk.

Sweet & Maxwell also provide group training if more than five staff need the same type of training. This can be held in-house in a meeting room; or it may be organised off-site at the premises of a specialist supplier.

1 What is the benefit for staff of the one-to-one sessions?
2 What are the equipment implications of organising group training sessions?
3 Consider other training options: vendor specific course, distance learning and CAL (computer assisted learning). Which of these might suit the Sweet & Maxwell staff? Which would suit you?
4 Refer to the OCR sample case study. Identify the training needs of the manager and staff. Make recommendations.

Location of technical information

Developments in IT happen daily and keeping up to date can be a problem. So, where can you locate the most up-to-date technical information?

Where you can find technical information depends of what form it takes.

- **Paper-based sources** of technical information may be supplied with a product. Some of these resources may also be found in a library, or bought at a bookshop. Books can also be bought online (Figure 1.5).

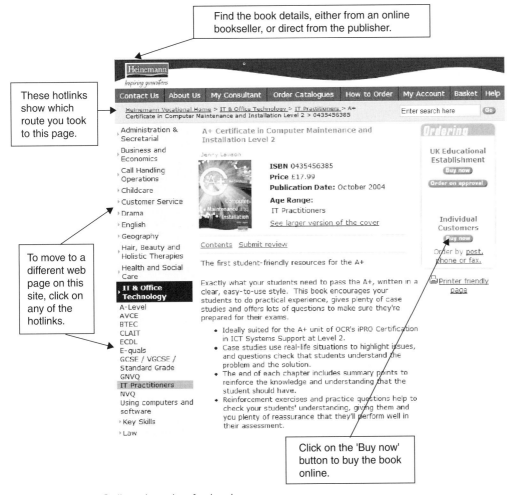

▲ FIGURE 1.5 *Online shopping for books*

- **CD-ROMs** are often used to supply software. This is easy to access and saves storage space. Some software houses provide the bulk of their technical information in this format. Updated CDs may be sent regularly. If you wanted to, you could print it out to produce a hard copy. However, the onscreen search options make the CD-ROM the most easily accessible form of information.
- **Online sources** include the Internet and online support within an application.

To access online **Internet sources**, you need the URL (uniform resource location), for example of a manufacturer's website.

Alternatively, you could search for such sites using a **web browser** such as Google (as used to search for books in Figure 1.5).

Within applications, the main menu usually includes a Help option – see Figure 1.1 on page 5. From there, notice other helpful features that may be offered, such as FAQs and hints and tips.

Some applications also provide an online link to further technical information. For example, the Windows *Office*® Assistant offers several topics that might answer your problem, but then offers a search of the web (Figure 1.6).

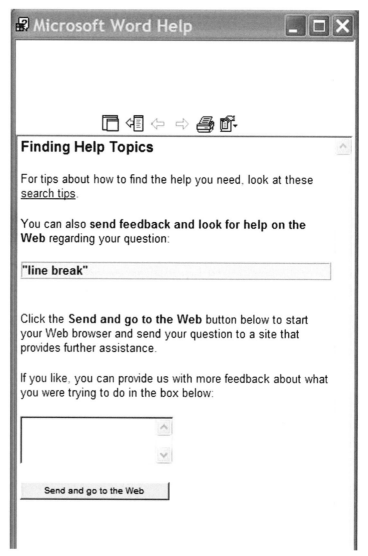

▲ FIGURE 1.6 *Help may be offered on the web*

Within Windows, support and help is also accessible from the Start menu. Clicking on Help and Support reveals a range of options (Figure 1.7).

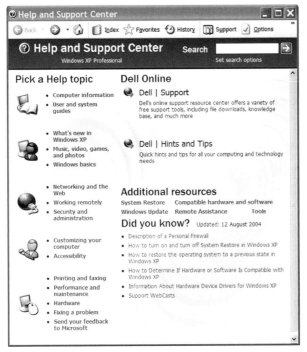

▲ FIGURE 1.7 *Help and Support Center on a Dell laptop*

A variety of sources of technical information are explained on pages 25–32.

Go out and try!

1 For each of three standard software applications, such as Word, Excel and PowerPoint, use the onscreen Help to find out how to do something you have not done before.

2 Working in small groups, choose individual topics to research, and make notes so that you can demonstrate this new skill to the others in your group.

3 Create a handout to explain how to do your task, including screen grabs of relevant toolbars. Use each other's handouts to check how useful the notes would be to a novice user.

Practical task

Refer to the OCR sample case study. List appropriate sources of technical information for the various end-users.

FAQs and hints and tips

Online help often supplies a list of FAQs (Figure 1.8). Providing answers to these FAQs, in this way, can solve the commonest of problems for users.

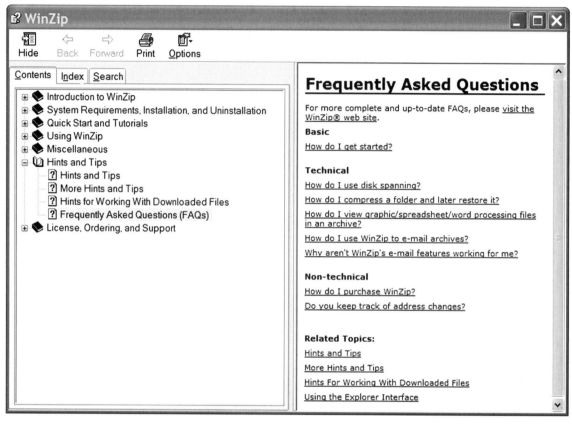

▲ FIGURE 1.8 *FAQs offered in WinZip*

Some software pages provide a useful hint or tip each time you open the application. For example, WinZip offers a tip, although you can prevent this happening (Figure 1.9).

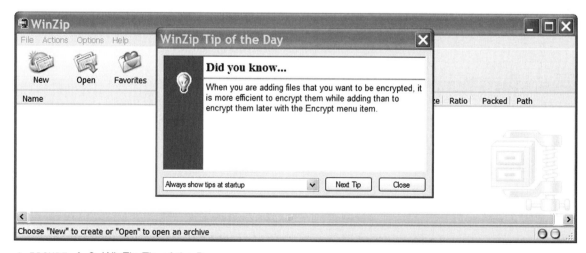

▲ FIGURE 1.9 *WinZip Tip of the Day*

Technical information can also be gleaned from the people around you. Often, colleagues at work, and friends outside work, can offer their experience in solving problems that you have just encountered. Knowing the right person to ask is the key to success. Sometimes, you may need to call on specialists: someone who is technically competent to a higher level. Such specialists may work within your organisation or may be contactable via a telephone help line.

Go out and try!

1 Explore WinZip to discover the answer to the FAQ: *How do I compress a folder and later restore it*? Follow the instructions given. How useful was the help given?

2 Working in a small group, agree on one software application or utility with which you are all familiar. Individually, write notes on 10 tips that you might give to a novice user. Compare your lists and show each other any tips that are news to any of you. Combine your lists into one list of the best 10 tips for novices.

3 Repeat task 2, but focusing on tips for more experienced users and for another software application.

Practical task

Refer to the OCR sample case study. Identify where the various end-users might locate FAQs, hints and tips.

Recording end-user requirements

You need to record end-user requirements that you have identified. You will develop and use the most appropriate method of recording requirements:

- You may decide to keep a manual log.
- You may use call logging software (page 16).
- You may use electronic submission of forms, e.g. to report an error (page 16).
- You may use verbal communication, both to find out the user's requirements and to give instructions as to how to fix the problem (page 20).
- You will also decide what information to record (page 22).

Manual logs

Manual logs, which are handwritten records of problems and how they have been solved, tend to be completed by the user. They may be on specially designed forms, or just in a notebook or diary.

The information written in a manual will be similar to that kept in electronic logs as discussed next; see, for example, Table 1.4 on page 24.

Call logging software

When the number of problems increases, a manual logging system to record these problems becomes unmanageable. The support team then need to use a software package to log the calls as they are made by users. The call logging system may also record what action is taken by technicians to solve the problem.

Electronic submission of forms

A **form** is a document that is used to collect data. Space is provided to enter the data, and information is provided so that the person filling it in knows what to write, and where to write it.

Before computers were invented, all forms were on paper. There was a stage when data entry was still on paper, but the data was keyed in and then processed electronically. To help the data entry clerks, the screen was designed to look like the paper version of the form. However, there is no option to scribble along the side of the form or on the reverse side of the page!

So, nowadays, much data entry is done straight to a screen, and forms on screen look similar to the old-fashioned paper-based forms. For example, interviewers who are conducting market research carry a laptop, and fill in the answers provided by the interviewee rather than noting the response on a questionnaire and then transferring this data to a computer at a later time.

There are advantages and disadvantages of using electronic forms (see Table 1.2).

Form-filling is also used a lot on the Internet (Figure 1.10).

- If you try to obtain a quote for car insurance, for example, you will be asked to complete a form giving all relevant details.
- Using a search engine, you effectively complete a form giving details of the key words that interest you.
- If you access a site to obtain information about train times or available flights, again you will be presented with an onscreen form to complete.

Advantages	Disadvantages
The data collection stage is cut short. This reduces the possibility of the data entry clerk misreading or miskeying data and introducing errors.	In planning the form, every possible input must be anticipated. For example, enough space must be allowed for the longest possible surname.
The data can be validated, as each item of data is keyed in. If the data is unacceptable, then the person filling in the form can be asked to re-enter the data, and guided to make sure it is correct.	To complete a form on screen, the person completing the form has to have access to a computer.
The data is immediately available for processing, which improves the currency of the data.	The storage of sensitive data electronically may increase the risk of fraudulent use of the data.
Entry requirements of data can depend on earlier data. So, if some data is not needed, the person filling in the form can jump to the next item that is needed.	

▲ TABLE 1.2 *Electronic forms: pros and cons*

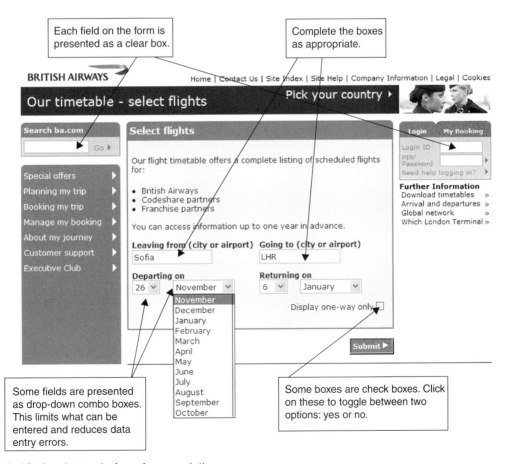

▲ FIGURE 1.10 *An electronic form for completion*

Forms may also be used for logging calls (page 23).

Data that is collected on a form tends to end up in a database.

- Each item of data is held in a **field**. These are usually shown as the columns of a table.
- Each group of data items that relate to a single form is called a **record**, and these are stored within one row of the table.
- In designing a form, some thought will be given as to what entries will be made, and perhaps how some data can be **coded**. This will relate directly to how the data will be stored electronically.

In *Access*®, as with any database, there is an option to generate forms to aid data entry. A Form wizard (Figure 1.11) is provided which can make the process even simpler. It is based on the tables that are set up to store the data, and so this becomes a two-way design process. You need to

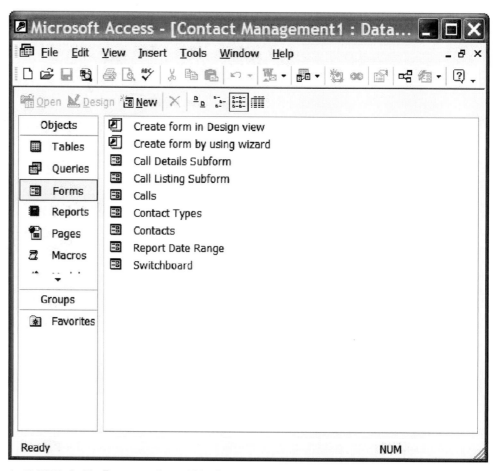

▲ FIGURE 1.11 *Form creation within Access*

think about how someone will enter the data, how it will be stored and then devise the best solution to suit both data entry and data processing requirements.

Rather than phone a help desk and have the operator log the call, some software vendors provide an option for the user to submit an error report electronically. For example, if a Microsoft product hangs up, the user may be given the option to report the problem to Microsoft (Figure 1.12). If the user accepts this option, special software sends relevant information to Microsoft automatically, before the software closes down.

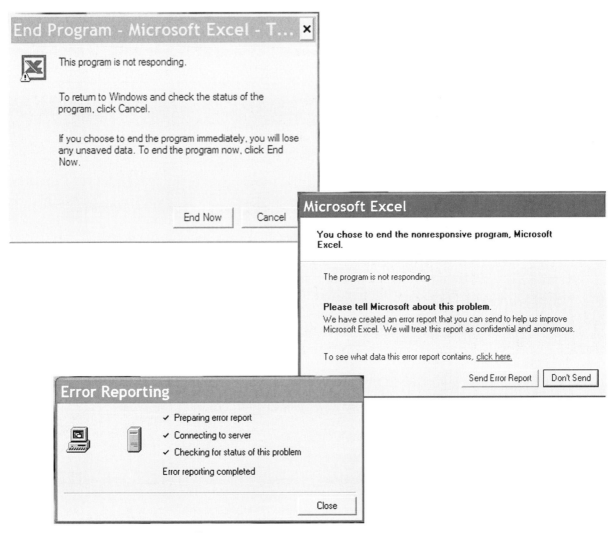

▲ FIGURE 1.12 *Microsoft offer to file an error report*

Staff at Sweet & Maxwell are encouraged to report errors to the IT support team by completing a log form (Figure 1.13).

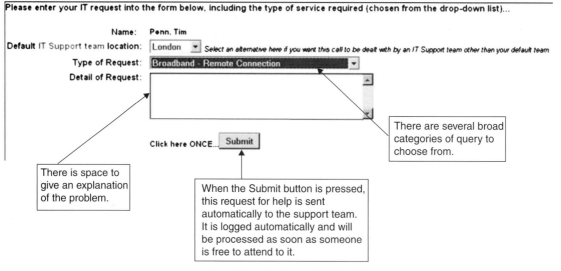

Please enter your IT request into the form below, including the type of service required (chosen from the drop-down list)...

Name: Penn, Tim

Default IT Support team location: London ▾ Select an alternative here if you want this call to be dealt with by an IT Support team other than your default team

Type of Request: Broadband - Remote Connection ▾

Detail of Request:

There are several broad categories of query to choose from.

There is space to give an explanation of the problem.

Click here ONCE... Submit

When the Submit button is pressed, this request for help is sent automatically to the support team. It is logged automatically and will be processed as soon as someone is free to attend to it.

▲ FIGURE 1.13 *Onscreen form*

In any one week, as many as 550 support requests are logged – nearly one per employee.

1 What are the benefits of recording requirements on a form, rather than telephoning the IT support team?

2 Look at the Sweet & Maxwell form. What information is required?

What flexibility is provided on the form?

3 In small groups, discuss any improvements you think could be made to this form design.

Verbal communication

People talk verbally (i.e. talk to each other) all the time:

- They greet each other.
- They exchange news.
- They express views.

Verbal communication is between two or more people.

- It may be one-to-many communication. The teacher talks to the class.
- It may be one-to-one communication. The shopper talks to the market stallholder.
- It may be many-to-many communication. The radio and TV broadcasters communicate with listeners or viewers 24 hours a day, 7 days a week, and some listeners or viewers may communicate back, with requests or comments on the content of a programme.

The communication between a technician and an end-user is not the same as everyday chatter. The technician needs to use the right terminology so that the user understands exactly what is being said. Also, the technician needs to show he or she is listening carefully to the user. This is called **active listening**.

- If the technician can maintain eye contact while the user is speaking, this shows that he or she is listening or at least gives that impression!
- Repeating what the user has just said, but rearranging it into a question and asking for confirmation, will convince the user that the technician has understood the problem. For example, 'So, the printer was turned on, but nothing printed?'
- **Body language** (Figure 1.14) by a listener can reinforce what the other person is saying. Nodding implies agreement. Head to one side, looking puzzled shows the listener is thinking about how to solve a problem.

▲ FIGURE 1.14 *Examples of body language*

Verbal sources of technical information are useful, but you may need to take notes if you are to remember the details of what has been said.

The technician may also need to **negotiate** with the end-user, for example to agree a convenient time to call and collect equipment that is faulty, or to deliver and install replacement equipment. Negotiation involves distinct skills: exchanging ideas; creating opportunities for others to speak; interpreting others' points of view; and listening and responding sensitively to others. The important thing to remember is that the aim of negotiation is to reach a decision by consensus. By the end of the negotiation, for it to have been successful, both sides must feel they have 'won': a win-win outcome. If either side feels they have given way or that the other is the 'winner', then the agreement may not last very long.

Check your understanding

1 List three types of communication, according to the number of people involved in giving and receiving information.

2 Explain what is meant by active listening.

3 Give two examples of body language that give the impression of active listening taking place.

4 Give two examples of body language which give the impression of a break down in communication between two people.

5 Explain how negotiation can happen between two parties.

Relevant information

Regardless of the method of recording, what kind of information might be relevant? What needs to be recorded?

You will need to collect and record relevant information. As with any management information system, it is important to retain all information that will help to keep track of progress in solving any particular fault that has been reported – and which may help to prevent similar problems happening in the future.

- **Dates/times** will be needed for each stage of the process: when the fault was first reported, when an engineer was assigned to the job, when the engineer visited the end-user, and so on until the final date/time when the problem was reported as fixed.
- You will need to identify which of the team of support staff were involved in each reported fault.
- The location of the user is essential! Otherwise, the engineer cannot visit the end-user.

- The nature of the problem is important. The engineer will need to know in advance, so that he/she can take necessary spare parts. It will also be important for analysis at later stages, to be able to categorise the faults.
- Hopefully, each fault will be solved, but whatever the outcome, this needs to be recorded.
- Sometimes, a fault cannot be solved. It may be necessary to refer the problem to a specialist. If so, details of who is now dealing with the client should be recorded, and the date it was passed on.

Table 1.3 lists some questions that the computerised call-logging system should be able to answer.

Question	What needs to be recorded
Who reported the fault?	Name and contact details
When was it reported?	The exact time as well as the date
Has someone been assigned to deal with this problem?	Who was assigned, and at what time it happened
Has the engineer decided on a course of action?	What action the engineer decided upon, and when this took place
What was the actual problem?	Categorise as end-user error/faulty hardware/faulty software, etc.
Has the problem been fixed?	How it was fixed
How much did it cost to repair?	Time spent by engineer, cost of replacement parts

▲ TABLE 1.3 *Questions that a call-logging system should answer*

Table 1.4 lists some possible entries in a call-logging system.

Additional information can be gathered by analysing the data:

- Are there any individuals who call in more regularly than others, and who could benefit from some extra training in the use of IT equipment and/or software?
- Are any items of hardware failing too often? Should an alternative hardware provider be found?
- Are the engineers coping with the flow of faults fast enough? Are additional support engineers needed?

Data field	Notes
Call ID	A unique reference number is used to identify this particular call and all subsequent action taken to resolve the fault.
Date and time of initial call	It is important to record the time as well as the date. Some faults will be reported and solved within the space of a couple of hours. Others may take longer.
Who initiated the call	The person who called may be noted by their name and department, or maybe an employee ID code, linked to other databases held by the company. This may allow HR to identify employees who regularly call for IT support, and may need to be given extra training.
Engineer allocated to supervise the solution	The call centre assistant will need to make an initial decision as to who best can help the caller. This will be based on information given by the caller, and the call assistant may have a questionnaire to complete which also helps to decide whether the fault is mostly hardware related, or mostly software related.
Date and time of passing information to engineer	A delay in passing details of the problem on to an engineer will mean the end-user might be waiting longer than he or she needs to. Keeping track of this data will ensure more efficient processing by the call centre assistant.
Report from engineer(s)	This may include information such as what equipment was repaired on site, what equipment was removed for repair, what loan equipment was given to the user as a temporary fix, or what replacement equipment was given to the user as a permanent fix. Each event needs a date and time of action so that progress can be monitored.
Error diagnosis	Details of exactly what went wrong and how it was fixed will help if other users call in with similar problems.
Costs (money)	Equipment that is supplied to replace faulty equipment can be charged to a particular reported fault.
Costs (time)	Time spent repairing equipment or just on-site with an end-user, trying to diagnose the problem, needs to be accounted for, and charged against each call.
Recommendations	Lessons learnt in solving a problem should be recorded and considered when making decisions about staffing levels within the support team, the equipment that is to be purchased in the future and training needs of support staff and end-users.

▲ TABLE **1.4** *Data stored in a call-logging system*

Practical tasks

1   Refer to the OCR sample case study. Identify the information that relates to hardware. Make notes.

2   Refer to the OCR sample case study. Identify the information that relates to software. Make notes.

Selecting technical information

You need to select technical information, and this can be from one or more sources:

- Some information will be online, accessible via your computer.
- Some information – such as manuals – will be written (page 27).
- You may use telephone help lines, or contact a manufacturer direct for advice (page 31).
- You may consult others in your team, and have verbal conversations with them, or with someone at the manufacturer's workplace (page 31).

Online sources of technical information

Nowadays, the majority of technical information is available online.

- **Websites** can be a very valuable source of technical information, given that a problem experienced in one workplace has probably happened elsewhere. There are many news groups where queries can be placed and speedy answers received. Some of these are provided by software houses. Most subject areas will be covered and there are groups for Microsoft application users, Windows users, Novell users (Figure 1.15), etc.

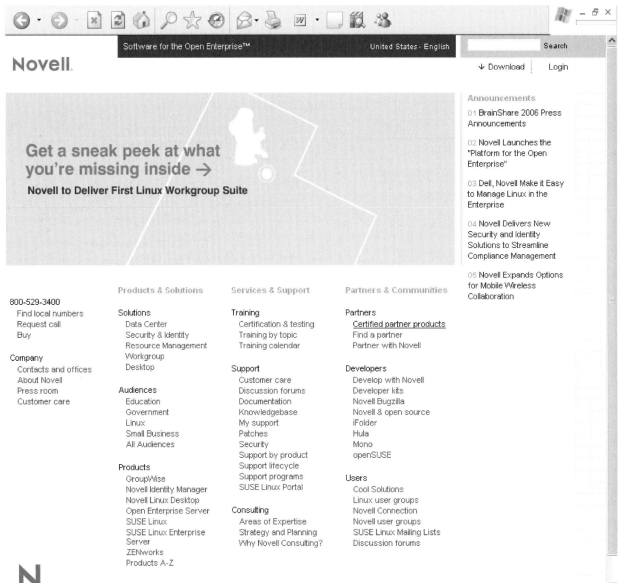

Software for the Open Enterprise™ | United States - English | Search

Novell.

↓ Download | Login

Announcements

01 BrainShare 2006 Press Announcements

02 Novell Launches the "Platform for the Open Enterprise"

03 Dell, Novell Make it Easy to Manage Linux in the Enterprise

04 Novell Delivers New Security and Identity Solutions to Streamline Compliance Management

05 Novell Expands Options for Mobile Wireless Collaboration

Get a sneak peek at what you're missing inside →

Novell to Deliver First Linux Workgroup Suite

800-529-3400
Find local numbers
Request call
Buy

Company
Contacts and offices
About Novell
Press room
Customer care

Products & Solutions

Solutions
  Data Center
  Security & Identity
  Resource Management
  Workgroup
  Desktop

Audiences
  Education
  Government
  Linux
  Small Business
  All Audiences

Products
  GroupWise
  Novell Identity Manager
  Novell Linux Desktop
  Open Enterprise Server
  SUSE Linux
  SUSE Linux Enterprise Server
  ZENworks
  Products A-Z

Services & Support

Training
  Certification & testing
  Training by topic
  Training calendar

Support
  Customer care
  Discussion forums
  Documentation
  Knowledgebase
  My support
  Patches
  Security
  Support by product
  Support lifecycle
  Support programs
  SUSE Linux Portal

Consulting
  Areas of Expertise
  Strategy and Planning
  Why Novell Consulting?

Partners & Communities

Partners
  Certified partner products
  Find a partner
  Partner with Novell

Developers
  Develop with Novell
  Developer kits
  Novell Bugzilla
  Novell & open source
  iFolder
  Hula
  Mono
  openSUSE

Users
  Cool Solutions
  Linux user groups
  Novell Connection
  Novell user groups
  SUSE Linux Mailing Lists
  Discussion forums

▲ **FIGURE 1.15** *Novell website home page*

- Help files are included within most software packages. The search facility has a base of information that can assist you in solving some of the most common problems. This can be a good tool to highlight to users and has the added benefit of being instantly available. The help file may include FAQs (page 14) and hints and tips.

Written sources of technical information

Some technical information will be supplied as hard copy (i.e. on paper).

- **Manufacturer's documentation** should be available for all hardware. This can be referred to if a component fails and you need to replace it. Manufacturer's documentation for software may be provided in various forms, according to who might read it.
- **Manuals** may be produced to provide detailed specifications for a piece of hardware or a software package. Because they contain so much detail, manuals may only suit the most technical reader.
- **Procedure guides and notes** tend to provide a more user-friendly source of help for non-technical users.

Manufacturers produce the hardware and software, so they should be the best source of technical information about their products and services.

- Most manufacturers put as much information as possible on their website. This cuts down the number of queries they might have to handle.
- Manufacturers will include FAQs (page 14) on their website. This again reduces the number of queries that might need to be handled. Many of the most common problems can be solved this way.
- Manufacturers supply **hardware compatibility lists (HCLs)** so you can check before buying extra components to upgrade your PC that they will work on your PC configuration (Figure 1.16).
- Manufacturers also make recommendations as to the minimum requirements needed before their software will run successfully on a particular PC.

Go out and try!

1 In a small group, look at a selection of hard copy manuals. Check how the information is presented. Decide on three advantages of having information available in this form.

2 The SpaceBall is an input device which offers a user the ability to manipulate 3D objects on the screen with simultaneous control of all six degrees of freedom.

Using a browser such as Google, search for information on Microsoft's HCLs to find out what versions of Microsoft Windows support this product, and any special requirements, e.g. hard disk space.

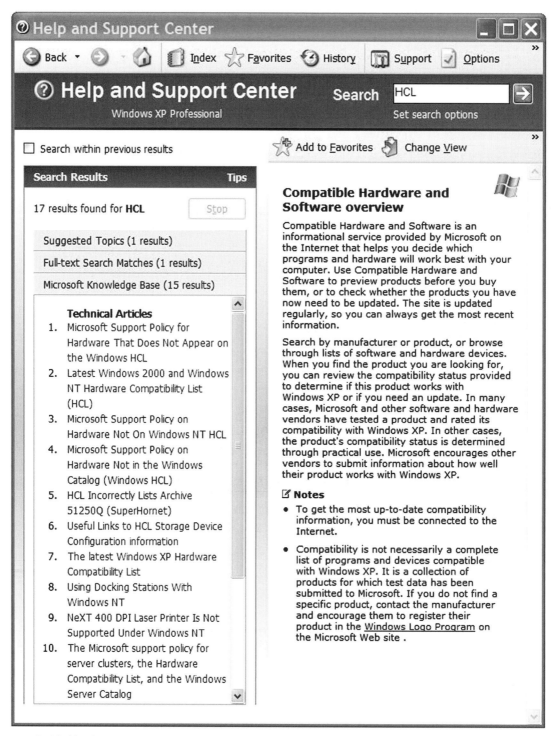

Help and Support Center

◉ Help and Support Center

Windows XP Professional

Search: HCL

Set search options

☐ Search within previous results

⭐ Add to Favorites   📋 Change View

Search Results   Tips

17 results found for **HCL**   Stop

Suggested Topics (1 results)

Full-text Search Matches (1 results)

Microsoft Knowledge Base (15 results)

Technical Articles
1. Microsoft Support Policy for Hardware That Does Not Appear on the Windows HCL
2. Latest Windows 2000 and Windows NT Hardware Compatibility List (HCL)
3. Microsoft Support Policy on Hardware Not On Windows NT HCL
4. Microsoft Support Policy on Hardware Not in the Windows Catalog (Windows HCL)
5. HCL Incorrectly Lists Archive 51250Q (SuperHornet)
6. Useful Links to HCL Storage Device Configuration information
7. The latest Windows XP Hardware Compatibility List
8. Using Docking Stations With Windows NT
9. NeXT 400 DPI Laser Printer Is Not Supported Under Windows NT
10. The Microsoft support policy for server clusters, the Hardware Compatibility List, and the Windows Server Catalog

Compatible Hardware and Software overview

Compatible Hardware and Software is an informational service provided by Microsoft on the Internet that helps you decide which programs and hardware will work best with your computer. Use Compatible Hardware and Software to preview products before you buy them, or to check whether the products you have now need to be updated. The site is updated regularly, so you can always get the most recent information.

Search by manufacturer or product, or browse through lists of software and hardware devices. When you find the product you are looking for, you can review the compatibility status provided to determine if this product works with Windows XP or if you need an update. In many cases, Microsoft and other software and hardware vendors have tested a product and rated its compatibility with Windows XP. In other cases, the product's compatibility status is determined through practical use. Microsoft encourages other vendors to submit information about how well their product works with Windows XP.

☑ **Notes**

• To get the most up-to-date compatibility information, you must be connected to the Internet.

• Compatibility is not necessarily a complete list of programs and devices compatible with Windows XP. It is a collection of products for which test data has been submitted to Microsoft. If you do not find a specific product, contact the manufacturer and encourage them to register their product in the Windows Logo Program on the Microsoft Web site .

▲ FIGURE 1.16 *Hardware compatibility lists*

In your local library, you should find a selection of **magazines**, **newsletters** and **articles**. These can be valuable sources of information on technological trends. 'How to' and 'How things work' articles contain lots of useful illustrations and diagrams.

The **trade press** for the IT industry, apart from advertising lots of products that you might be tempted to buy, also run articles which can help the technician to select an appropriate item of hardware, or the manager decide on what software to use in the office.

When you buy software, sometimes the vendor offers a free subscription to a newsletter which can be sent via email (Figure 1.17).

April 2004

HP Newsgram

» Recording live TV
» Block web ads
» Spring-cleaning projects

» Household helpers
» Timely tax tips
» iTunes for Windows

It takes just a moment to ensure you're getting the most useful content from HP.

» **Update your preferences**

Product support
» Update your product

Always prime time
» **Recording live TV**
Easily capture your favorite television programs using your HP Media Center PC. This quick demo shows you how.

Stop the pop
» **Block web ads**
Discover two different methods to stop online ads-known as "pop ups" - from cluttering your desktop.

Feature articles & offers
» Customize this section

Happy returns
» **Timely tax tips**
During the time of year when we're all "deep in the heart of taxes," these handy tips can help ease the burden.

Rock on
» **iTunes for Windows**
Visit HP Music to download the revolutionary Apple jukebox software that's sweeping the nation—free!

Protect your HP products

Let HP Total Care protect your HP and Compaq products with award-winning support—then relax. Discover your options.
» **Learn more**

Quick tip: PC protection
If you want more control of your kids' computer use, you can use passwords to keep them from using the PC unsupervised.
» **Find out more**

Creative projects

Like craft projects? Get more creative projects and photography ideas delivered straight to your e-mail every month.
» **Update your preferences**

Clean sweep
» **Spring-cleaning projects**
The flowers are in bloom, but your house is a blooming mess. Swing into spring with these printable checklists and labels.

Ship-shape
» **Household helpers**
Use these dishwasher magnets, labels, menu planners, and chore charts to organize your kitchen and more.

Tell us more

How do you get your photo prints?

○ Print pictures at home
○ Take the memory card to a photo lab
○ Upload photos to an Internet order site
○ Use traditional film processed at a photo lab
○ Don't print photos at all

Share with a friend
If you think this is helpful, someone else might too.
» **Pass it on!**

About your Newsgram
» Update your preferences
» Change your e-mail
» Privacy policy
» Unsubscribe

HP destinations
» Projects and tips
» Support
» Find a local retailer
» Buy online

▲ FIGURE **1.17** *HP newsletter for owners of HP products*

Some magazines are also available on the Internet (Figure 1.18).

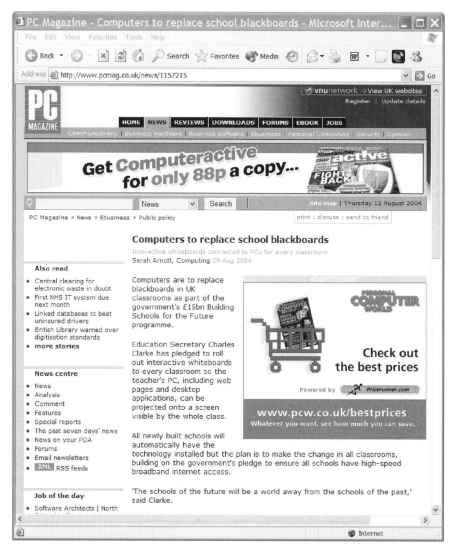

▲ FIGURE 1.18 *PC Magazine*

Logbooks, if kept by technicians and users alike, can be a source of useful information. A logbook should include details of what was done to fix particular problems. The technician or user can then refer to this if something happens that they have seen before. This can save time and provide an instant source of 'history' to a particular piece of hardware/software that has been installed.

Go out and try!

1 Follow the links from www.heinemann.co.uk/hotlinks to the website of *PC Magazine*. Find out what advice it has to offer for anyone thinking about buying a digital camera. Compare your research findings with others in your group.

2 Follow the links from www.heinemann.co.uk/hotlinks to locate other trade press online magazines. Share your findings with others in your group.

Telephone help lines

An organisation may arrange to have access to a help line, so that employees can call if they are experiencing difficulty. For these organisations, there will be many interactions between a help-desk analyst and the end-user over the telephone. The end-user will most likely be upset because the computer has failed, and stressed because pressure of deadlines may be worsened by the non-availability of the computer. So, the technician's ability to communicate verbally is critical.

- He or she must be able to solve problems, but being remote from the computer user means that their choice of language must be clear, confident and at the right pace.
- Patience and focusing are vital because some end-users may need more guidance than others. For example, a technician speaking to a first-time computer user will need to use more simplistic language when guiding them through a set of instructions.

CASE STUDY – Requesting support

Sweet & Maxwell staff can send a support request direct to the internal IT support team field by completing a form (Figure 1.13 on page 20). To meet the needs of the 600-plus employees at the London office, a team of 6 work a shift pattern: early shift (8 am until 4 pm); from 9 am until 5 pm – the normal office hours that most staff work; or late shift (10 am until 6 pm). Some projects need to be done outside office hours, so the team also share night working as the need arises.

1 What are the advantages of having an in-house team available at the end of a telephone?

2 What are the disadvantages of offering a telephone help line? What alternative methods of logging faults might be offered?

Verbal sources of technical information

Making a telephone call to the help desk is an example of a verbal source of technical information (page 20). Another is a **face-to-face discussion** with the support technician.

- This may be during a site visit – perhaps because the workstation is not working and the user is waiting for a technician to arrive and fix it.
- It may be during a scheduled training session.

During face-to-face discussions, the body language can give more information – or contradict what the person is saying. Figure 1.14 on page 21 gives examples of body language. However, it is also important to listen to what is being said – and what is not being said – and to use active listening techniques (page 21).

The technician may guide the conversation by asking questions. There are two main types.

- **Open questions** invite the other person to say whatever they like. Open questions are useful to start off a conversation, and may relax the user. Asking: 'So, when did things start to go wrong?' may trigger lots of useful information, apart from the date.
- **Closed questions** expect simple answers, such as YES/NO. Closed questions can be used to pin down facts: 'Are you using Windows 95 operating system?'

There is a third type of question that may prove useful when talking to a user.

- A **rhetorical question** need not be answered but will confirm that you have understood the problem: 'So, am I right in thinking that you need a replacement printer within the hour?' The user will, most probably, say 'Yes' and feel reassured.

Go out and try!

1 With the sound turned right down, watch a video of an interview (e.g. recorded from a news programme). Make notes on the body language of both the interviewer and the interviewee. Watch the interview again with the sound turned up. Does the body language shown reinforce what was being said, or does it contradict it?

2 Imagine you are visiting a client whose computer has broken down. Practise how you would introduce yourself and talk for a maximum of two minutes to reassure the client, starting with the words: 'Hello, my name is … and I am from …..' Work out how many words you might say in two minutes and then write that many words.

- With three or four others, practise your two-minute presentations.
- While the others are giving theirs, make notes about their delivery. What was good about it? What could have been improved?
- When everyone has 'introduced' themselves, compare notes and decide how you could each improve on what you said.

3 Repeat the role play of task 2, while being videoed. First though, look again at your text and rehearse it, taking into account your body language. Watching yourself in a mirror can help.

Then, within a small group, repeat the introduction activity. As well as listening to others while they speak, notice their body language. When it is your turn, watch the body language of those listening to you.

Videoing the activity means you can study each others' body language. Notice in particular any mannerisms, like fidgeting, that you will need to overcome if you are to appear more confident during a presentation.

1.2 Identifying potential improvements

For this element of the unit, you will assist others in reviews to identify potential improvements for users. You will focus on two aspects: the resources available to the user, and the automated procedures they might use. So, this section considers two questions, and provides answers to them:

- *What improvements can be made in hardware and software provision?*

You will find out how to gather information about existing hardware and software, how to report hardware provision and software provision (page 42) and then how to identify potential areas for improvement (page 44).

- *What improvements can be made in the use of automated procedures?*

You will find out how to produce and use information gathering resources for identifying usage of existing automated procedures (page 46), identify those that are frequently used and then identify areas where potential improvements could be made (page 47).

Hardware and software resources

This section aims to identify improvements that can be made in the provision of hardware and software. This is broken down into three stages:

- First, you need to consider how you might gather information about the current provision of hardware and software.
- Second, you will learn how to report on your findings, and what information to include.
- Finally, you will identify areas where potential improvements could be made.

To find out the usage of existing hardware and software, you need to identify how you will find appropriate information. You might ask one person for the answers to all your questions, but it is likely that this person will need to refer to other sources to find the information for you.

Sweet & Maxwell installed Adobe *Acrobat Professional*® on the workstations of all marketing personnel so that these staff could check the accuracy of marketing literature by reading on screen the PDF files supplied by the Design Studio. Any corrections are then marked up on screen, and the PDF files sent back to the Design Studio as an attachment to an email.

Penny needs to arrange training for all staff who may need help in using this new software, and to schedule that training to suit all staff involved. A trainer is available for one-to-one training every day for one week – and there are 40 people who may need training.

1 In small groups, discuss how the training might be provided.

2 How can Penny find out who needs training?

3 How can Penny match the availability of the trainer with meeting the needs of all those who do need training?

You then need to collate the information that you have collected. There are several methods of collating the required information:

- You may devise a questionnaire (see below).
- You may set up an audit trail (page 37).
- You may refer to the various logs available on a system, such as network access logs, application access logs, Internet/email access logs and support logs (page 40).

Questionnaires

A questionnaire is a form (see page 16) designed to ask questions to find out information. It limits the responses that a person can make, so does not offer the same amount of flexibility as a one-to-one interview. Sometimes, interviews may be based on a questionnaire, especially when the interviewer needs to be reminded of the questions to be asked, and the kinds of answers to expect.

Table 1.5 compares the two ways of collecting information.

The questionnaire needs to be carefully designed.

- A poorly designed questionnaire may confuse the person who is filling it in.
- Well-designed questionnaires are straightforward to complete and are easy to read.

	Questionnaires	Interviews
What to decide	Who should complete it? What questions should be asked? How should the responses be collated? What analysis is needed?	Who should be interviewed? Where will the interviews take place? Who will be the interviewer? What questions should be asked? How should the responses be recorded?
Advantages	Many people can be asked identical set of questions. It is a cheap method of finding out information from a large number of people. Because the person who completes the questionnaire may not need to give their name, more honest answers may be given.	A rapport can be built up between the interviewer and the interviewee. The questions can be adjusted according to the answers to previous questions. Additional questions can be asked to find out more information.
Disadvantages	Careful design is necessary. Questions must be simple and easy to answer. Questions must not be ambiguous. People may not bother to complete and return a questionnaire.	Interviews take time, and cost more. Poor interviewing can produce poor results, so it depends on the skill of the interviewer. If there are too many people to interview it becomes impossible within a sensible time span.

▲ TABLE 1.5 *Questionnaires versus interviewing*

The format of the questionnaire should include an introduction to explain why you are asking the questions, and to thank the person who is filling it in.

There are then two main types of question on a questionnaire:

- **Closed questions** offer a list of possible answers, such as YES/NO.
- **Open questions** let the person write whatever they like.

For each question, there must be enough space to write the answer. With open questions, this is more difficult to judge!

Before deciding on the questions, think carefully about how the answers are to be used.

- If a question does not help with the analysis, it is probably not worth including.
- If the data being collected will be confidential, you may not need to ask the person's name.
- If the answers are needed for a calculation, the question must make this clear so that a number is given as the response.

Having designed your questionnaire, ask yourself these questions:

- Are the questions in a sensible order?
- Is it quite clear what each question means?
- Is there is enough space to write each answer?

CASE STUDY – Questionnaires

Sweet & Maxwell create questionnaires to obtain feedback from delegates on courses, and analyse this data automatically to produce a report.

Figure 1.19 shows two questionnaires.

QUESTIONNAIRE

Training course title..

Date .... Name ....

Please provide feedback on the course attended.

1 How useful did you find the course?
  Circle your answer.
  very useful   quite useful   OK   not very useful   not useful

2 How would you rate the trainer?
  Circle your answer.
  excellent   good   average   poor   not to be used again

3 What did you particularly enjoy about the course?
  ....
  ....
  ....
  ....

4 Would you recommend it to others?   Yes [ ]   No [ ]

5 What did you not like about the course?
  ....
  ....
  ....
  ....

6 What changes would you like to be made?
  ....
  ....
  ....
  ....

7 Any other comments
  ....
  ....
  ....
  ....

Many thanks for your cooperation.
Joyce Smith, Training Coordinator

▲ FIGURE **1.19** *Sample questionnaires*

(Continued)

CASE STUDY – Questionnaires *(Continued)*

QUESTIONNAIRE

Training course title ....

Date .... Name ....

Please provide feedback on the course attended.

1 Pre-course communication/arrangement?

....

....

2 Venue, and other housekeeping arrangement?

....

....

3 Your trainer (would you recommend we re-use – or change?):

....

....

4 Training facilities?

....

....

5 Any suggestions?

....

....

Many thanks for your cooperation.
Joyce Smith, Training Coordinator

▲ FIGURE 1.19 *(Continued)*

1. Study the first questionnaire, and note the good design points.
2. Working in pairs, list things that you would change about the second questionnaire, so that the answers to the questions could be analysed more easily.
3. Compare your notes with other pairs, and between you, produce a well-designed questionnaire.
4. Trial it on each other. Analyse your results.

Trialling your questionnaire on a few people will help you to see whether your design works.

Audit trails

An audit trail is a record of everything that has happened: all events like users logging on and off, files being accessed and/or modified. An audit trail therefore provides an opportunity to track potential security problems, helps to ensure user accountability, and provides evidence in the event of a security breach. So, how do you set up an audit trail?

Within Windows XP, the audit trail feature is available as part of the Administrative Tools available from the Control Panel.

- You first decide your audit policy (Figure 1.20): the categories of events you want to audit. For example, you may want to note each time a user logs on and logs off a workstation within a network. When you first install Windows XP Professional, no categories are selected, and therefore no audit policy is in force. Computer Management lists the event categories that you can audit. For each, you must specify the objects to which you want to monitor access and amend their security descriptors accordingly. For example, if you want to audit any attempts by users to open a particular file, you can set a Success or Failure attribute directly on that file for that particular event.

From the Control Panel, select the Administrative Tools and then click on the Local Security Policy icon.

Choose Audit Policy...

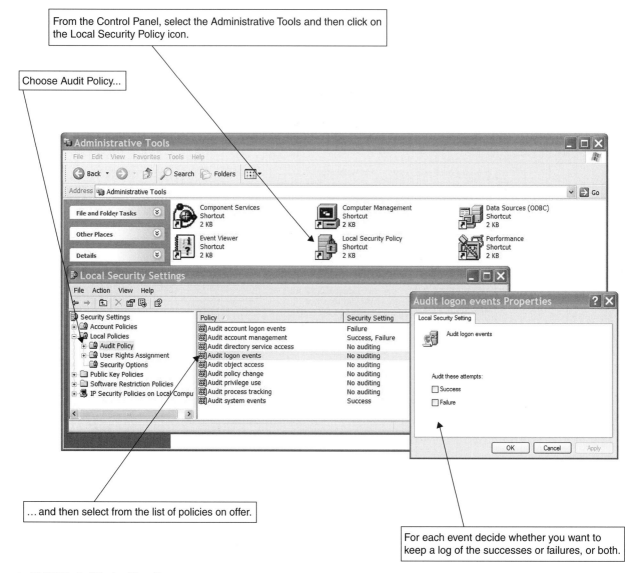

... and then select from the list of policies on offer.

For each event decide whether you want to keep a log of the successes or failures, or both.

▲ FIGURE 1.20 *Audit policy*

- The next step is to set the size and behaviour of the security log. How much history will you keep? The longer the history, the greater the size of the space needed for the log. Access this through the Event Viewer of the Administrative Tools (Figure 1.21).

From the Control Panel, select the Administrative Tools and then click on the Computer Management icon.

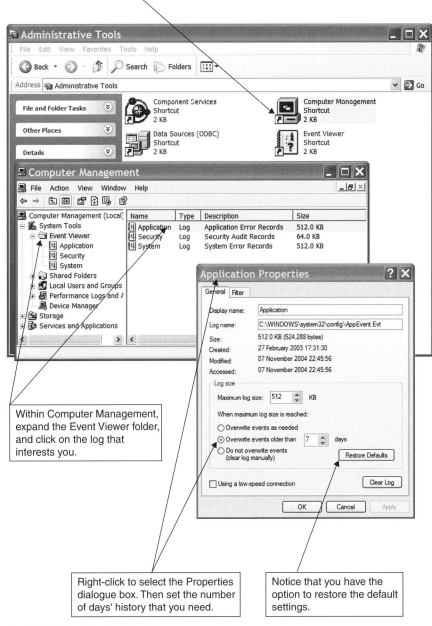

Within Computer Management, expand the Event Viewer folder, and click on the log that interests you.

Right-click to select the Properties dialogue box. Then set the number of days' history that you need.

Notice that you have the option to restore the default settings.

▲ FIGURE 1.21 *Audit history*

Log files

There are many different log files on a system.

- **Network access logs** are used to record which users log on and when they log on and off. Using the audit trail options, a network administrator can therefore monitor access to the network. A firewall log (Figure 1.22) will show attempts to access the system and give details of the IP address of the blocked attacker.

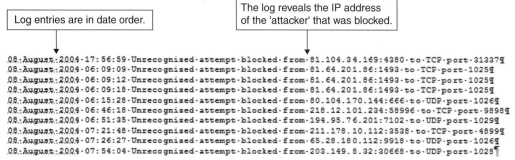

| Log entries are in date order. | | The log reveals the IP address of the 'attacker' that was blocked. |

```
08.August.2004-17:56:59-Unrecognized-attempt-blocked-from-81.104.34.169:4380-to-TCP-port-31337¶
08.August.2004-06:09:09-Unrecognized-attempt-blocked-from-81.64.201.86:1493-to-TCP-port-1025¶
08.August.2004-06:09:12-Unrecognized-attempt-blocked-from-81.64.201.86:1493-to-TCP-port-1025¶
08.August.2004-06:09:18-Unrecognized-attempt-blocked-from-81.64.201.86:1493-to-TCP-port-1025¶
08.August.2004-06:15:28-Unrecognized-attempt-blocked-from-80.104.170.144:666-to-UDP-port-1026¶
08.August.2004-06:46:18-Unrecognized-attempt-blocked-from-218.12.101.234:58996-to-TCP-port-9898¶
08.August.2004-06:51:35-Unrecognized-attempt-blocked-from-194.95.76.201:7102-to-UDP-port-1029¶
08.August.2004-07:21:48-Unrecognized-attempt-blocked-from-211.178.10.112:3538-to-TCP-port-4899¶
08.August.2004-07:26:27-Unrecognized-attempt-blocked-from-65.28.180.112:9918-to-UDP-port-1026¶
08.August.2004-07:54:04-Unrecognized-attempt-blocked-from-203.149.8.32:30668-to-UDP-port-1028¶
```

▲ FIGURE 1.22 *Access log example*

- An **application access log** can record which users are using which applications. This is important for keeping track of compliance with software licensing conditions.
- **Internet/email access logs** can keep track of all incoming and outgoing correspondence, and the sites visited by each user.
- Support logs are created by diagnostic tools like **Dr Watson**, a **program error debugger** (Figure 1.23). These tools detect information about system and program failures, and record the information in a **support log** file. In the event of a program error, Dr Watson starts automatically, but you can access it via Start/Run; the program to run is called drwtsn32. Although Dr Watson cannot stop errors happening, the information it saves (like memory dumps) can help the technical support team to work out what went wrong and – perhaps – prevent similar problems arising in the future.

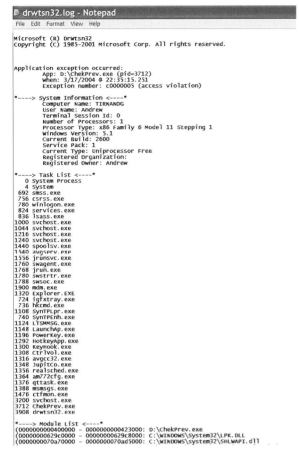

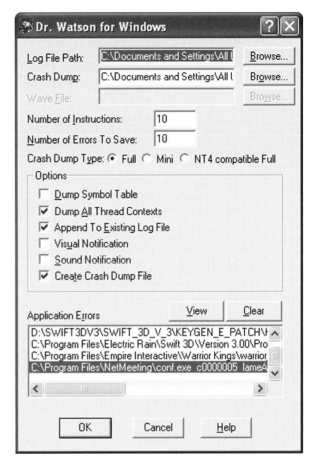

▲ FIGURE 1.23 *Dr Watson*

Go out and try!

1 Experiment with using Dr Watson. Find out what information is recorded in the log file.

2 Find out what shortcut keys are available for use within the Help viewer of Dr Watson.

Practical task

Refer to the OCR sample case study. Invent forms that you might have used to collect the information that has been provided.

Check your understanding

1 Why might a questionnaire be used to support the interviewer in a face-to-face interview?

2 Explain the difference between open and closed questions.

3 Define these terms: audit trail, network access log, support log.

Reporting existing hardware/software provision

You will produce reports detailing existing hardware provision and existing software provision.

When collecting information about an existing situation, it makes sense to have a form that you can complete. For a technician, who has to maintain a number of PCs, each of them slightly different, the form shown in Figure 1.24 could be completed to keep a record for each individual PC.

PC Identification Form

Name .... Number ....

CASE Manufacturer: .... No of bays: 3.5 inch................. 5.25 inch ....

MOTHERBOARD   From factor? AT/ATX

                 Manufacture: ....   Model: ....   Bus speed: .... MHz

CHIPSET   Manufacture: ....   Model: ....

BIOS   Manufacture: ....   Model: ....

CPU   Manufacture: ....   Model: ....   Speed: .... MHz

                 Socket/Slot?   No of CPU socket/slots:............................

PSU   AT/ATX/Other ....   Wattage: ....

EXPANSION SLOTS

                 No of ISA slots: ....   No of PCI slots..............................

                 No of EIDE connectors: ....   AGP slot?   YES/NO

                 No of floppy connectors: ....   No of serial ports:...........................

                 No of parallel ports: ....   No of USB prots: ....

                 Any other ports or slots: ....

MEMORY   No of memory slots: ....   Max memory supported: ....

                 Fastest memory supported: ....

MEMORY INSTALLED

                 30-pin SIMMs: ....   72-pin SIMMs: ....

                 168-pin DIMMs: ....   160-pin RIMMs: ....

                 184-pin RIMMs: ....   Other:...............................

HARD DRIVE   Manufacturer: ....   Model: ....   Size: ....

                 Cylinders: ....   Heads: ....   Interface type: IDE/SCSI

CD-ROM   Manufacturer: ....   Model: ....   Speed: .... MHz

                 Interface type: IDE/SCSI

FLOPPY DRIVE   Manufacturer: ....

MONITOR   Manufacturer: ....   Model: ....

VIDEO CARD   Manufacturer: ....   Model: ....

                 Memory: .... MB   ISA/PCI/On board

SOUND CARD   Manufacturer: ....   Model: ....

                 ISA/PCI/On board

MOUSE   Type: PS/2/Serial/USB

KEYBOARD   Connector: 5-pin DIN/6-pin mini DIN/USB

                 Matches connector on motherboard? YES/NO

▲ FIGURE 1.24 *A PC identification form*

When investigating the current hardware and software provision at a client's site, you need to ask questions so that you find out all relevant information:

- What hardware is installed? How many workstations are there? How are these workstations networked together?
- Are there any standalone computers?
- What peripherals are connected?
- What consumables are available to users? Where are these stored? How is the distribution of consumables controlled?

The hardware report should then include all relevant information.

The report detailing existing software provision should focus on the software that has been installed on the network and/or standalone computers:

- What operating system is installed for each workstation? What networking operating system is installed?
- What applications have been installed on each workstation? What applications are installed centrally, for all to share?
- Which particular components of applications have been installed? What components, if any, of those applications have not been installed?
- Which versions of each application have been installed?
- What licence arrangements have been made?
- What utilities – this includes virus checkers, email, Internet access – have been provided for the users? What protection is in place against viruses?
- What facilities are available for using email and Internet browsers?

Go out and try!

1 Working in pairs, investigate the current hardware and software provision available to your partner.

2 Record the details that you think are important and prepare a report.

3 Read each other's reports and comment on their accuracy and usefulness.

Practical task

Refer to the OCR sample case study. Write a report detailing existing hardware and software provision.

Recommending potential improvements in hardware/software resources

You need to produce recommendations for potential improvements. So, you will need to identify areas where potential improvements could be made.

- You may consider additional hardware or software that would improve productivity or security. This may include special forms of keyboard or additional input devices (like a microphone) to help people who have special requirements.
- You may identify that some individual employee lacks basic IT skills and needs further training. For these people, you would need to identify what they already know and can do, what they need to be able to do with confidence, and hence the gap in the skill profile that needs to be addressed through training.
- There may be large numbers of staff who are not making the most efficient use of their time, due to inexperience in making the best use of power user techniques.

CASE STUDY - Improving resources

To have ready access to toolbar buttons in Adobe *Acrobat Professional*®, additional toolbars – apart from those that appear by default when the software is first installed – need to be opened: the Commenting, Advanced Commenting, Advanced Editing. From these, an additional two toolbars become available: Drawing and Highlighting.

To open a toolbar, most staff followed the route View/Toolbars and then checked the one to be opened. This has to be repeated for each new toolbar.

1 A quicker route to the drop-down list of available toolbars is to right-click the mouse when the cursor is positioned in the toolbar area.

   Investigate other uses for the right-click option, either within Adobe *Acrobat Professional*®, or some other application. Compare your findings with others in your group.

2 Review the configuration of your PC. Suggest additional hardware and/or software that would improve your productivity. Provide cost details and reasons to justify your recommendations.

(Continued)

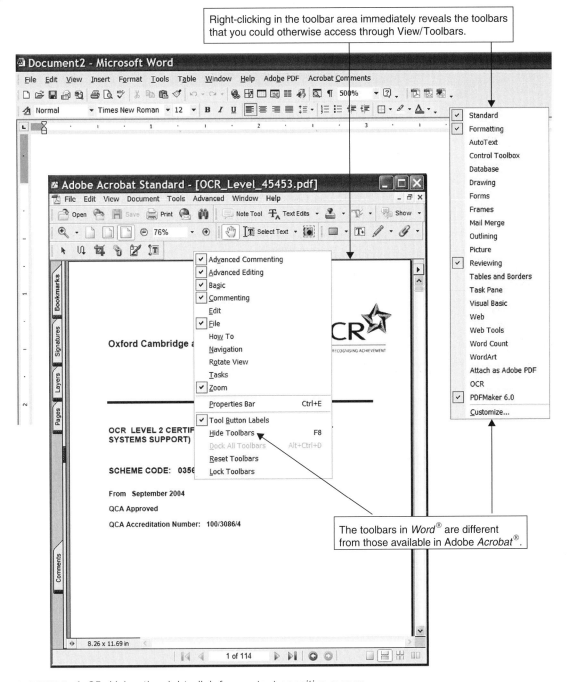

Right-clicking in the toolbar area immediately reveals the toolbars that you could otherwise access through View/Toolbars.

The toolbars in *Word*® are different from those available in Adobe *Acrobat*®.

▲ FIGURE 1.25 *Using the right click for context-sensitive menus*

3 Identify one contact who you think would benefit from some one-to-one tuition on making better use of his/her PC. Interview this person – and/or observe them working – to establish what they already know, and what you might help them with. Discuss your findings and suggestions with this person and negotiate some targets for the training you will provide. Prepare two 30-minute training sessions to meet the needs of this person.

One major area where improvements can be made is in the use of automated procedures, which is the topic of the third and final section of this unit (page 64). In preparation for that, consider now how you could produce and use information gathering resources to identify usage of any existing automated procedures.

Information gathering

Apart from devising a questionnaire (page 34), and talking face-to-face with the end-user (page 31), there are two other ways of collecting information about how the user works.

- You may use **observation**. This involves sitting beside the user, and watching him or her working. This **walkthrough** activity allows you to see exactly how they do their job. From this, you may see possibilities for improving their methods.
- It is possible to use **keystroke monitoring**, an automated way of finding out exactly how the end-user achieves particular effects on the computer. Do they use shortcut keys (see page 69) for speed? Or do they rely on context-sensitive menus by right-clicking with the mouse?

Which of these methods – or which combination of methods – is used ought to depend on the circumstances: the amount of time you have available, the number of people you might need to observe, and the budget for this stage of the work. Table 1.6 summarises the pros and cons of each method.

Method	Advantages	Disadvantages
Questionnaire	Offers a structured guide to the respondent Can aid an interviewer Can be used for many people at once	Takes time to prepare Needs to be trialled Respondents may decide not to complete and return a questionnaire
Interview	Questions can be adapted to suit the respondent Personalised approach can give more detailed responses	Time-consuming Time constraints may limit the sample size Takes up the time of the respondent
Observation/Walkthrough	Personalised approach can provide more detailed observations Need not interrupt the normal working time of the observed person	Time-consuming Time constraints may limit the sample size
Keystroke monitoring	Automated	Needs to be carefully planned
Audit trail	Automated	Monitoring systems need to be set up

▲ TABLE 1.6 *Fact-finding methods*

Identify frequently used automated procedures and improvements

Your objective in studying how the user works is to find aspects of their work that you feel could be improved by cleverer use of the PC, or higher skill levels on the part of the user. You should identify whether your user is making the best use of the most frequently used automated procedures. This section questions whether a user is making the best of a range of procedures:

- utilities (page 48)
- email (page 50)
- Intranet/Internet (page 55)
- backups (page 59)
- data transfer (page 60)
- macros (page 61) and
- menus (page 62).

You may be able to think of other topics to consider for your particular user.

Utilities

Is the user making full use of utilities? Some utilities are supplied by specialist vendors, like **anti-virus software** which checks for the presence of viruses, worms and trojans. Some utilities – like Disk Cleanup and Disk Defragmenter (page 68) – are supplied with Windows, and may be found in the System Tools (Figure 1.26).

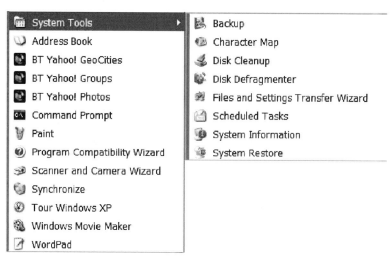

▲ FIGURE 1.26 *Utilities in System Tools*

If the task requires no intervention by the user, an **automatic scheduled task** could be set up. Using Scheduled Tasks (Figure 1.27) from the System Tools menu, you can schedule a task to run daily, weekly, monthly, or at certain times. This is discussed in greater detail in section 1.3 (page 64).

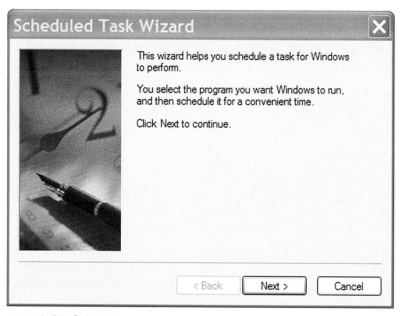

▲ FIGURE 1.27 *Scheduled tasks wizard*

Utilities that need to be running all the time, such as the anti-virus software, would best be started as soon as the computer is turned on, and so a user should include the opening of this software in the Startup menu (Figure 1.28).

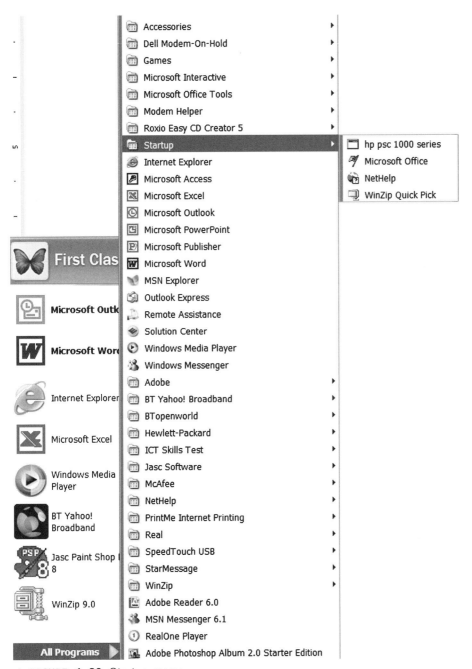

▲ FIGURE 1.28 *Startup menu*

You have already met WinZip (page 14). This utility is used to compress files, to make them smaller. Compressed files are then quicker to transfer, for example as email attachments. Before looking in more detail at emails, complete the following tasks.

Go out and try!

1 Explore the Accessories menu to see what other utilities are available.

2 Choose one particular utility, such as the calculator, and write brief notes on its usefulness.

3 Find out what programs are in the Startup menu. Consider adding other programs, or deleting some. Discuss this with others in your group.

Email

Some users may be familiar with how email software works, but are they using it most efficiently and effectively?

Email was once seen as a boon: a quick and easy way to communicate. Nowadays, the downside is beginning to be realised. Email traffic is on the increase and users have to cope with email overload.

- Some users complain that downloading emails takes forever. And then, when they open the inbox, it is full of spam.
- Some users regularly send email messages to a group of friends or colleagues, but individually select the recipients, which takes time.
- Some users return from holiday to find an inbox with hundreds of emails, and then have problems working out what to look at first.

Emails are used to communicate electronically and are best used for brief informal messages. Although it is possible to write a long letter using email, the formatting features are limited (or may not be acceptable to the recipient). Instead, if you want to communicate a more complex structure of information (such as a business letter, diagram or table), it would be better prepared using the most appropriate software, saved in a document and then sent as an attached file.

For example, you may need to prepare some material for a project planning meeting. You could produce a schedule using spreadsheet software, a map explaining how to reach the meeting using graphics software, and a covering letter including the agenda using word processing software. All three can be saved separately and then attached to one email – addressed to all those who are invited to attend the meeting.

However, emails with attachments will take longer to upload and download. Zipping a file before attaching it does reduce the size of the attached file, and so cuts down the upload/download time (Figure 1.29).

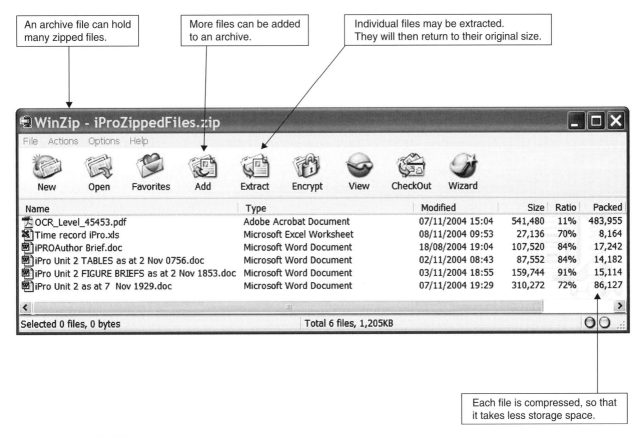

An archive file can hold many zipped files.

More files can be added to an archive.

Individual files may be extracted. They will then return to their original size.

Each file is compressed, so that it takes less storage space.

▲ FIGURE 1.29 *Zipped files*

There are two main ways of accessing emails:

- You can access them through the Internet. This is particularly useful when away from your normal place of work, and the only access available to you may be through an Internet café. However, it is relatively slow, and you have to be online while processing your emails.

- You can have your emails downloaded into software that is resident on your PC, such as Microsoft *Outlook®*. You only need to be online for as long as you are receiving or sending emails and can work offline otherwise. However, unless you filter your emails in some way, anything that is sent to you will be downloaded, and this can take a long time.

Most email software providers include features to cut down on spam. Yahoo, for instance, puts any mail that might be spam into a Bulk Mail folder (Figure 1.30).

▲ FIGURE 1.30 *Bulk inbox in Yahoo*

Even if your emails are normally downloaded into an Outlook inbox, this bulk mail is not downloaded until you look at it and confirm that it is not spam. So, you should aim to do this regularly – say once a week – just in case there is a bulk mailing that you do want to receive, for example from a club that you belong to, which needs to send legitimate bulk mailings to all members.

Bulk mailing does have its advantages for those sending emails. Setting up a **distribution group** (Figure 1.31) to include all the people to whom an email needs to be sent, can save time if this group often has to be sent an email.

If incoming emails are from different clients, or colleagues working for the same organisation, it is possible to have separate inboxes, one per client or maybe one per project. Then, by setting up **rules**, incoming mail can be automatically redirected (Figure 1.32) from the main inbox into specific inboxes, according to the sender (and/or the content).

As mail arrives, the user can therefore prioritise the emails – simply by opening the inboxes of the most important colleagues and clients before looking at those of contacts whose emails may not be so urgent.

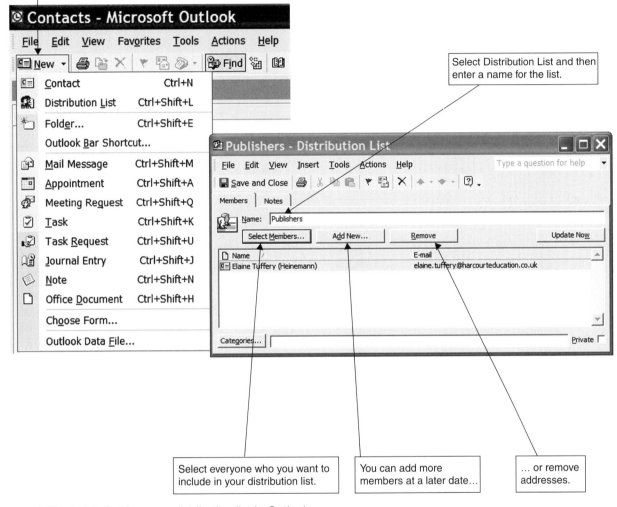

In Outlook, drop down the New menu to reveal the Distribution List.

Select Distribution List and then enter a name for the list.

Select everyone who you want to include in your distribution list.

You can add more members at a later date...

... or remove addresses.

▲ FIGURE 1.31 *Setting up a distribution list in Outlook*

Users could set up their own **spam filter**, by setting up a rule that sends unwanted mail straight to the Deleted files folder. For example, if you are being bombarded with emails offering you a degree, you could automatically transfer emails which have the word 'degree' into the Deleted Items folder. However, before you permanently delete the emails in the Deleted folders, you should glance through them to make sure there is nothing of interest to you.

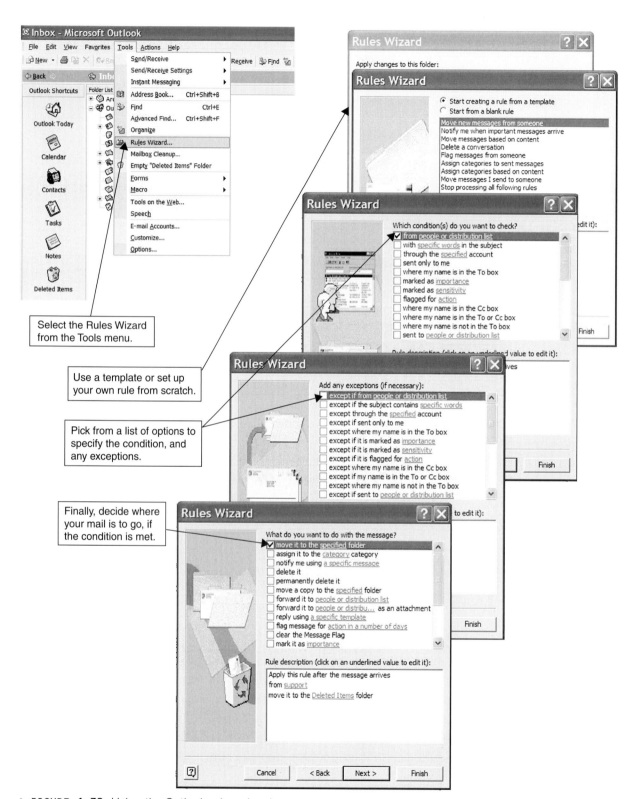

Select the Rules Wizard from the Tools menu.

Use a template or set up your own rule from scratch.

Pick from a list of options to specify the condition, and any exceptions.

Finally, decide where your mail is to go, if the condition is met.

▲ FIGURE 1.32 *Using the Outlook rules wizard*

CASE STUDY – Using protective software

There are 600 workstations in the Sweet & Maxwell network. Every employee has email software to allow them to communicate internally with colleagues, and also with external contacts such as freelance designers and typesetters.

Emails received from external contacts may have attached files, and, potentially, these could contain viruses which could affect the whole network.

1 Sweet & Maxwell has anti-virus software to prevent such damage. In a small group, discuss the importance of anti-virus software being used to screen incoming emails. What other ways might a virus be introduced to the system? How can this be avoided?

2 Sweet & Maxwell also has a firewall to block hackers. Explain the term 'hacker'. Find out what a firewall is, and what purpose it serves. Write brief notes.

Internet/Intranet

Does the user make the best use of the Internet/Intranet options?

The **Internet** is a global network of millions of computers. Each computer is linked so that anyone who is connected can access information and communicate with other users on the Internet.

The **World Wide Web** is a software application which allows users to access the many millions of web pages that have been set up on the Internet. The web pages are written in a special language called HTML (hypertext markup language) and users need a browser to access these websites and interpret the HTML.

An **Intranet** is similar to the Internet, except that its users are confined to a smaller group of people, usually those working for the same organisation. Your school or college may have an Intranet, so that everyone within the organisation can communicate with each other electronically, and share information. However, those outside the organisation cannot access or communicate on the Intranet – unless they gain access illegally, that is hack their way into the system.

To use the Internet (or an Intranet) efficiently and effectively, you need to be able to locate websites of interest as quickly as possible:

GLOSSARY

URL (uniform resource locator) is the address of a web page.

- For sites that you have visited before, you need to retain the URLs so that you can visit them again.
- To discover new and relevant sites, you need to search the Internet using a search engine, like Google.

A **search engine** supplies a **hit list** of sites (Figure 1.33) that might suit, based on a **search key** that you enter. It will also show **sponsored links** – sites that pay to be included whenever particular key phrases are used in a search.

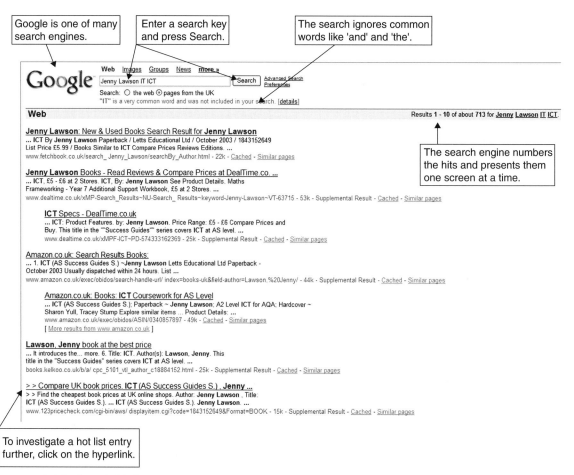

Google is one of many search engines.

Enter a search key and press Search.

The search ignores common words like 'and' and 'the'.

The search engine numbers the hits and presents them one screen at a time.

To investigate a hot list entry further, click on the hyperlink.

▲ FIGURE 1.33 *Google hit list*

- Entering a single word will probably result in too many hits for you to sensibly find what you want.

- To **narrow a search** down, you may use a plus sign (+) or the word AND to link words. Using quotation marks around a phrase will have the same effect, requiring that *all* the words in the phrase are found.

- When entering more than one word in the search key, put the most important word(s) first. If you have not linked the words (with + or AND or " " as above) then the sites found may have one or more of the key words, not necessarily all of them. This is a good way to **widen a search**. It has the same effect as using the word 'OR' between them and is particularly useful if you don't know exactly what term might have been used to describe something.

While surfing the net, you may use the **Back button** and/or **Forward button** to revisit web pages that you have visited during this particular session (Figure 1.34). A trace of all sites visited is retained in the History folder, so if you decide to refer back to sites you have visited recently, you can access these sites through the **History folder** (also shown in Figure 1.34).

Each page that is visited is also saved as a **temporary file**, so you do not need to download the page again; it is simply displayed from memory. This does, however, mean that memory is taken up storing these pages and, over time, the space taken up by these temporary files can adversely affect the performance of your PC. So, you need to regularly delete these files, using the **Disk Cleanup utility** (see page 68). It also means that the version of the page you view is the same as the one viewed the first time you downloaded it. If there is data on the page which is being constantly updated, then your displayed page could be out of date already. To avoid such problems, you may use the **Refresh button** (see Figure 1.34 again) to download the latest version of the web page.

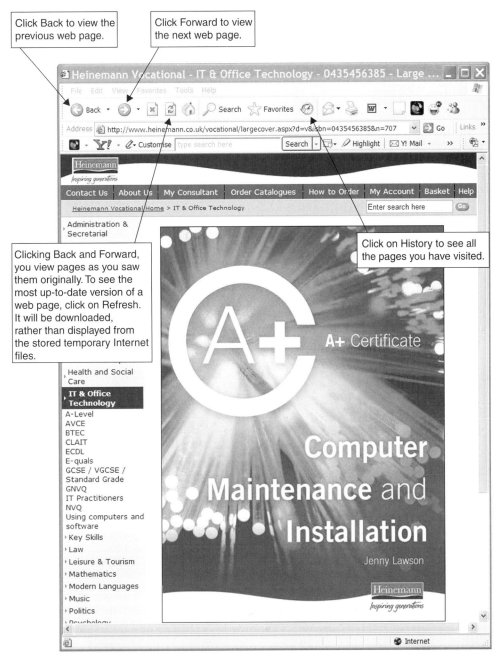

Click Back to view the previous web page.

Click Forward to view the next web page.

Clicking Back and Forward, you view pages as you saw them originally. To see the most up-to-date version of a web page, click on Refresh. It will be downloaded, rather than displayed from the stored temporary Internet files.

Click on History to see all the pages you have visited.

▲ FIGURE 1.34 *Surfing the net*

Within a hit list, the URLs of the sites are shown, either in a different colour or underlined. Double-clicking on these **hotlinks** (Figure 1.35) will open up the web page. URLs are sometimes provided on sites; having found one site that is useful, it may point you to another. In this way, you **surf** the Internet to find whatever information you need.

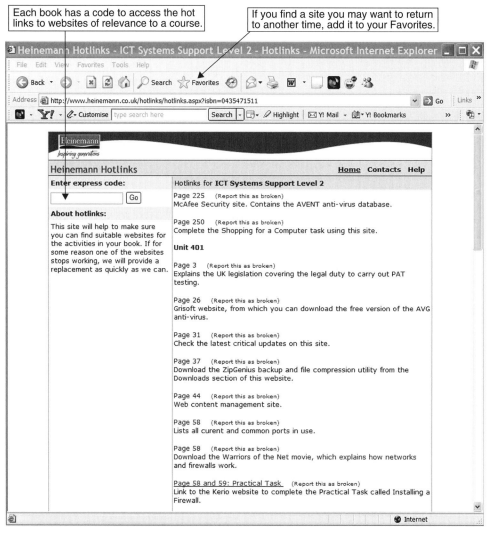

▲ FIGURE 1.35 *Hotlinks on the Heinemann site*

A **bookmark** is a reminder of a page that you might want to refer to again.

● In a paperback, the bookmark may be a physical strip, maybe of cloth. Or you may turn the corner of the page over, so that it is noticeable when you close the book.
● For the Internet, a bookmark is the URL of a particular page, remembered with other URLs of interest to you. To note the bookmark, click on Favorites star, and then use Add Favorite (Figure 1.35). Organising the Favorites into folders of related websites can also speed up the time taken to locate these sites at a later date.

You can control how far back in time the URLs are retained. You need to compromise between retaining useful information, and wasting space on details that you may never refer to again.

Go out and try!

1 Locate the Disk Cleanup and Disk Defragmenter utilities in the Accessories menu. Investigate what they do.

2 You have done some research on the Internet, e.g. looking up details of the SpaceBall (page 27) and digital cameras (page 30). Look in your History folder to locate the URLs of these sites – or any other sites you have visited recently – and add one as a favourite.

Backups

Does the user take backups regularly?

A backup is a copy of data taken at a particular time as a security measure.

- A **full backup** is a copy of all files.
- A **partial backup** – or **incremental backup** – is a copy only of those files that have changed since the previous backup.

The purpose of taking a backup is to be able to **restore** data should there be some disaster: a corrupted hard disk, a PC that just stops working, a fire, or theft.

The software needed to do a backup may be provided as a utility (page 48) or you might buy a specialist package from a specialist vendor.

It is important that the process of taking backups is done in a systematic way, and that the saved data is easily retrieved in the event of any disaster.

- To minimise the amount of time taken during the backup process, you should choose a medium that has fast read/write times, such as another hard drive, a CD or a zip drive.
- To reduce the amount of data that has to be saved, incremental backups could be taken each day, with the full backup being done, say, weekly.
- The timing of the backup can be chosen so that the disruption to other work is minimised, that is scheduled for when little other work is being done, maybe late at night or at the weekends.
- To automate the backup procedure an automated scheduled task should be set up; see page 48.

Data transfer

Does the user transfer data in the most efficient and effective way?

Data transfer is the movement of data from one computer system to another.

- In setting up a website, the individual pages are uploaded to the Internet site.
- Suppliers of software, for example, may provide information on a website, which interested customers may download.
- For organisations with many shops, individual shops may send end-of-day data to the head office on a daily basis, as soon as the shop has closed.
- For some organisations, data needs to be downloaded before the start of business. This may give the closing balances from the previous day, from which decisions today may be made.

The speed at which data can be transferred depends on how the link between the two computers is set up, and this is determined by the service you select from the telephone company that you employed. There are a number of choices available as to the hardware involved, the technology used and what type and amount of data that you expect to transfer. Faster, more exclusive links tend to be more expensive!

At Sweet & Maxwell, Internet access is currently maintained using a networked service that provides a 2 megabyte/sec connection. This is soon to be upgraded to one which offers 8 megabyte/sec.

At present, the London office is the hub for all other locations within the UK via leased lines, and there is also a VPN to allow connection with the Dublin office. This star network design will soon be replaced by a mesh network.

This will mean any two sites can communicate and there is not such a reliance on communications going through the London office. However, it is a more complex system.

1 Find out how your school/college maintains Internet connections.
   What speed of connect is provided?
   What type of network are you working on?

2 Discuss with others in your group how their home computers link to the Internet. You might devise a questionnaire to find out the most common methods being used.

3 Research the Internet for unusual uses of Internet access, e.g. during the Round the World sailing events, and share your findings with others in your group.

4 Investigate the best way of uploading web pages onto the Internet. Find out about FTP (file transfer protocol).

Macros

Does the user have macros set up to perform simple tasks?

A macro is a short piece of code, which performs a simple task. If you find you need to perform a particular task repeatedly within a single software application, it could be productive to create a macro.

Go out and try!

1 In a small group, share your previous experiences with using macros.

2 Share your experiences of creating macros.

3 For three Microsoft common applications, look at the Help information about creating macros, and make brief notes.

Creating the macro will take a little time, but you should save a lot of time thereafter. Details of how to do this are given on page 74.

Menus

Does the user make the best use of menus?

Windows applications offer a huge range of features and these are grouped for ease of access into menus. The main menu appears at the top of the screen, similar to the one shown in Figure 1.36; see also Figure 1.1 on page 5.

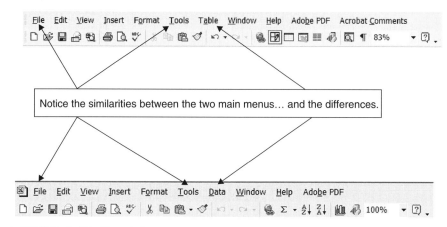

▲ FIGURE 1.36 *The static menu*

This is an example of a **static menu**, offering a set of choices that applies throughout the application. Depending on the application, it may appear along the top of the screen or down the left-hand side. On websites, the static menu bar is called a **navigation bar**.

A **pull-down menu** only appears when the user feels ready to make a decision. It drops down below the main menu bar if you select one of the items on the menu bar; it also disappears when you move the cursor away. Any options in the pull-down menu that are not currently available are 'greyed' out. To speed up menu selection, options which have been used recently appear at the top of the menu, and the double-down arrows at the bottom indicate that more options are available; clicking on the double arrow reveals the complete list of options.

Sub-menus offer yet more choices. To fit all options on a single drop-down menu may be impossible, so grouping into sub-menus makes sense (Figure 1.37). Notice the small triangle alongside some options; this means that a sub-menu is available for this option.

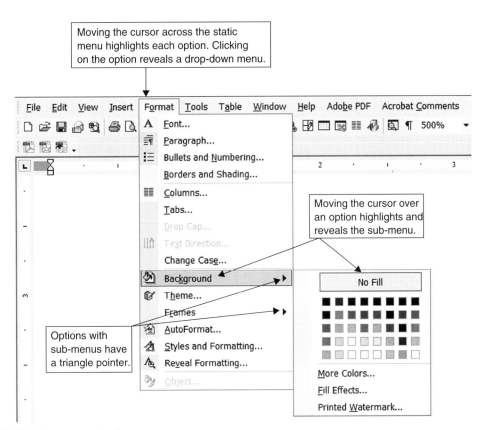

"Moving the cursor across the static menu highlights each option. Clicking on the option reveals a drop-down menu."

File Edit View Insert Format Tools Table Window Help Adobe PDF Acrobat Comments

500%

Font...
Paragraph...
Bullets and Numbering...
Borders and Shading...
Columns...
Tabs...
Drop Cap...
Text Direction...
Change Case...
Background
Theme...
Frames
AutoFormat...
Styles and Formatting...
Reveal Formatting...
Object...

"Moving the cursor over an option highlights and reveals the sub-menu."

No Fill

More Colors...
Fill Effects...
Printed Watermark...

"Options with sub-menus have a triangle pointer."

▲ FIGURE 1.37 *A menu and sub-menu*

A **pop-up menu** appears when you right-click the mouse. It is similar to a pull-down menu, but may appear anywhere on the screen, wherever there is room. It is **context sensitive** in that it offers options that relate to an object on the screen, wherever you have positioned your cursor. Figure 1.25 on page 45 shows two examples of pop-up menus.

Finding your way about an application means you need to be familiar with what features are available and where to find them. This comes with practice, but is helped by the fact that many applications adopt the same menu structure.

Go out and try!

1 For one particular Microsoft application, explore the menus to check that you are aware of all the features on offer. Notice the sub-menus and how these may lead on to additional menus and dialogue boxes.

2 For another Microsoft application, compare the menus. What features are common to both applications?

3 Experiment with right-clicking the mouse when in different positions on your desktop, to see what context-sensitive options are offered.

Finally, you need to produce a report of your recommendations for potential improvements.

1.3 Creating routine and complex automated procedures

In this element of the unit, you will create routine automated procedures and then assist others to create more complex automated procedures.

- You will need to identify existing system configurations which may be affected by the development of automated procedures.
- Then, on your own or with others, you will develop the automated routine and install it, ready for testing. Creating your procedure may involve you writing some code, or editing some existing code or following a wizard. Make sure you plan in advance what you are going to do, and make notes that you can refer to.
- Testing of your automated procedures will follow an agreed plan. You need to keep full records of testing. This will include the actual outcome of the test, the data that you used and any remedial action that needs to be taken.
- You will develop documentation for the automated routine which may assist in future end-user support. The better your documentation is, the more likely that it will prove helpful during any future end-user support. So, be sure to include as much detail as possible.

Automated procedures include routines written for everyday procedures. Keeping track of what has to be done, especially tasks like backups that may need to be done daily, weekly or monthly, is best done electronically.

Some software applications, such as Microsoft *Outlook*®, incorporate a calendar (Figure 1.38) or diary with scheduling options.

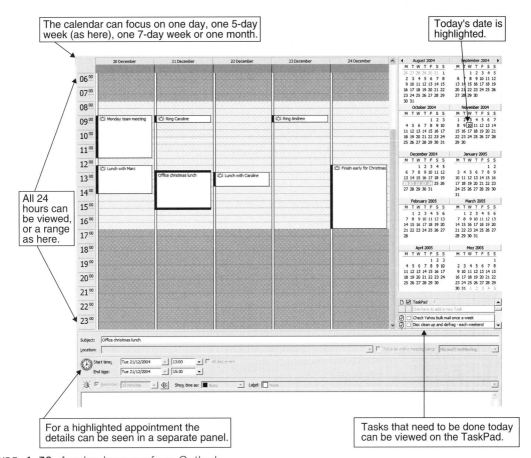

The calendar can focus on one day, one 5-day week (as here), one 7-day week or one month.

Today's date is highlighted.

All 24 hours can be viewed, or a range as here.

For a highlighted appointment the details can be seen in a separate panel.

Tasks that need to be done today can be viewed on the TaskPad.

▲ FIGURE 1.38 *A calendar page from Outlook*

You can use these tools to plan events and to co-ordinate meetings with others within the same organisation. However, these tools simply remind you about what has to be done, rather than doing it for you. A user could also be encouraged to include a reminder in a task list, say within Microsoft *Outlook*® (Figure 1.39).

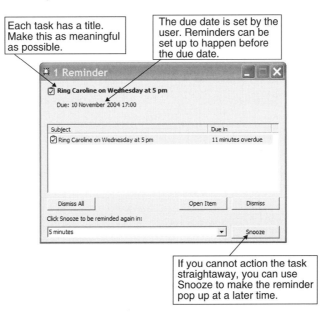

Each task has a title. Make this as meaningful as possible.

The due date is set by the user. Reminders can be set up to happen before the due date.

If you cannot action the task straightaway, you can use Snooze to make the reminder pop up at a later time.

▲ FIGURE 1.39 *A reminder from Outlook*

Automated scheduling is a more powerful tool, and most useful for essential tasks like taking backups.

The Windows operating system provides a **task scheduler** (Figure 1.40), which allows you to schedule tasks to run at a time that is most convenient for you. The task scheduler software starts each time you start Windows, and runs in the background.

You can set up tasks to run at a time that is convenient for you.

A wizard will help you to add a new scheduled task.

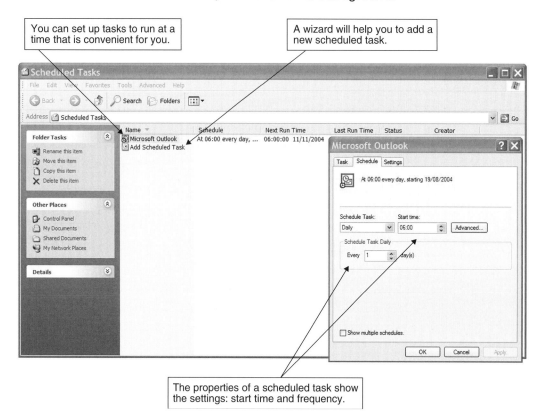

The properties of a scheduled task show the settings: start time and frequency.

▲ FIGURE 1.40 *Task scheduler*

- You can schedule a task to run daily, weekly, monthly, or at certain times (such as system startup).
- You can change the schedule for a task.
- You can stop a scheduled task.
- You can customise how a task runs at a scheduled time.

Go out and try!

1 Explore Task Scheduler to see what tasks have already been set up on your computer.

2 There are other products which provide scheduling options. Follow the links from www.heinemann.co.uk/hotlinks to find examples of how one software product expects to meet the needs of its clients.

3 Start thinking about what procedures you might want to automate. Discuss this with others in your group.

Routine automated procedures

On your own, you will create and test routine automated procedures. Here are some examples.

- Backing up should be part of your routine procedures. You may automate this; see below.
- You could also schedule other utilities such as virus scans, disk scanning and defragmenting; see page 66 for more details.
- You could set up new shortcuts to suit a particular user. Shortcuts are particularly useful for the power user; see page 69 for more details.
- Hyperlinks allow navigational jumps within a *PowerPoint*® presentation, or within a website, or from one website to other websites. Hotlinks, incorporated into a document, are discussed on page 72.

You may be able to think of others, and need to choose ones that suit your client.

Automatic backups

The Windows operating system provides software so that you can back up files on your hard disk, either on to floppy disks, a tape drive, or another computer on your network. If your original files are damaged or lost, you can restore them from the backup. The backup software can be found in Start/Programs/Accessories/Systems Tools (Figure 1.41).

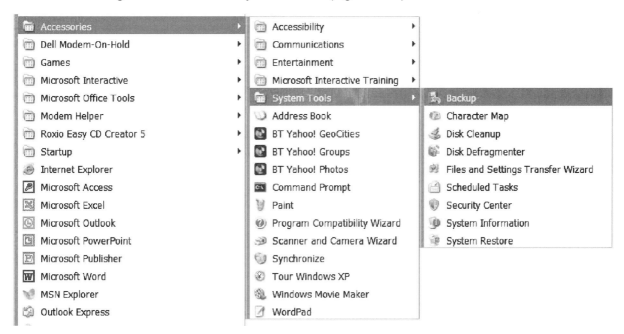

▲ FIGURE 1.41 *Backup software*

Alternatively, you may install another version of backup software, from another vendor.

Scheduled utilities

Utilities like Disk Cleanup and Disk Defragmenter (Figure 1.42) should be
used regularly, to rid the memory of unneeded temporary files and tidy up
how files are stored within the hard disk.

Disk Cleanup is used to free up space
by deleting unwanted files.

Disk Defragmenter is then used to tidy
up the disk to create patches of free space.

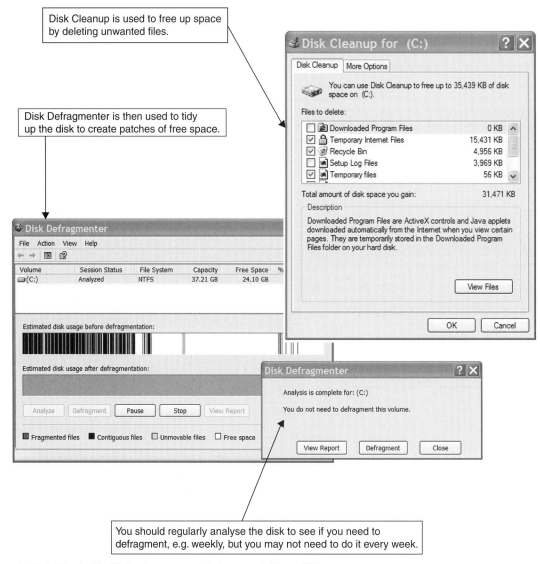

You should regularly analyse the disk to see if you need to
defragment, e.g. weekly, but you may not need to do it every week.

▲ FIGURE 1.42 *Disk cleanup and defragmentation utilities*

- **Disk Cleanup** scans disks to identify files that could be deleted, thus releasing much-needed space.
- **Defragmentation** unites clusters of files that were separated on first saving due to lack of space long enough to take the whole file.

For details of these and other tools used to organise files, see Unit 4 (page 306).

Go out and try!

1 Review the virus scanning software installed on your computer. What options are in force?

2 Use the Disk Cleanup and Disk Defragmenter utilities on your computer.

Shortcuts

Shortcuts are particularly useful for the power user.

You should be familiar with the placement of the alphabet and number keys in the QWERTY keyboard (Figure 1.43), but do you use the other keys to good effect?

GLOSSARY

Power user techniques involve making better use the keyboard.

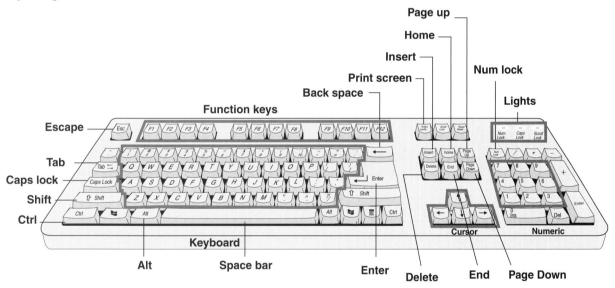

▲ FIGURE 1.43 *Keyboard*

At the top of your keyboard, there is a row of function keys. Each of these has a specific function if pressed alone. Table 1.7 shows the effect of the function keys within *Word*®.

F1	Get Help or the Office Assistant
F2	Move text or graphics
F3	Insert an AutoText entry (after Microsoft *Word*® displays the entry)
F4	Repeat the last action
F5	Choose the **Go To** command (**Edit** menu)
F6	Go to the next pane or frame
F7	Choose the **Spelling** command (**Tools** menu)
F8	Extend a selection
F9	Update selected fields
F10	Activate the menu bar
F11	Go to the next field
F12	Choose the **Save As** command (**File** menu)

▲ TABLE **1.7** *Function key effects within Word*

If pressed with the Alt key depressed – or the Ctrl key, or the Shift key – these functions may have other effects. To help you to remember these effects, you could create a strip to place on your keyboard as shown in Figure 1.44.

Elsewhere on the keyboard, additional keys – used in combination with other keys to form **hotkeys** – can also speed up your work.

- The Shift key (the one placed either side of the QWERTY keys) can be used in conjunction with the letter keys to produce upper case letters, or with the function keys to give another 12 features, or with other keys, like the arrow keys, to give accelerated features.
- The Alt key extends the features of the functions keys as well, but also gives access to options on the main menu.
- The Ctrl key can also extend the features of the functions keys, and provides shortcuts to actions like embolden and italicise.

GLOSSARY

A **hotkey** – or **keyboard shortcut** – is a key which initiates some action. It may be a single key (such as the F1–F12 keys along the top of the keyboard) or a combination of keys may be needed (such as Ctrl-B for bold).

CTRL		Print Preview	Cut to the Spike	Close window	Restore document window size
ALT	Next field		Create AutoText	Quit Microsoft Word	Restore program window size
SHIFT	CS Help/Reveal formatting	Copy text	Change case	Repeat a Find or Go To action	Move to the last change
	Help	Move text or graphics	Insert Auto Text	Repeat last action	Go To
WORD	F1	F2	F3	F4	F5

▲ FIGURE **1.44** *Keyboard strip*

Look at the main menu bar shown in Figure 1.45.

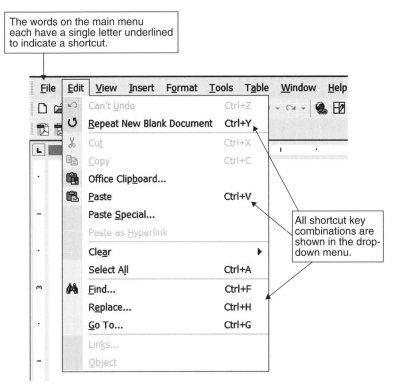

The words on the main menu each have a single letter underlined to indicate a shortcut.

All shortcut key combinations are shown in the drop-down menu.

▲ FIGURE 1.45 *Ctrl key options*

You can use the Alt key with the underlined letter to reveal the drop-down menu for each of the main menu groupings. So, Alt-F has the same effect as using the mouse to move the cursor to the main menu and clicking on File – but is much quicker.

Having revealed a drop-down menu, each of the options within it also has a letter underlined. Keying that letter will select the option or, if it has a triangle indicating yet more options, it will reveal the next level of choices that you need to make.

So, power users make the best use of the keyboard, using it instead of the mouse where this speeds up their work. They also make the best use of software features, for example to navigate through a document.

Next window	Move	Size	Insert empty field	Maximise document window	Lock a field	Open file
	Next error	Run a macro	Switch: all find codes/results	Maximise program window	Display Microsoft VB code	
Previous pane or frame	Thesaurus	Shrink a selection	Switch: field code/result	Display shortcut menu	Previous field	Save file
Next pane or frame	Spelling	Extend a selection	Update selected fields	Activate menu bar	Next field	Save as
F6	F7	F8	F9	F10	F11	F12

▲ FIGURE 1.44 *(Continued)*

- You can set up **hotlinks** within a document and then use Edit/GoTo/Bookmark to jump to wherever you want.
- If you double-click on the current page number at the base of the screen, the GoTo dialogue box opens and you can enter the page number you need.
- If you were to set up the headings of your document using the standard levels of styles, you could navigate by viewing the document in Outline View and Ctrl-clicking on the heading you want to jump to.
- You can insert an automatic contents list (using Insert/Reference/Index and Tables). This allows you to jump to a section and to see what page numbers each section starts on.

There are other 'tricks' that will improve the efficiency of data entry.

- Word offers features such as **autotext** to speed up data entry.
- You can turn on the Autocorrect feature, so that any silly typing errors are fixed – probably before you even notice them on the screen.

Toolbars provide another quick way of choosing a feature, using the mouse. Buttons can be created to perform macros, speeding up processing even more. See page 74 for details of how this can be done.

Batch files (page 78) also offer the opportunity to make you a power user, and becoming one may allow you to run circles around point-and-click friends and colleagues.

Go out and try!

1 In Word, press Alt-T W and check that it leads you to the Word Count dialogue box being displayed and data relating to your current document being displayed.

2 Use Microsoft Help to identify the complete range of shortcut keys available within one particular standard application, like *Word*® or *Excel*®.

3 Create a keyboard strip to show what the function keys, in conjunction with Shift, Alt and Ctrl, do in one application.

4 For a document that runs to more than ten pages, experiment with navigating using Outline View, and setting up an automatic contents list.

5 Review your notes on shortcuts. Having learnt about them, have you started using them in your own day-to-work work? If not, why not?

Hyperlinks

On a web page, a hyperlink is a hotspot that links it to other another page on the same website, or a page on another website; see Figure 1.5 on page 11.

A hyperlink may also be created within a document or from one file to another. Within *Word®*, if you create a table of contents, the page numbers are links to the actual pages within the document (Figure 1.46). This can provide a quick route to a page, especially during the writing stage of a document when the page numbers may change.

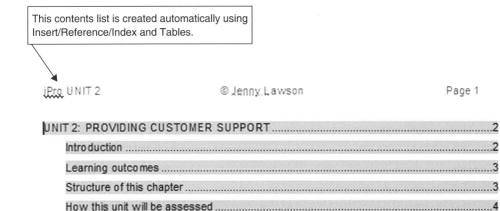

This contents list is created automatically using Insert/Reference/Index and Tables.

iPro UNIT 2   © Jenny.Lawson   Page 1

UNIT 2: PROVIDING CUSTOMER SUPPORT 2
   Introduction 2
   Learning outcomes 3
   Structure of this chapter 3
   How this unit will be assessed 4
  2.1   Providing technical information and support 4
   Determining end-user requirements 5
   Recording end-user requirements 13
   Selecting technical information 18
  2.2   Identifying potential improvements 23
   Hardware and software resources 23
   Automated procedures 30
  2.3   Creating routine and complex automated procedures 39
   Routine automated procedures 40
   Complex automated routines 44
  REVISION POINTS 50

To jump straight to a section within the unit, while holding down the Ctrl key, click on the entry.

▲ FIGURE 1.46 *Using the contents list to move through a document*

Go out and try!

1 Explore how hyperlinks can be set up within a website.

2 For a document with more then 10 pages, and different sections, set up a table of contents. Use the links to jump straight to a section.

Complex automated routines

With others, you will assist with the creation and testing of more complex automated procedures. These procedures should meet the needs of end-users, as identified by you.

This section looks at four examples:

- Macros are discussed on this page.
- Network/workstation log-in screens can be found on page 77.
- Batch files are considered on page 78.
- Templates are on page 82.

You may be able to think of other examples, ones that suit your client.

As with simple automated routines, you must adopt the correct approach:

- First, identify existing system configurations which may be affected by the development of automated procedures.
- Then, develop the automated routine and install it, ready for testing. Plan in advance what you are going to do, and make notes that you can refer to.
- To make sure it works, test your automated procedure, following an agreed plan. Keep full records of your testing: the actual outcome of the test, the data that you used and any remedial action that needs to be taken.
- Finally, develop documentation which may assist future end-user support.

In developing a complex automated routine, you will most probably be working with others. Make sure that you contribute to the process, and that your contribution is clear and well documented.

Macros

Macros help you to automate routine tasks, so as a support technician you should encourage end-users to think about using macros to increase their productivity.

Macros are available in many software applications. The language used for macros within Microsoft applications is Visual Basic (Figure 1.47). You could learn how to write Visual Basic code, but macro wizards are supplied to make the macro writing as simple as possible.

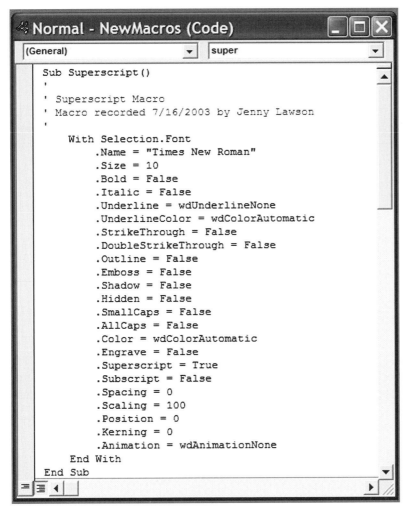

```
Normal - NewMacros (Code)

(General)                          super

    Sub Superscript()
    '
    ' Superscript Macro
    ' Macro recorded 7/16/2003 by Jenny Lawson
    '
        With Selection.Font
            .Name = "Times New Roman"
            .Size = 10
            .Bold = False
            .Italic = False
            .Underline = wdUnderlineNone
            .UnderlineColor = wdColorAutomatic
            .StrikeThrough = False
            .DoubleStrikeThrough = False
            .Outline = False
            .Emboss = False
            .Shadow = False
            .Hidden = False
            .SmallCaps = False
            .AllCaps = False
            .Color = wdColorAutomatic
            .Engrave = False
            .Superscript = True
            .Subscript = False
            .Spacing = 0
            .Scaling = 100
            .Position = 0
            .Kerning = 0
            .Animation = wdAnimationNone
        End With
    End Sub
```

▲ FIGURE 1.47 *Screen grab of VB code process*

In *Word*®, a macro will replace a series of *Word*® commands to do the following:

- Speed up routine editing and formatting, e.g. to change the case of a selected piece of text to 'all caps'
- Replace a series of commands, for example to insert a table with a specific size and borders, and with a specific number of rows and columns
- Increase the accessibility of an option in a dialogue box
- To automate a complex series of tasks

Within *Word*®, there are two ways to create a macro:

- For people with more expertise, the code for a macro can be written in **Visual Basic** code – literally, as if writing a program – using the Visual Basic Editor.
- The easier way is to use the **macro recorder**, a bit like a tape recorder with on, pause and stop buttons (Figure 1.48).

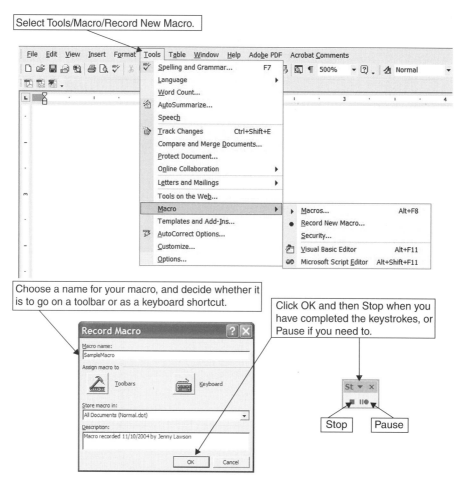

Select Tools/Macro/Record New Macro.

Choose a name for your macro, and decide whether it is to go on a toolbar or as a keyboard shortcut.

Click OK and then Stop when you have completed the keystrokes, or Pause if you need to.

Stop   Pause

▲ FIGURE 1.48 *The macro toolbar*

The macro recorder monitors the keystrokes made. When activated, it records every mouse click for commands and options, but not mouse movements within the document window. If you need to include movement, for example to the next line, or cell in a table, you must use the keyboard, for example the arrow keys, to record these actions.

The Pause button allows you to temporarily stop recording and then, later, resume recording where you stopped. The Stop button is used to end the macro sequence of commands. Running the macro 'plays back' the commands that were recorded. Simple!

Before you record or write a macro, it makes sense to plan the steps and commands you want the macro to perform. If you make a mistake when you record the macro, any corrections you make are also recorded.

Apart from the main menu, there are other toolbars offered as standard that you can reveal. You can also create your own menu items to go on the main menu, and your own toolbars.

The macro can be assigned to a toolbar or a menu so that you can select it by clicking with the mouse, and/or you can decide to assign shortcut keys to action the macro. Then, running the macro is just a case of clicking the toolbar button or menu command or pressing the shortcut keys. Alternatively, you can use Select Tools/Macro to run a macro.

So far, in this section, the examples have been of macros within Microsoft *Word*®. However, macros are available in other applications too.

- With *Excel*®, you can also record macros. Visual Basic stores each macro in a new module attached to a workbook. As well as assigning a macro to a toolbar, menu or shortcut key, you may assign a macro to a graphic object on a worksheet.
- In *Access*®, a macro can be written to perform a particular operation, such as closing a form or previewing a report, or a sequence of operations. Macros within a database can be more complicated, for example only being run if a certain condition is met. You may need to refer to the macro by name so it makes sense to name all your macros in a particular way, for example all starting with Mcr_ and followed by the action it does, for example Mcr_CloseEmployeeForm. Grouping your macros can also make later development of a database easier.

Macro support is also provided within *PowerPoint*®, but not all other applications.

Go out and try!

1 Set up a macro within *Word*® using the macro recorder. Look at the VBA code it generates. Change something within the code to change the macro.

2 Set up a macro within another application, such as *Excel*® or *Access*®. In what ways does the recording process differ? Make notes.

3 Start thinking about what macros might be useful for a user. Discuss this with others in your group.

Network/workstation log-in screens

When two or more computers are networked together, several users may be given access to the system and they could work from any workstation on the network.

To identify who is working at a particular workstation, the user has to log on, giving their **user name** and a **password**.

The network administrator will set up new users so they can access the network, and assign an initial password. The first time a user logs on, he or she may change the password, and then keep it secret.

The information about which user is logged on can be used in many ways.

- The header or footer of a document may include autotext of the username.
- Error logs may show which user was using the workstation when the problem occurred.
- Some software may use the user name dynamically, for example to create an 'APPROVED' stamp in Adobe *Acrobat Standard*® (Figure 1.49).

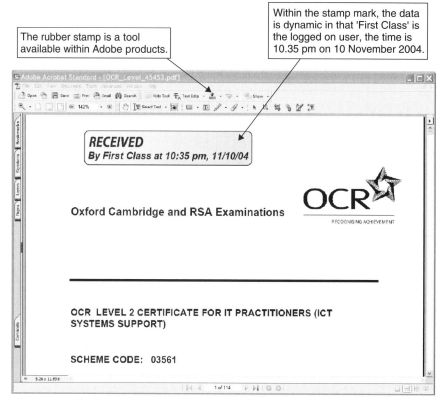

▲ FIGURE 1.49 *Dynamic data*

Go out and try!

1 Within your group, discuss other situations where dynamic data is used.

2 In a *Word*® document, include examples of dynamic data within a header and a footer.

Batch files

The term 'batch file' dates back to the early days of computing when programmers would write a series of system commands to carry out a variety of processes.

Within the code of a batch file, as in all other programs, any of the three program constructs can be found:

- Sequencing presents the instructions that are to follow one after the other. In Basic, line numbers are used to sequence the instructions; in some other languages, a semi-colon or full stop is used to show the end of a command. In batch files, a carriage return (using the Enter key) shows where one command ends and another starts.
- Repetition – or looping – can be achieved. The instructions within the loop are executed a given number of times or until an end condition is met.
- Conditioning – or branching – allows a test to be taken and, depending on the result, one course of action to be taken as opposed to another. In batch files, a line of code may be given a label and the goto command can then be used to jump to the labelled command.

The commands used in a batch file might be operating system commands, or special batch file commands. Table 1.8 lists some of these, together with some operating system commands that might be called from the batch file.

	Command	Notes
Operating system commands	cd	Changes the active directory
	cls	Clears the screen
	copy	Copies files
	dir	Lists the contents of a directory
	md	Makes a new directory
	rd	Removes an existing directory
Operating systems programs	chkdsk	Checks the integrity of disk
	deltree	Deletes an entire directory structure (called a tree)
	fdisk	Formats a disk
	format	Formats a drive
	ipconfig	Provides network settings
Batch file commands	:	Label
	%1	Command line input
	call	Calls another batch file
	echo	Displays a message
	echo off	Stops system output
	goto	Jumps to a label
	pause	Waits
	rem	What follows is a comment – not to be actioned

▲ TABLE 1.8 *System configuration commands*

Many batch files are simple sequences of commands. Figure 1.50 shows the commands needed to copy all files with a particular file extension into a new directory.

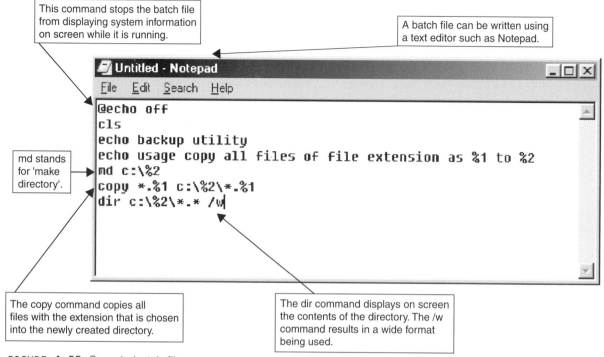

This command stops the batch file from displaying system information on screen while it is running.

A batch file can be written using a text editor such as Notepad.

md stands for 'make directory'.

The copy command copies all files with the extension that is chosen into the newly created directory.

The dir command displays on screen the contents of the directory. The /w command results in a wide format being used.

▲ FIGURE 1.50 *Sample batch file*

On your computer, within any folder, a batch file can be identified by the .BAT file extension, as in AUTOEXEC.BAT.

AUTOEXEC.BAT contains OS (operating system) commands. It is an optional file, but can be used to specify how a computer system is to be each time it is powered up:

● to determine what system prompt is to appear
● to specify what user startup menus are to appear
● to load a device driver, for example for a particular make of mouse.

When creating batch files, it makes sense to store them all in one place. So, you might create a directory called BATCH for your own creations. This may be on the C: drive or elsewhere, within your own user area.

To make your computer execute these batch files on power up, you need to include a PATH command in the AUTOEXEC.BAT file:

PATH C:\;C:\DOS; C:\BATCH

Note that the entry for C:\BATCH needs to appear before any paths to applications.

To edit batch files, using 'RUN sysedit' from the Start menu opens AUTOEXEC.BAT and three other files used during the startup process, allowing them to be edited. You can also open batch files using *Notepad®*. You could even use *Word®*, but make sure that when you save the batch file you save as plain text (Figure 1.51). You would then need to rename the file to change the file extension to BAT.

Set up a directory to hold your batch files.

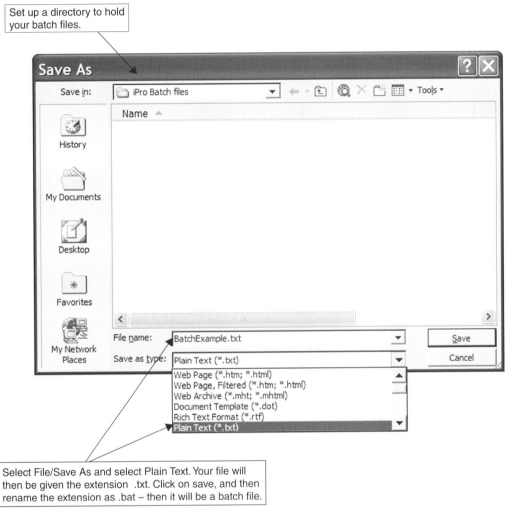

Select File/Save As and select Plain Text. Your file will then be given the extension .txt. Click on save, and then rename the extension as .bat – then it will be a batch file.

▲ FIGURE 1.51 *Saving as plain text in* Word®

Go out and try!

1 Use sysedit to open the files that are used during startup. Print out these files and study the commands being used.

2 With others in your group, compare the batch files. Look for similarities and differences between the startup files.

3 Create a batch file similar to the one shown in Figure 1.50. Save your file with a .BAT extension.

Templates

A template is a master document, created to specify the main features of all documents of a given type, such as acknowledgement slips and invoices. The template shows what should and should not be included, as well as how the document should look. There are a limited number of standard documents:

- Business letter
- Sales invoice
- Purchase order
- Memo
- Fax cover sheet
- Reports
- Web pages

When creating a new document in *Word®*, if you select File/New, you are offered all available templates on your system (Figure 1.52). There are many standard templates to choose from, all conveniently grouped by type.

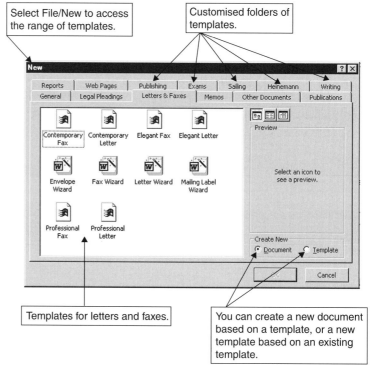

▲ FIGURE 1.52 *File/New*

Notice that you have two options:

- to create a new document using a selected template
- to create a new template, basing it on one that is already available.

For example, having set up a template for headed stationery, you could use the same template, with extra material, to create all other business document templates for an organisation.

Another option is to start with a blank document, create all the styles that you need, decide on things like paper size, margins and so on, and then use 'Save As', selecting 'Template document' (Figure 1.53). As soon as the 'Save as type' is selected the Templates folder is offered as the place to save the file. When you next select File/New, the newly created template will be on offer.

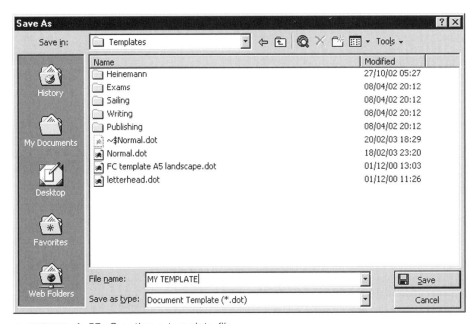

▲ FIGURE 1.53 *Creating a template file*

You can also use template files to copy styles (and menus and toolbars).

- In some versions of *Word*®, selecting Format/Style and clicking on the Organiser button, reveals a list of styles in use in this document and you can then copy style from other documents, or more likely, from other document templates.
- In other versions of *Word*®, the route to the Organiser is via Tools/Templates and Add-Ins.

A template should determine the basic structure for a document (paper size, orientation), special formatting and styles for that particular type of document, and contain document settings such as AutoText entries (date, filename in footer), key assignments, macros and menus.

Sweet & Maxwell has a series of templates (Figure 1.54) that are used by the Design Studio team to create brochures and leaflets.

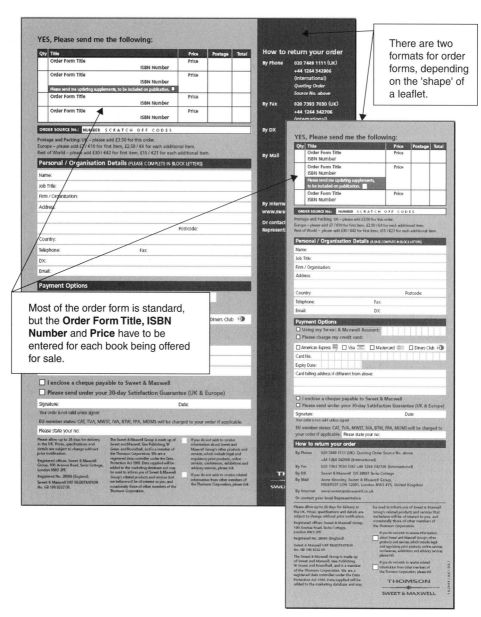

There are two formats for order forms, depending on the 'shape' of a leaflet.

Most of the order form is standard, but the **Order Form Title, ISBN Number** and **Price** have to be entered for each book being offered for sale.

▲ FIGURE 1.54 *Templates for an order form*

1 What are the benefits to Sweet & Maxwell of having a series of templates available?

2 Look at the standard templates available within *Word*®. Choose one and customise it to suit yourself.

3 Set up a new template – from scratch – to meet the needs of a particular user.

Testing

It is important, whatever change you make to a system, that you thoroughly test the system, to make sure that your improvement works and that you have not introduced a problem with how other parts of the system work.

Testing is an activity that requires planning – and it is important that you follow that plan, and document your findings.

- If you find nothing wrong, you must be sure that that you have tested every possibility and there is nothing wrong. You must not overlook anything!
- If you do find something that does not work, you may or may not have time to fix the problem. However, you should document what you know about the problem, and how you believe it could be fixed. Then when you do have time, you will not need to investigate the fault all over again.

Go out and try!

1 Select one of the changes that you have made. Familiarise yourself with what you were trying to do. Draw up a test plan, and carry it out. Document your testing, showing the results you obtained.

2 Working with a partner, test each other's work. Discuss your findings.

Practical tasks

Refer to the OCR sample case study.

1 Develop a test plan to test the automated procedures that you have developed, both on your own and with others.

2 Carry out your test plans and produce test documentation.

Documentation

Some improvements seem so simple when you are doing them that the extra effort of writing any documentation to support them may seem like a waste of time. Surely, you will remember what you did and why, when you next look at the system?

Well, this theory breaks down on two counts:

- How you solve a problem today may not be the same way you solve the problem in three months' time. You will learn new techniques, have different, better, skills and see things differently. In a year's time, or sooner, you will have forgotten the thought processes you went through to arrive at your solution. Writing comments within your code, or producing some technical documentation while your solution is fresh in your mind will save you time in the long run.

- You will move on, change jobs, get a promotion. The job of maintaining the system will fall to someone else and without some documentation to explain your changes, they will have no indication as to what you did, or why. It will save your successor a headache trying to make sense of what you have done, if you document your work.

Practical tasks

Refer to the OCR sample case study.

1 Select one of the changes that you have made. Familiarise yourself with what you were trying to do. Develop full documentation for the work you did.

2 Working with a partner, read each other's documentation for a given improvement. Discuss your findings.

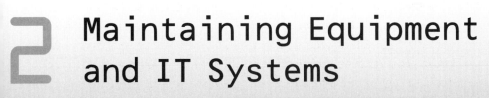

2 Maintaining Equipment and IT Systems

INTRODUCTION

In this unit, you will develop your skills in recognising common faults with computer systems and understand how to complete a systematic problem-solving process, including all required documentation.

Learning outcomes

In completing this unit, you will achieve these learning outcomes:
- Carry out routine preventative maintenance and remedial maintenance procedures for equipment components and sub-assemblies.
- Identify and locate common types of faults on communications systems to system or equipment level.
- Understand available repair options and the factors to consider when evaluating the most appropriate option.
- Take actions to rectify faults, including referral, and confirm that faults have been rectified.
- Bring repaired equipment back into service.
- Check the effectiveness of preventative and remedial maintenance procedures.

How this unit will be assessed

This unit is assessed through practical activities by your local assessor and externally moderated. You need to complete the tasks covering all the assessment objectives and you need to show evidence that the objectives have been achieved. For this, you will need to complete OCR forms showing where and how the objectives have been met.

> Carry out routine preventative maintenance for equipment components in accordance with manufacturer's and health and safety guidelines

Why do you need to carry out routine preventative maintenance?

You very likely know what it feels like when suddenly the computer freezes, or a blue screen appears, just as you are busy working on the computer, typing that important assignment, emailing your best friend ... .

▲ FIGURE 2.1 *Computers can be very temperamental*

The nature of the technology makes computers prone to failure. However, many of the problems can be prevented by simple routine maintenance.

For example, if you keep your car well maintained, it will continue to run well. To do this you would have to:

- change the oil regularly
- ensure the radiator has anti-freeze in winter
- ensure the tyres have a legal tread and are fully inflated
- have the car serviced annually
- check there are no cracks and 'chips' in the windscreen
- ensure the CD auto-changer and speaker system is working properly!

Some of these are legal obligations required to maintain the safety of yourself and others on the road; others are sensible precautions.

The maintenance of computers is also crucial, particularly as failure can affect the lives of so many people who depend on the computer to perform vital functions. For example, in the case of a company with a computerised payroll system, a failure in that system could affect people's income for the month in which the failure occurred.

To prevent computer failures occurring, there are recognised maintenance practices to follow. These include:

- checking that the technology is adequate for the task
- regularly backing up the data
- maintaining quality and quantity of the storage
- ensuring that there is a regular stock of consumables
- running diagnostic programs
- PAT testing
- checking the system for viruses/trojans/worms, etc.
- applying critical software updates
- ensuring you keep in touch with the user, as they may notice a fault long before you do.

Practical task

Look at the computers at your centre of learning. Some may have a small sticker on the plug, monitor or base unit, showing when they were last PAT tested.

- Why have they been PAT tested?
- Read the label carefully and identify the date of test.

Different types of preventative maintenance

Given that technology affects a major part of our lives, with many of us depending on it for our livelihood and often our personal safety, preventative maintenance of computers is essential.

There are, of course, many pieces of equipment we rely on in our lives that need to be maintained in good working order so they don't break down or fail.

- You should have your car serviced regularly by a garage.
- You need to ensure that the tyres on your bike are fully inflated.
- You should employ a central heating engineer to check your home's system before the onset of winter.
- You need to regularly run disk maintenance programs on your computer.

The type of preventative maintenance you need to carry out on a computer includes:

- simple non-destructive testing of the computer system
- the completion of an agreed periodic inspection of the computer system
- pre-planned maintenance tasks.

Testing of the computer system is covered in section 4.3 (page 293).

You may have a job in which you have to carry out preventative maintenance for external customers (those outside your organisation) or for internal customers (colleagues in other departments). This may involve a periodic inspection of a computer system, so you can spot a problem before it becomes an issue. This can be achieved by the use of *diagnostic* software.

A useful technique in diagnosing problems is to use a benchmark utility.

In the computer industry, **benchmarking** involves taking a snapshot of a computer system so that you can see what is running, and what memory and processor resources are being used.

Computer professionals use benchmarking to:

- diagnose any performance issues with the local computer
- identify trojans (see page 251) or unwanted processes that require removal from the computer. (Adware is a good example of an unwanted process.)

Benchmarking your computers at regular intervals is to be recommended. If the computer is benchmarked when new, and then benchmarked at least once a year afterwards, you can identify any problems or issues with the computer through a measured drop in the performance.

The common benchmarking tasks include:

- speed measurement of the processor
- display performance for the graphics card
- read/write access times for the hard drives (this can also include CD/DVD technology)
- read/write access times for the system memory
- measurement of access times for the network connection.

Practical task

Here you will download and install a diagnostic application, FreshDiagnose, and use it to create a report on the profile of your computer.

1 With the permission of the computer owner, go to www.freshdevices.com and download and install the *FreshDiagnose* application (Figure 2.2). *FreshDiagnose* is managed by a simple menu system to access information and benchmarks on all major system components.

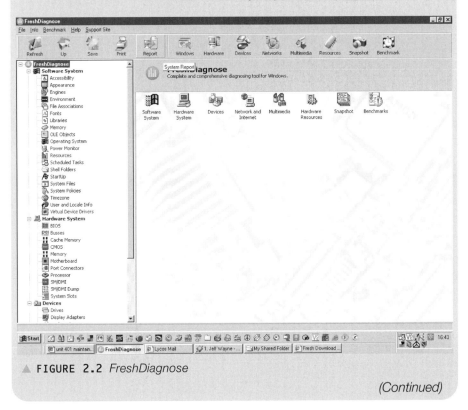

▲ FIGURE 2.2 *FreshDiagnose*

(Continued)

2 Click on the Report button and you will have the opportunity to build a comprehensive report on all system features associated with your computer.

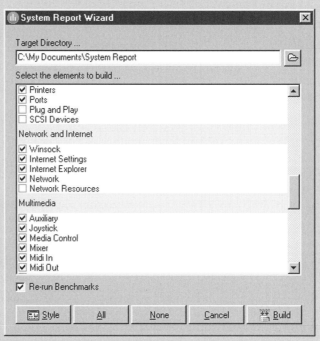

▲ FIGURE 2.3 *System report and feature*

3 Once you have compiled your report, *FreshDiagnose* will save it as a web page. Retain this as part of your employer's system management policies (Figure 2.4).

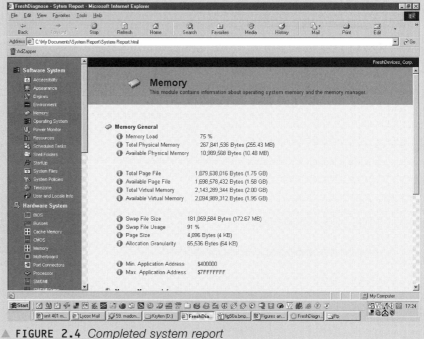

▲ FIGURE 2.4 *Completed system report*

Go out and try!

There are many other commercial computer diagnostic systems. Using an appropriate search engine, carry out some research into the popular brands of computer diagnostic applications.

Different preventative maintenance products

To do preventative maintenance or carry out a repair job on a computer, you need the tools, skills and resources.

In dealing with computer systems, you cannot cover every eventuality or problem that may occur; all you can do is prepare for dealing with most of the problems. The common resources you are likely to require include:

- computer tools, including a size 1 and 2 screwdriver, an anti-static wristband, a compressed air canister, lint-free cloths and anti-static bags
- licensed copies of common operating system software, so you can complete and update or install/reinstall system components
- licensed copies of common applications for installation or reinstallation
- driver and utilities disks for common cards and external devices
- replacement components (hard drives, floppy drives, CD-ROMs, CD-burners, DVD-ROMs, memory sticks, network cards, USB cards, graphics cards, etc.)
- emergency boot disks, to restart the computer
- anti-virus software, including a 'magic bullet' disk (see page 254)
- diagnostic software.

What ESD (electrostatic discharge) can do

Static electricity is caused by a physical process called **triboelectrification**. All atoms have electrically charged elements called electrons that will jump from one atom to another. This builds up when electrons jump back and forth between these atoms, and the result is **static electricity** (Figure 2.5).

NOTE!

Your personal skills, knowledge and experience are the most important requirements without which you cannot attempt any repair or complete any maintenance.

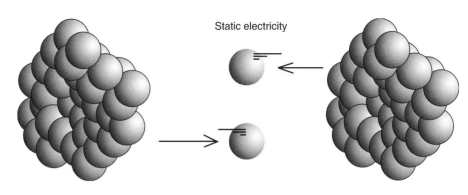

Static electricity

▲ FIGURE 2.5 *Triboelectrification – electrons jump from one atom to another*

It takes static electricity to build up to a charge of over 1000 V before we may notice that our hair stands on end or a small spark jumps from an object to ourselves. Static electricity is harmless to humans; you can endure discharges of over 10,000 V.

Computer processors, motherboards and associated circuitry will normally operate at a maximum of +/-5 V. So an electrostatic discharge (ESD) of 1000 V will wipe or blow many of the sensitive components of a computer.

A range of ESD protective devices can be used to protect the computer from you, not to protect you from the computer (Table 2.1).

When you are working with the components inside a computer you must always connect yourself to an electrostatic wristband and ensure that it is earthed. You must also do this when handling any computer components, even when they are not connected to the computer.

If you have any 'spare' components that you are not using, ensure that they are kept in an anti-static bag. This will protect them from misuse by others and against damage.

If a computer component has been subjected to ESD, it is beyond economic repair. In most circumstances, it is less costly to replace the component with one that is undamaged. A motherboard costs £25–£200, and any ESD damage can make void any warranty agreement between yourself and the supplier, which means the purchaser has to pay the cost of the damage. So, ESD has cost implications and should be avoided (Figure 2.6).

GLOSSARY

The **earth** in an electrical circuit is the point which is connected to the earth, to where the excess electricity flows. A building, for example, will have a copper strip or rod that is driven into the ground and connected to every plug.

GLOSSARY

A **warranty** is a legal agreement whereby a supplier or manufacturer will replace any faulty goods within a given period (normally one year unless you purchase or negotiate an extended period).

Device	Purpose
Wrist strap	This elasticised wristband with a metal pad fits next to the skin. The cable runs to a ground connector that may fit into a plug that connects to the earth in the mains, or it may connect to a specially fitted earth circuit. 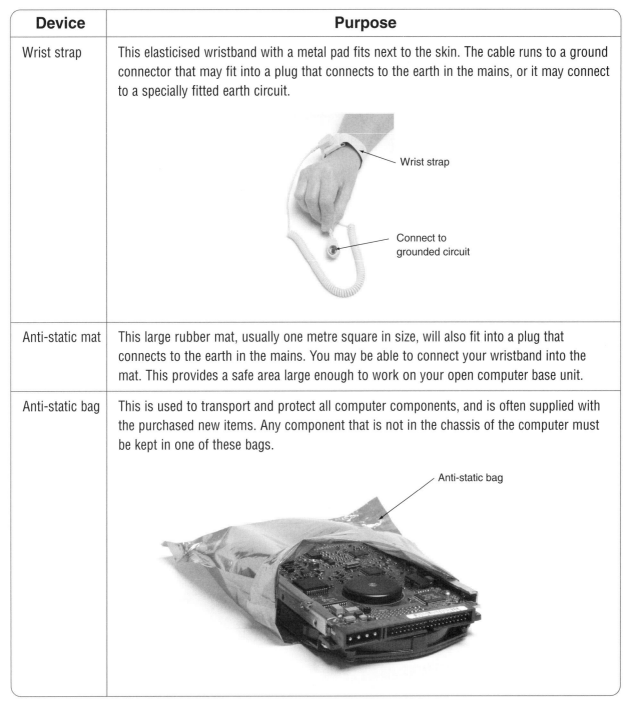
Anti-static mat	This large rubber mat, usually one metre square in size, will also fit into a plug that connects to the earth in the mains. You may be able to connect your wristband into the mat. This provides a safe area large enough to work on your open computer base unit.
Anti-static bag	This is used to transport and protect all computer components, and is often supplied with the purchased new items. Any component that is not in the chassis of the computer must be kept in one of these bags.

▲ TABLE 2.1 *Electrostatic discharge protective devices*

▲ FIGURE 2.6 *An ESD warning sign*

> ## Carry out routine remedial maintenance for equipment components in accordance with manufacturer's and health and safety guidelines

Looking after computer equipment before it goes wrong is an important part of the computer maintenance process. As mature humans, we exercise a choice in maintaining our own health. Either we go to the doctor when we are ill or we go to the doctor for regular 'check-ups' or screenings. In the case of pregnancy, a woman will have routine checks to ensure that she and the baby are well in the time leading up to birth (Figure 2.7).

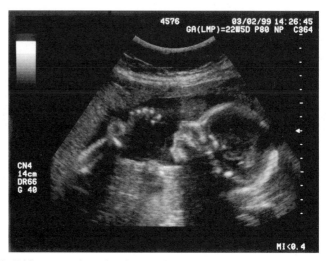

▲ FIGURE 2.7 *Ultrasound to check on unborn baby's health*

Hazards and risks

The biggest **hazard** in any workplace is YOU! Most accidents occur due to negligence or irresponsible behaviour. When working with computers in the workplace, there are many hazards:

● electric shock from the computer chassis or monitor

- computer cases posing a 'cutting' hazard where the metal has not been turned properly
- manual handling or lifting hazards
- chemical hazards, especially from laser printer toner.

Most hazards can be avoided through common sense or safe practices. Often, simply being aware of the hazards is enough to prevent accidents from occurring.

A **risk** is an activity or venture that may lead to danger. The difference between a hazard and a risk is illustrated here:

- A mountain is a hazard: some people may climb it successfully, and some people may die from trying to do so.
- A mountain climber takes a risk climbing the mountain (Figure 2.8). They know that it is a hazard and they are aware they may (or may not) die in the attempt.

▲ FIGURE 2.8 *A mountain is a hazard and climbing it is a risk*

When you open up a computer that is still connected to the electricity supply, you take a risk because there is an obvious hazard. You can reduce the risk by disconnecting the computer from the electrical outlet. Naturally, it is essential that you make every reasonable effort to minimise or remove the risks that you are taking when carrying out any computer maintenance task.

In working with computer systems, it is important that you are aware of the common hazards and risks, and that you know what to do to avoid or minimise them.

- You need to take care in your use and maintenance of equipment such as printers, monitors and computer base units.

- The clothing or jewellery that you choose to wear, may pose risks:
  - A tie should be clipped or tucked into your shirt so that it does not get trapped in the roller assembly of a printer.
  - Dangling metal jewellery is an electrical safety hazard.
  - Your hair may also be a hazard if it is long and is not tied appropriately.
  - Flowing garments are generally unsafe.
- Your use of materials or substances has to be carefully managed. For example, the toner in a laser printer cartridge is a known carcinogen.
- All working practices and behaviour must conform to the employer's health and safety procedures.
- Accidental breakages and spillages must be cleaned up in a safe and effective manner.
- You need to avoid environmental hazards.
- You need to safely store equipment and resources on shelves.
- The power and data cables need to be laid safely.
- All computer power supplies handle an incoming (from the electricity supplier) hazardous voltage of 240 V, whereas monitors and laser printers can operate at a range of over 1000 V.

Being safe and sensible

Everything done in the workplace is governed by the **Health and Safety at Work Act 1974**, whereby all employees are responsible for their own personal health and safety as well as that of everyone else working around them. Any serious breach of the Act can lead to criminal prosecution and those found guilty may have to serve a prison sentence.

This Act covers a number of other Acts and is supported by a wide array of legislation to ensure that employees can work safely. As a computer maintenance professional, this law applies to you.

Another law that affects you directly as a computer maintenance professional is the **Control of Substances Hazardous to Health Regulations 2003**. The foam that you may use to clean monitors, printers and computer base units and the toner for laser printers is controlled under this legislation.

- Under the **Health and Safety at Work Act 1974**, you have four main responsibilities:
  1 to work safely
  2 to cooperate with your employer in any work safety systems
  3 to report any hazardous conditions
  4 not to interfere with safety systems for any reason.
- You also have **other legal responsibilities**:
  1 to be aware of fire procedures and evacuation
  2 to carry out accident reporting procedures

3 to be aware of any special safety features in your workplace (this may be especially important if you work for a manufacturing organisation)

4 to know what actions are to be taken in an emergency.

In a computer maintenance and support role, you will often lift computer base units and monitors. Do this the wrong way too often and you could damage yourself and suffer long-term back problems (Figure 2.9). The lifting of heavy objects is commonly referred to as manual handling and there is a correct technique for doing this.

To lift a heavy object safely, bend your knees and lift the object in a straight upward direction. If the object is too big or heavy, ask for help. A trolley or some other form of wheeled carrier should be used to move equipment any distance.

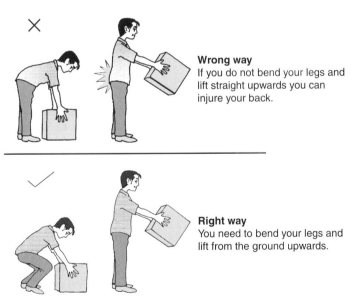

Wrong way
If you do not bend your legs and lift straight upwards you can injure your back.

Right way
You need to bend your legs and lift from the ground upwards.

▲ FIGURE 2.9 *The right and wrong ways of lifting an object manually*

A fire extinguisher is designed to combat small fires. If the fire is too big, or you believe it is too big, for you to tackle, then raise the alarm, retreat to safety and ensure that others around you are also safe.

If you are tackling a fire with a fire extinguisher, make sure you are using the right one for the type of fire and aim it at the base of the fire (Figure 2.10).

There are five types of extinguisher, only three of which can be used to fight a computer or monitor on fire:

1 **Powder** works on most kinds of fire, including electrical fires.
2 **Water** works on wood, paper, textiles. If you use this on an electrical fire then you will make the situation worse as well as endanger yourself.
3 **Aqueous Film Forming Foam (AFFF)**, like water, cannot be used on an electrical fire.
4 **CO_2 (carbon dioxide)** works best on electrical fires.
5 **Chemical foam** can be used on a range of fires.

Aim the fire extinguisher at the base of the fire

▲ FIGURE 2.10 *The safe use of a fire extinguisher*

Hazards with laser products

You are likely to encounter lasers in printers, fibre optic networking and telecommunications systems, and CD/DVD technology. Each of these systems has specific hazards that you need to be aware of.

You may find in the line of your work that you have to work with laser technology. While DVD and CD technology rely on lasers, these are often referred to as low risk and, unless you are continuously exposed to such a laser for more than an hour, you are unlikely to come to any harm.

In the networking and telecommunications sector, fibre optics use multiple light sources which include lasers. The type of laser used for 'single-mode' fibre optic technology is powerful enough to burn the back of the eye if exposed to it for less than one second. Remember, this is invisible light so you will not see it.

Safety is therefore paramount when working with any laser device. You **must**:

● ensure that the device is disconnected from any power source
● NEVER look directly at the end of a data cable
● NEVER look directly at any reading mechanism
● NEVER point the device at anybody else.

Hardware items containing lasers should be marked with the following symbol ☀. This tells the user to avoid looking at or allowing any part of their body to come into contact with the laser beam.

Go out and try!

There are many types of laser used in computer systems. Using a well-known search engine, identify the common classes of laser.

The laser in laser printers (Figure 2.11) is only dangerous if it is exposed while the printer is running. You are more likely to be harmed by the fuser/roller, which operates at 350°F, and other developer components which can reach −2000 V DC.

▲ FIGURE 2.11 *A laser printer*

There are two types of fibre optic systems: multimode uses a LED (light emitting diode) to transmit data and therefore is harmless, and single mode uses a high specification laser to transmit data at high speed over greater distance. Unfortunately, you may not be able to tell the difference, as both systems can use the same connectors. If you look down the cable of a single mode fibre, you will see nothing, even when it is running. This is because the laser light is outside your visible range. Nevertheless, the brief exposure to the laser has already burnt the cells at the back of your eye; you will now have a permanent blind spot (Figure 2.12).

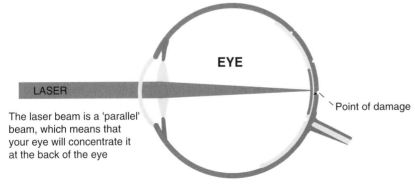

EYE

LASER

Point of damage

The laser beam is a 'parallel' beam, which means that your eye will concentrate it at the back of the eye

▲ FIGURE 2.12 *Eye damage caused by a laser beam*

CD/DVD readers and writers use a lower quality of laser, which is unlikely to be a problem as these only operate while the CD/DVD is clamped in the reader, with the head over the media.

There are four classes of laser use:

Class 1 is often used on CD/DVD technology – avoid direct exposure to eyes.

Class 2 for example is used in laser printers. Do not stare into beam or allow others to do so, as prolonged exposure may cause damage. Warning labels should be placed on the product.

Class 3 is used in fibre optic cables. A beam stop should be used to stop the beam without scattering; lasers should not be used by unauthorised persons.

Class 4 is military or medical use – to be used by licensed organisations in scientific application and research.

Remember, lasers can cause extensive damage to eyes as well as to exposed areas of the skin.

Cleaning a computer system and fault resolution

In the use and management of computer systems, many components are prone to failure due to dust or dirt. This is a major source of faults in:

- input devices, such as scanners, keyboards and mice
- output devices, especially inkjet and laser printers
- internal components of computer base units
- external surfaces such as cases and monitor screens.

To clean a computer you need some cleaning products (Figure 2.13):

- *Air dusters* come in a compressed air canister and can be used to remove dust, without your needing to touch the computer component. It ensures that you do not cause ESD.
- *Anti-static cleaning foam* is a neutral solution used in the cleaning of computer cases and monitors.
- *Lint-free cloth* will not 'fluff' and leave material behind in the cleaning process.
- *Cotton buds* are very useful in cleaning keyboards and mice only. Do not be tempted to use the cotton bud to clean 'awkward' parts of the computer as you may leave potentially damaging fluff behind.
- *Non-static vacuums* are portable vacuum cleaners used in your kitchen at home. As the 'nozzle' is plastic, it is neutral and will not act as an earth if you make contact with the computer assembly.

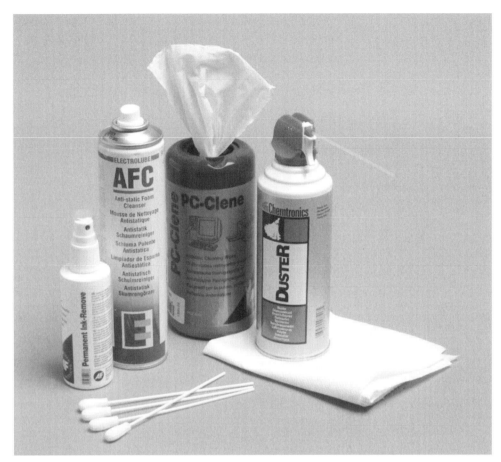

▲ FIGURE 2.13 *Computer cleaning products*

Pages 103–7 explain how to clean computer components and why it is important to do so.

Scanners

A scanner (Figure 2.14) is a digital device that can convert a printed picture or photo to a computer-stored digital image. With appropriate software, it can read in printed text and convert it to a format understood by Microsoft *Word*®.

All flatbed scanners have a glass plate on which to lay the document or image to be scanned. In time, this plate will collect dust, paper fragments and finger prints. This will impair the quality of the image and may corrupt any text that is being read in to a Microsoft *Word*® document.

To clean the scanner glass plate, use ordinary window cleaner, and a lint-free cloth. Apply a very small quantity of the window cleaner and gently rub the glass, ensuring that there are no smears. For home and ordinary office use, you will only need to do this occasionally; in a publishing/graphics environment, you may need to do it monthly.

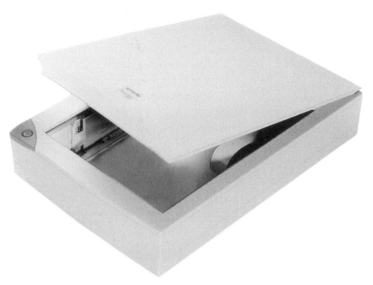

▲ FIGURE 2.14 *A scanner*

Go out and try!

You can obtain cleaning materials for computers from various websites. Using a suitable search engine (e.g. Google) find at least five prices for lint-free cloth. (This may also be called computer cloth or computer wipes.) Compare each for value.

Keyboards

Keyboards collect dirt from:

- hands that are not clean
- dust
- tea/coffee/soft drinks being spilled
- food crumbs.

In time, this may affect the performance of the keyboard.

You may have to clean two areas of the keyboard: the surface and inside.

To remove surface dirt, use anti-static cleaning foam. Only use the foam with the keyboard disconnected from the computer:

- Spray a small quantity of the foam on a lint-free cloth.
- Scrub the keyboard keys 'aggressively' with the cloth.
- Keep adding small quantities of foam until the keyboard is clean.

For more on cleaning products, see page 102.

▲ FIGURE 2.15 *The surface of a keyboard*

You will have to clean the inside of the keyboard (Figure 2.16) if you spill drink or drop crumbs between the keys.

Never try to lever out the keys with a screwdriver. This is what you need to do:

● Disconnect the keyboard from the computer.
● Open the back of the keyboard by removing the screws (some low-cost keyboards have snap tight lugs).
● Carefully extract the keyword membrane.
● Spray a small quantity of the foam on a lint-free cloth.
● Clean the membrane gently.
● Use a compressed air canister to 'blow away' any dust, if there is any.
● Replace the membrane.
● Replace the back of the keyboard.
● Reconnect the keyboard to the computer.

▲ FIGURE 2.16 *An open keyboard*

Mouse

There are two types of computer mice in common use: optical and opto-mechanical.

Optical mice are easy to clean (Figure 2.17) because there are no moving parts; the underside of the mouse is a small LED (light emitting diode) and a light sensor. You can use a single cotton bud to remove any collected dust or dirt.

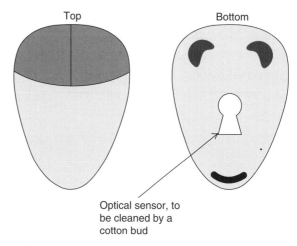

Top   Bottom

Optical sensor, to be cleaned by a cotton bud

▲ FIGURE 2.17 *Cleaning an optical mouse*

Opto-mechanical mice have been the standard in mouse technology for over ten years. Because the mechanical process (see Figure 2.18) relies on the mouse using rollers to connect to the ball that rolls across your desk, the system is prone to collecting dust, dirt and hair.

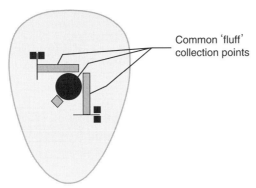

Common 'fluff' collection points

▲ FIGURE 2.18 *Cleaning an opto-mechanical mouse*

Here is the way to clean an opto-mechanical mouse:

- Remove the mouse ball cover and extract the ball.
- Clean the ball with a lint-free cloth.
- Clean the three rollers with a cotton bud.
- If the 'fluff' is solid, you may need to use a small craft knife to cut way the debris.
- Replace the ball.
- Replace the mouse ball cover.

Mice are now very low cost items; a new opto-mechanical mouse can be purchased for as little as £0.69 at www.ebuyer.co.uk.

Printers

The method of cleaning printers differs with the type and model of printer. Not only do you have the toner or ink to deal with, you may need to move paper from the roller assembly.

An **inkjet printer** operates using disposable/refillable printer heads. The need for cleaning varies according to manufacturer and the quantity of the cartridges. The main reasons for cleaning is too much ink being discharged (e.g. printing large quantities of one colour may cause this) or the printer having been left unused for some time.

Some printer manufacturers will include a head-cleaning routine with the printer software. However, this often involves using excessive quantities of ink. Some printers include software that includes a cartridge cleaning and conditioning process.

This is how to clean an inkjet cartridge:

- Remove the cartridge from the printer.
- Wipe the head with a tissue, until some ink appears.
- Replace the cartridge.

Laser printers conduct high voltages while in operation. So, a complete cleaning of any assembly must be done by qualified professionals. The manufacturer may recommend recognised companies that can provide this service.

There are only two areas of a laser printer that you may clean successfully and, with instruction, safely:

- Cleaning the toner can be done with a small brush, such as a make-up brush, although most printers will include a small brush as part of the kit on purchase. Only clean the printer if any toner was spilt from the cartridge on insertion or removal.
- You can remove trapped paper from most laser printer models, which allow easy access to the roller assemblies. Refer to the manufacturer's instructions to find out how this can be done without damaging the rollers.

Computer base unit

Being the main part of the system, the **computer base unit** must be kept clean.

Go out and try!

With the permission of your employer, tutor or the person who owns the computer, open the base unit and see how much dust and fluff has collected.

Over time, the power-supply and processor fans suck large amounts of dust and fluff into the computer case. This will cause the motherboard to heat up and may degrade the performance of the computer system. Dust will also collect in the various ports which, if any additional cards are added, may cause the connection to the device to fail.

Removing the dust from inside the base unit must be done carefully because you can easily damage any of the components. Here is what to do:

- Disconnect the base unit from the mains and any other devices.
- Connect yourself to an ESD wristband and ensure that it is connected to an appropriate earth.
- Unscrew the lid of the base unit.
- Remove the surface dust with a compressed air canister.
- Remove the dust from any fans using a make-up brush.
- Replace the lid and ensure that it is screwed in correctly.
- Correctly reconnect the base unit to the mains and any other devices.

Monitor

Under no circumstances will you need to open a monitor (Figure 2.19) to clean it.

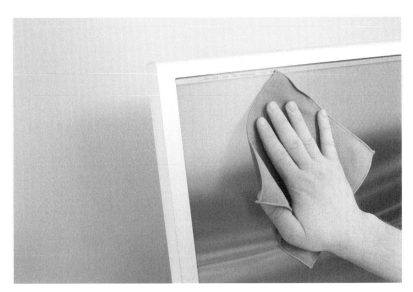

▲ FIGURE 2.19 *Cleaning a monitor*

Cleaning computer monitors is no longer straightforward. There are laptop/TFT monitors as well as CRT (cathode ray tube) systems, and the process for cleaning each is very different.

The advice for cleaning a laptop/TFT is to use a dry lint-free cloth. Make sure you clean off the dust and marks without applying too much pressure, otherwise you will cause damage to the LCD (liquid crystal display).

You need to clean a CRT monitor in two separate stages:

1 Spray glass cleaner onto a lint-free cloth and clean the screen thoroughly. (*Note:* If the monitor has an anti-glare mesh on the screen, it will be impossible to clean.)

2 Use a separate, dry lint-free cloth to clean the rest of the case. Try to squeeze the cloth into the gaps for the rear ventilation.

Practical task

Cleaning computers and their components is an essential role of any computer support specialist.

To complete this task, you will need these items:

- lint-free cloth
- tissues
- screwdriver
- compressed air canister
- glass cleaners
- cotton buds
- small craft knife or similar tool
- ESD wristband.

If you are doing this task for the first time, ensure that you have suitable permission before you start.

Using the guidelines for cleaning in the last section, clean these items:

- monitor
- keyboard
- mouse
- inkjet printer (or a laser printer if one is available)
- computer base unit.

Disposal of hazardous resources

Given the speed at which computer technology changes and the need to dispose of the components that have been replaced by the latest developments, legislation is in place to govern that disposal in a way that does not damage the environment. You are responsible for disposing of:

- batteries
- cathode ray tubes (the technical term for the monitor, with a vacuum tube)
- toner kits/cartridges
- chemical solvents
- compressed air canisters
- sharps, such as needles and fibre optic cable shards.

Batteries

Batteries contain many different metals, some of which are poisonous to the environment, animals and humans. These include lead, cadmium, lithium, alkaline manganese and mercury. Mercury, which is commonly used in the manufacturing of batteries, is extremely toxic and harmful to humans. Remember, the metals used in batteries do not decay and will remain in the environment for many years, causing damage if they are not disposed of safely. Large batteries must not be disposed of by incineration (burning) as they may explode. You may find that your local authority provides facilities for the safe disposal of batteries.

Batteries are required on the motherboard (Figure 2.20) to manage the CMOS and clock, and a rechargeable battery is required for laptops.

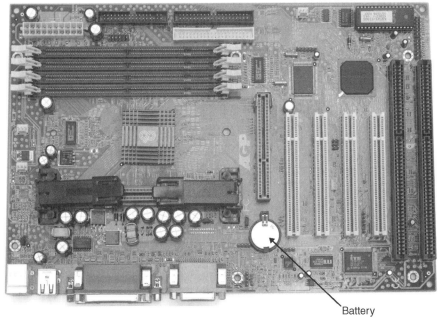

Battery

▲ FIGURE 2.20 *A battery on a motherboard*

Go out and try!

Since 2002, the UK and the European Union have regulated the disposal of batteries. Visit http://www.envirogreen.co.uk/services_battery.html and list how each type of battery is made environmentally safe.

Cathode ray tube

A monitor with a cathode ray tube (CRT) must always be handled with care because of the potentially lethal voltage that is maintained, even after they are switched off, and because of the potential of the vacuum tube to implosion if subjected to any impact. CRTs also contain glass, metal, lead, barium and rare earth metals. Some CRT monitors contain as much as 1.8 kg (4 lbs) of lead.

Most of the components of end-of-life CRT monitors can be salvaged or recycled. If your employer, school or college has to dispose of a monitor or television, they must order a special 'waste skip' from a local supplier into which they place the equipment for disposal.

Toner and ink cartridges

Used toner and ink catridges (Figure 2.21) can be damaging to the environment, because of the chemicals used for the 'ink'. Laser printer toner cartridges can be recycled. When a new toner cartridge is purchased, some suppliers will take the old cartridge for a discount. It is cleaned, recycled and reloaded with toner, then resold. You can also do the same with inkjet cartridges; some manufacturers offer a DIY solution, but this tends to be very messy and time-consuming.

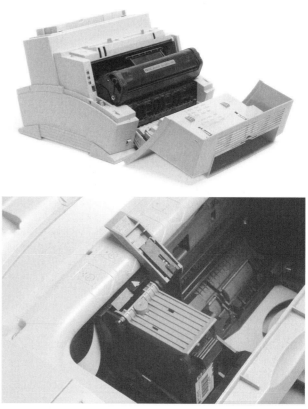

▲ FIGURE 2.21 *Toner cartridges*

Chemical solvents and compressed air canisters

The chemical solvents and compressed air canisters used to clean computers are also potential problems for the environment. You cannot simply 'dump' the contents of a can down the sink and wash it away.

Technically, all cans and bottles are hazardous waste. If you try to burn (incinerate) canisters, they may explode when exposed to the heat. Most cans can go into ordinary waste, but you must check with local authority guidelines (see pages 232–3).

Sharps

Sharps, such as needles and fibre optic cable shards, can be very hazardous if the shards are breathed in or if they go into the skin/eyes. Some companies expect their computer hardware professionals to work on fibre optic equipment; you may be expected to 'terminate' a fibre optic connection. The core of the fibre optic cable is less than 0.5 mm in diameter. When cut, the remains must be placed in a yellow sharps bin (Figure 2.22), along with the syringe needle used for the glue to make the connection. This bin will then be disposed of and burnt.

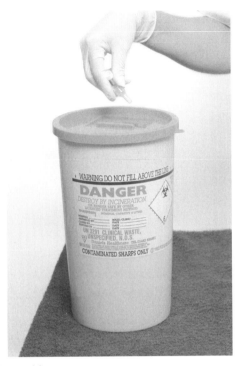

▲ FIGURE 2.22 *Sharps bin*

Complete relevant documentation to a professional standard

Why do you need to keep accurate records?

Accurate records enable you to keep your colleagues informed, especially if any of them has to take over your role or has to work on a problem on a computer maintained by you.

It is important that you contribute to maintaining records of:

- preventative maintenance carried out on a system, including when, where, and who completed the maintenance
- benchmarking that may have occurred and the results
- hazards within the terms of your responsibility.

You should also keep a journal of hazardous resources disposed of, when, and by whom.

MSDS (material safety data sheet) records

A material safety and data sheet (MSDS) is an information sheet that provides information about substances. It should include information on hazardous elements that can affect personal health, as well as fire hazards and possible first-aid requirements. It will refer to chemical reactivity and include spill, leak, and disposal guidance, along with protective measures for the safe handling and storage of materials.

An MSDS may include:

- name of the material/substance
- physical properties of the material
- hazardous ingredients contained
- reactivity, fire and explosion information
- spill or leak advice
- special precautions
- potential health hazards
- requirements for special protection.

To determine if a material used in preventive maintenance is classified as hazardous, you must consult the manufacturer's MSDS.

Go out and try!

Visit www.msdssearch.com and find information on a variety of products, then compare the results with www.envirogel.co.uk/material_safety_datasheet_env.html, which provides an example for silica gel, which is often found in computer packaging.

Check your understanding

1 What does the term 'benchmarking' mean in the computer industry? What do professionals use benchmarking for?

2 List some of the hazards that you could face as a professional. What do you need to do to avoid or minimise the risks posed by these hazards?

3 How would you clean a scanner? A keyboard? A mouse? A printer? A monitor?

4 How would you dispose of batteries? Cathode ray tubes? Toner or ink cartridges? Chemical solvents or compressed air canisters and sharps?

5 Why do you need to keep accurate records of the work you do on a computer? What information should you include in these records?

Locate and document common types of faults on systems

Being able to locate common faults on any computer system comes with experience and practice. To do this successfully, you need to develop the skill of **troubleshooting**.

In section 2.3 (page 153) you explore troubleshooting and repair options.

Following a manufacturer's instructions/health and safety guidelines

Devices such as printers and scanners, which have moving parts, often come with troubleshooting guidance. You must take note of the guidance to avoid the risk of devices causing you or others harm. As you become more experienced, you will be able to remember how to carry out tasks, particularly how to install, fix and configure a variety of complex systems. However, if you have any doubts as to how to do something, you should seek advice from colleagues or help from a manufacturer's guidelines.

Many of the problems with computer systems and the devices that you may attach to them are known and documented by the manufacturers. If you have a recurring problem that you are unable to solve, you can:

- read the manufacturer's manual provided
- consult online help
- look at the read.me file.

Motherboards, printers, scanners, digital cameras, etc. all have a printed manual. In some cases, it may be on a CD that contains a large PDF or *Word*® document. This gives a guide to installation, configuration, troubleshooting and potential problems.

Windows has a useful facility called Help. If you press the F1 key, you will activate the Windows context-sensitive help system. For all applications or Windows features, there are related Help files (Figure 2.23).

> **GLOSSARY**
>
> The term **troubleshooting** originated in the days of the American Wild West. Where there was no law enforcement, a professional gunfighter would be hired to deal with anyone who broke the law or was creating problems. In technology, it means the systematic process of solving a technical problem, often based on personal technical experience.

> **GLOSSARY**
>
> **PDF (portable data format)** is a standard created by Adobe for web-based or CD-based documents that cannot be edited.

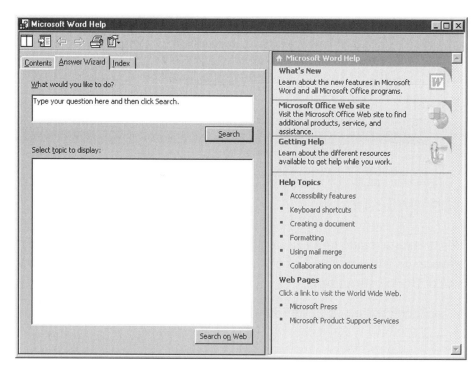

▲ FIGURE 2.23 *Windows context-sensitive help*

You can search through the Help facility by typing in the required key phrases to identify your problem.

Some help systems are web-based. You will be led through a system on your CD or hard drive that will link to the latest help on a manufacturer's website. Most manufacturers will duplicate this help on their website so that you are able to resolve any issues with their products.

Practical tasks

1 Using the Windows help, search for assistance on 'printer problems'. You should obtain a link to the printer and network troubleshooters.

2 Go to www.hp.com, and type in the search field 'LaserJet 2200 problems'. You should find a series of links to support and driver pages. Find the page that lists all known issues.

On some older, smaller or less commercial applications, you will encounter read.me or readme.txt files. These are simple documents that can act as a guide to the application. They are just as useful as professional manuals/help guides, and tend to contain the same quality of information.

Common faults

This section describes common faults and their likely causes. Refer to the page shown for each item.

- Processor (page 118)
- Memory (page 119)
- Operating system (page 120)
- Mouse (page 121)
- Floppy drive (page 124)
- Parallel ports (page 125)
- Hard drive (including LBA) (page 126)
- Sound card/audio systems (page 130)
- Monitor/video systems (page 130)
- Motherboards (page 133)
- Modems/NICs (page 134)
- BIOS, CMOS, CMOS battery and POST audio/visual error codes (page 137)
- Power supply (page 138)
- Slot covers (page 139)
- CD-ROM/DVD (page 140)
- USB (page 142)
- Cables (page 143)
- Keyboard (page 144)
- Peripherals (i.e. printers) (page 146)

To identify some of the faults and repair them, the computer will need to be taken apart. A variety of standard tools are required (see page 95 and Figure 2.24):

- a size 1 Phillips screwdriver (the crosshead variety)
- a torx screwdriver (6 spokes, used rarely but sometimes required)
- an anti-static mat and wristband, earthed.

> **NOTE!**
>
> Many computer systems use standard tools. It is becoming less common for manufacturers to expect you to use 'specialist' tools within their specific guidelines. However, this is not always the case. You may have to use a specialist fitting and ensure you have read and understood the manufacturer's health and safety guidelines.
>
> An example is working with laser printers. Some parts on some systems have specialist tools to prevent unqualified repair. Often, to ensure the safety of the individual, because of the immense electrostatic charge stored by the printer, you have to follow the guidelines exactly, for your own safety.

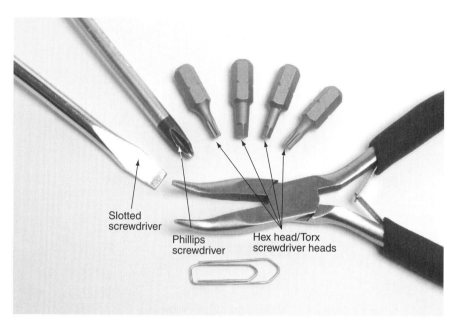

▲ FIGURE 2.24 *Types of screwdriver*

Processor faults

Processor faults are often catastrophic in nature. The processor is a complex array of transistors (a transistor is a small electronic switch), of which there are millions on the microscopic circuitry of the processor. This means that the processor:

● will generate a considerable quantity of heat in relation to its small size
● is prone to immediate failure if exposed to any voltage greater than its design voltage.

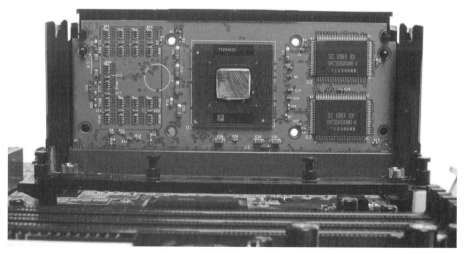

▲ FIGURE 2.25 *Processor*

Therefore if the processor fan, which is used to cool the processor, is not working, the computer may boot up but freeze in under five minutes.

If there is a power surge from the power supply, or when the computer was built the motherboard was set to the wrong voltage for the processor, the computer system will not start. Basically the processor has been 'fried'.

Memory faults

Memory faults often go undetected for some considerable time as many computers have more than one memory card. When memory fails due to age, quality or exposure to an unexpected voltage, the memory card will be rendered useless.

This means that if you have a computer with 512 MB of memory, based on two memory cards of 256 MB apiece and one of the memory cards fails, you may not notice that there is a problem until the computer starts struggling with the applications/operating system you are running.

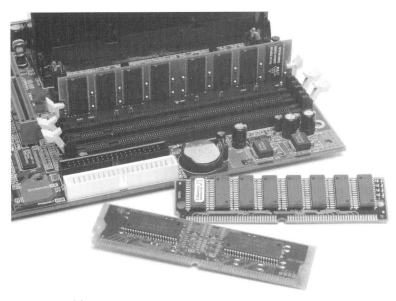

▲ FIGURE 2.26 Memory

The only way you may be able to show that this is a problem is by opening the computer to see how much memory is installed and checking this against what the operating system is reporting. Computer systems do complete a memory check on startup, but current technology is so fast that you may not have time to capture this information unless the BIOS (see later in this section) reports the total memory.

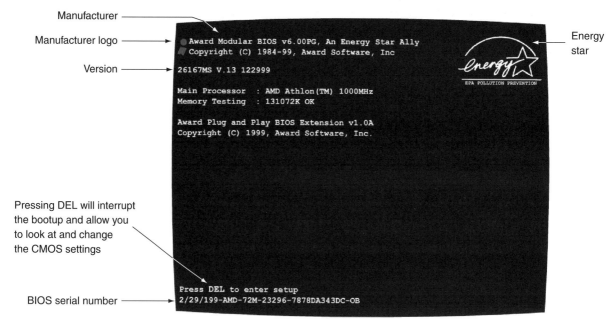

Manufacturer

Manufacturer logo

Version

```
 Award Modular BIOS v6.00PG, An Energy Star Ally
 Copyright (C) 1984-99, Award Software, Inc

26167MS V.13 122999

Main Processor  : AMD Athlon(TM) 1000MHz
Memory Testing  : 131072K OK

Award Plug and Play BIOS Extension v1.0A
Copyright (C) 1999, Award Software, Inc.
```

Energy
star

Pressing DEL will interrupt
the bootup and allow you
to look at and change
the CMOS settings

```
Press DEL to enter setup
2/29/199-AMD-72M-23296-7878DA343DC-OB
```

BIOS serial number

▲ FIGURE 2.27 *Onscreen display during bootup*

Sometimes the only problem with memory is that there is not enough, as the computer is now below the specification required to run the operating system or selected applications. The best solution is to add new memory. If the motherboard has spare slots you can add new memory or replace existing memory cards. Additional memory will release the operating system's processes, so that it can carry out a greater variety of tasks. At the time of publication, the average minimum was 256 MB of memory, but you could upgrade to 512 MB at a very low cost.

Practical task

Memory used to be an expensive resource in a computer system, however since the late 1990s the price per unit has dropped dramatically. Most motherboards have three slots for memory.

Why does a computer need memory and what sizes of memory are required for current computer systems? Consider the impact of cost and the quantity of memory slots available.

Operating system

The operating system is responsible for the management of the entire computer system and provides you with access to all the resources of the computer.

An operating system can easily become out of date for the task required, as any new developments that occur immediately after the release of the operating system will render it outmoded. A classic example is Windows 95, which was released at the start of Pentium technology. The first systems to run Windows 95 were 75 MHz. By the time Windows 95 had ceased to be current, the processor speed was 233 MHz (three times the speed), the Internet boom had arrived and USB technology was commonplace, resulting in seven versions of the operating system.

You can 'service-pack' more recent operating systems, where the vendor will produce hardware and software updates to attempt to keep the system as current as possible. You can install a completely new operating system; this is fraught with problems as the hardware may not be able to support the new system. (Windows XP, for example, ideally needs a base system of 700 MHz with 256 MB of RAM to operate effectively, regardless of the manufacturer's declaration that it can run on a 266 MHz system.)

Other faults tend to be more complex: you may need to reinstall the operating system, carrying out a detailed repair of specific resources or look at upgrading the system, if the specification of newly purchased hardware is not compatible with the operating system. Many operating system vendors offer detailed training on their operating systems.

Go out and try!

Visit v5.windowsupdate.microsoft.com (note the deliberate lack of www) as shown in Figure 2.28. Scan your computer and version of Windows for updates. You may find that the website has discovered that your computer requires many or no critical updates.

Mouse

The mouse is an integral part of our everyday use of computer systems. If there is a fault with a mouse it tends to fall into one of three categories:

- hardware of the mouse
- operating system configuration of the mouse
- communication between the mouse and the computer system.

Cleaning an opto-mechanical mouse (Figure 2.29) will often solve the problem of the ball causing the cursor on screen to jump erratically.

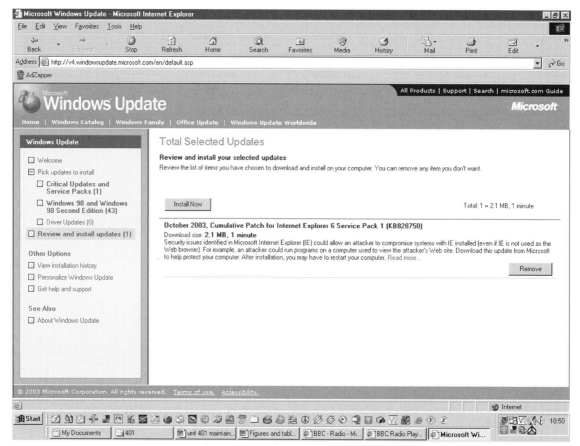

▲ FIGURE 2.28 *Windows update*

Practical task

Take the time to open an opto-mechanical mouse and identify the internal components. Look at where dust and debris will gather and clean away any that has accumulated.

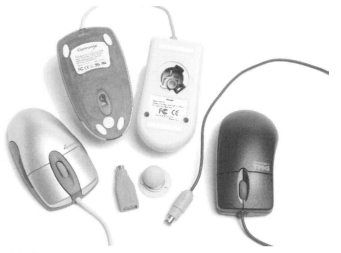

▲ FIGURE 2.29 *Opto-mechanical and optical mice*

Optical mice are predominantly fault-free. If one fails, you have to replace it outright. Optical mice can be used without a mouse mat on a range of surfaces. When the mouse cursor starts 'shuddering' you will have to:

- check if any dirt/fluff has collected in the light sensor, and remove it with a cotton bud
- provide a mouse mat as the surface is changing the angle of reflection of the light emitted by the sensor (Figure 2.30).

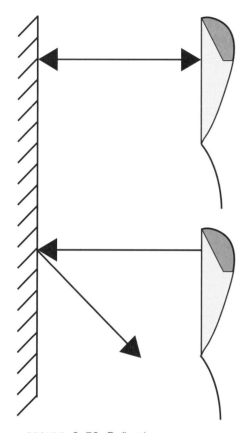

With normal reflection the light sensor sees the original light source

With an increased angle of reflection (on a shiny surface) the light sensor will not see the original light source

▲ FIGURE 2.30 *Reflection*

Windows and other operating systems allow you to calibrate the mouse to your own personal use. While this is not a fault, a user may calibrate the mouse in a way that renders it useless to others.

The way Windows controls mice is the same, regardless of the technology used to control the mouse.

Some users may have problems with using the mouse if the controls are too sensitive or restrictive, thus preventing them from being able to use the mouse effectively.

Practical task

1 Select Start/Settings/Control Panel and open the mouse icon (Figure 2.31).

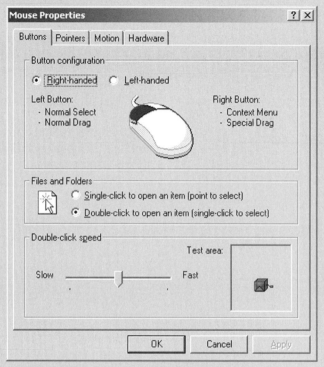

▲ **FIGURE 2.31** *Mouse control in Windows*

2 Using the buttons and motion tab, calibrate the motion and click speed of the mouse that you are using.

Floppy disk drive

Floppy disk drives remain popular for these reasons:

● They cost less than £4.
● It is an excellent backup system to use to boot the computer if all else fails.
● Many users retain data stored on floppy drives that they may wish to access.
● It is a quick and effective mechanism for moving small quantities of data.

Floppy disk drive faults can involve both the mechanism and the media, and changing the floppy disk may be the solution. In everyday use, you will encounter these common faults:

● You may be unable to insert the floppy disk.
● You may be unable to remove the floppy disk.
● The floppy disk is damaged or unreadable.
● Your computer is unable to write to the floppy disk.
● The floppy disk drive makes a crunching sound.

▲ FIGURE 2.32 *Floppy disk drive*

Like CD/DVD technology, floppy disk drive technology is now so low cost that it is less costly to dispose of a faulty item rather than repair it. If you encounter problems with a drive:

● eject a stuck floppy disk by gently sliding a knife from left to right to left inside the bottom and top sides of the disk thus releasing it from the catch inside the drive
● check if the 34-pin cable is the correct way around in the case
● check to see whether the write-protect lug is closed on the disk
● confirm whether the disk is full, by using Windows *Explorer*®.

To confirm if the disk is damaged or corrupt, use *scandisk* or Windows *Explorer*®.

Parallel port

The parallel port (Figure 2.33) is the connection between the computer and higher specification data devices. It was once commonly used for printers, scanners and other specialist devices, but is now being replaced by USB (see later in this section).

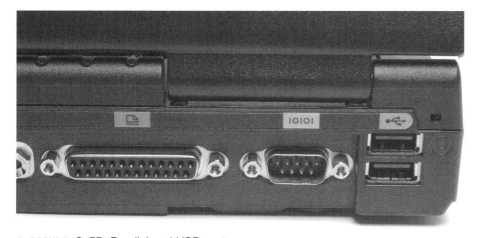

▲ FIGURE 2.33 *Parallel and USB ports*

The parallel port is an older standard and is not serviceable by many engineers. The 25 pins enable the data to be sent simultaneously. Each bit is sent down the line separately, unlike serial connections where the data is sent in sequence.

If you are trying to resolve a problem involving a printer that is not working and you have managed to eliminate the printer (because it works on another system), the problem may lie with the software or another component. Carry out more tests to identify the source of the fault.

Hard drive

The hard drive (Figure 2.34) is the main storage medium for the operating system and all personal files and applications. Therefore the failure of a hard drive tends to cause the greatest consternation among users and computer technologists. The failure may lead to the loss of work.

> **NOTE!**
> Under no circumstances must you ever attempt to open a hard drive. Doing so will damage the hard drive as you will let dust into the delicate system; also you will invalidate the warranty.

▲ FIGURE 2.34 *Hard drive*

> **GLOSSARY**
> A **warranty** is an agreement that guarantees that the manufacturer will repair faulty products for a period of time after the item is sold. Companies like PC World offer extended warranties to increase the length of repair cover for a computer system.

Hard drives are complicated and delicate systems, which can fail through age and wear and tear. You will not be able to solve all hard drive faults; no computer professional can. However, there are many specialist companies that provide hard drive recovery services.

> **Go out and try!**
> Using a popular search engine (such as *Google*), search the web to find three companies that offer hard drive/data recovery services. Compare the fees they charge and the products they offer.

When dealing with hard drive faults, it is likely that you will encounter these problems:

- a head crash, which occurs when the hard drive has completely failed and the read/write head has locked or hit the magnetic platter
- a driver motor failure
- the boot sector being corrupted
- the computer not booting due to a fault with the ATA, IDE or SCSI bus
- the BIOS not detecting the hard drive
- the operating system incorrectly installed
- the **LBA (logical block addressing)** used to control drives between 0.5 GB and 8 GB not correctly referencing the hard drive's cylinders (a storage unit used on hard drivers with more than one disk)
- the hard drive having corrupt sectors or tracks.

GLOSSARY

ATA (advanced technology attachment), **IDE (integrate drive electronics)** and **SCSI (small computer system interface)** are commonly used to transfer data from storage devices to the main computer system.

If a hard drive is near its capacity, check whether the customer has saved resources on the hard drive that are best placed on a CD-ROM or DVD-ROM. It is possible that you need to carry out a disk cleaning exercise to remove a variety of temporary files from the system.

Replacement hard drives are easy to install, and cost from at least £40 for an entry-level solution (60 GB in 2004). You can add an additional hard drive into a computer, in which there should be an additional IDE channel (see page 190). In this way you can move non-essential files over to the second hard drive.

You can resolve some hard drive problems by:

- replacing the IDE or SCSI cable, if the hard drive is not communicating with the rest of the system
- ensuring that the hard drive is switched to master or slave, according the hardware configuration (see page 190)
- running *scandisk* or *defrag* to complete operating system repairs on the structure of the hard drive
- installing (or reinstalling) the operating system if there is no boot sector.

If you install a new hard drive on an old system and the system does not recognise the size of the hard drive, you may need to upgrade the BIOS. To flash upgrade the BIOS, go to the manufacturer's website and follow the instructions given there.

Practical task

In this task, you will use the version of Windows available on your own computer to complete a comprehensive analysis of the integrity of your hard drive.

1 To access *defrag*, click on Start/Programs/Accessories/System Tools/Disk Defragmenter.

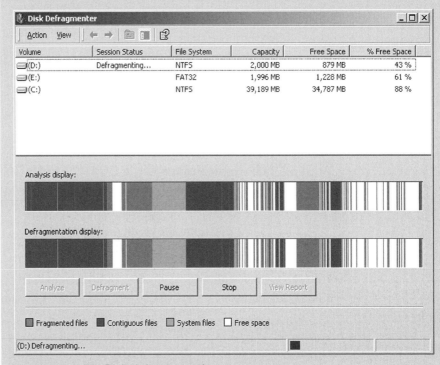

▲ **FIGURE 2.35** *Disk defragmentation*

Note that Windows 95/98 has a different version of *defrag*, although the operation is similar.

Once you have started defrag, click on the Defragment button.

2 Scandisk has been available since DOS version 5 and was a feature in Windows 95/98. It checks your hard drive if you do not shut down your computer correctly.

In older versions of Windows, find *scandisk* by entering run/scandisk (Figure 2.36). Otherwise, in Windows 2000, etc. run an older command called CHKDSK (Figure 2.37). Access this by entering run/cmd and then typing chkdsk.

(Continued)

GLOSSARY

Defrag is a tool that rearranges (tidies) all the files on the hard drive to create more space for larger files. You could have 2 GB free on a hard drive, but because the free blocks are all less than 100 MB in size it is difficult to save large files.

Practical task (Continued)

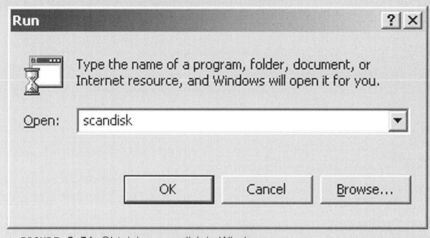

▲ FIGURE 2.36 *Obtaining scandisk in Windows*

▲ FIGURE 2.37 *CHKDSK*

1 With the permission of your tutor or the person who owns the computer you are working on, restart the computer, press Del or F2 and enter the BIOS.

2 Each BIOS is slightly different, however you can always find the same information. Find the section that detects hard drives. Run this utility and identify:

- the storage capacity of the hard drives on the system
- the number of cylinders on the hard drive (i.e. the number of drive platters)
- the number of sectors that are on the hard drive.

3 Does this utility detect the number of CD-ROMs or other media?

Sound card or audio system

The sound card or audio system is now standard technology on all computer systems. Some computer professionals will install better sound cards in the pursuit of quality; this is important for musicians and music technology specialists.

As in the case of many other computer components, it is more economical to replace rather than repair a sound card that has failed. What is more costly is when the sound card system is embedded into the motherboard; then you need to replace the whole motherboard.

Some sound card faults occur when the driver is incorrectly installed or there is a device conflict on the system. **Latency** is a fault in more expensive sound cards used for music and media technology. In such cases, the computer system hardware and operating system needs to be reconfigured so that it is compatible with the sound card.

Monitor and display adapter

There are two components that control your ability to see 'what is going on' with the computer. The **monitor** display, or VDU (visual display unit), is attached to the **display adapter** (or graphics card).

If a fault occurs on the video board you may initially suspect that you have a fault with the monitor or the motherboard. The only symptom of a fault with a display adapter is that you see nothing. This may be due to many things:

- the video board not starting, so the computer system is not active
- the video output being faulty and the monitor not receiving a signal
- the display adapter not being compatible with the monitor used
- the operating system not having the correct drivers for the card used
- the operating system not having the correct drivers for the AGP port
- the video settings being out of range for the display adapter in use
- the 3D effects required for the game/application not being compatible with the display adapter available.

GLOSSARY

Latency explains a delay in communication between different technical systems. You may notice latency on a web video, where the sound is not synchronised with the video.

GLOSSARY

AGP (accelerated graphics port) is a slot on a computer's motherboard that allows the display to have a faster connection to the system's processor resources. This is designed to improve the speed and quality of the graphical output.

Video cards can be very problematic due to the many likely solutions to a problem:

- You may need to replace the monitor if you had installed the wrong type, i.e. one which is not compatible with the resolution of the video board.
- The SVGA socket may be damaged on the video board and you may not need to replace the video board.
- The SVGA plug on the monitor may have damaged pins, and the solution may require the replacement of the monitor (on a sealed unit) or the monitor cable.
- If the operating system is not using the correct drivers for the video board, you may need to install manufacturer-specific drivers. Go into safe mode and download the drivers from the manufacturer's website. (*Note:* Most video boards will work on 660 x 480 with 256 colours.)
- If the AGP or PCI bus is not recognising the video board (or vice versa, the video board is not recognising the AGP or PCI slot), you may need to update the drivers on your operating system to manage the AGP or PCI system.
- If there is no output at all, replace the monitor first. If there is no success, then replace the video board. If you still have no success, the problem is the motherboard.

There are two types of monitor in common use and the faults can be very different. This section investigates common faults found with CRT and TFT monitors. These both suffer from the following problems:

- All monitors are vulnerable to the whims of the motherboard and video board and the result may be no apparent display.
- If there is a fault with the connector, the monitor may display a tinted colour scheme (in purple, green or blue).

CRT monitors are more complex than TFT ones. They can have a wide range of visual faults, as demonstrated in Figure 2.38.

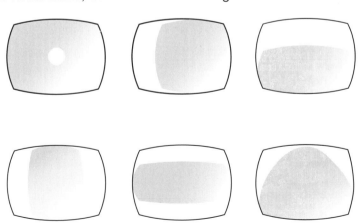

▲ FIGURE 2.38 *Common problems with a CRT monitor*

Each fault is caused by problems with the equipment, which directs the electrons to the front of the monitor.

The TFT monitor's only likely fault is when the screen has been damaged. The liquid crystal system is a delicate structure that is easily ruptured, producing a rainbow effect in the damaged area of the monitor.

(a)

(b)

▲ FIGURE 2.39 *(a) CRT and (b) TFT monitors*

Monitors are computer resources that may last for years or run briefly and then fail. If you identify that the monitor is at fault, **do not** attempt to repair it. You are unlikely to succeed. Instead, send it to a specialist to repair. If it is still under warranty, send it to the manufacturer or the retailer from whom you bought it.

The only fault you can solve is by unbending bent plug pins, often caused by someone putting the plug in the wrong way. Use a pair of tweezers to straighten the pins and then replace the cable.

Practical task

For this task, use an old unused monitor. You will need a small screwdriver and a small pair of tweezers.

Take the D-type plug that connects to the PC from the monitor and bend back one pin using the small screwdriver.

- How does this affect the image being displayed on the monitor when it is plugged into the PC?
- How many pins do you need to bend and which pins do you need to bend to change the image colour?
- To what colours does the monitor change?

Once you have completed this task, make sure that you repair the damage, using the small tweezers to straighten the monitor cable pins.

Motherboard

The motherboard (Figure 2.40) is the skeleton on which the entire computer system operates. It is a collection of many complex systems and is therefore prone to failure and fault.

▲ FIGURE 2.40 *Motherboard*

The symptoms of a motherboard failure include:

- computer not starting
- computer starting but the system sending a series of beeps via the onboard speaker
- devices such as your modem, network card or soundcard not working because the PCI bus has failed (see pages 316–17)
- hard drive, CD-ROM or floppy drives not working because the IDE data bus is not operational (see pages 316–17)
- video board of monitor not operational
- your not being able to use the USB port
- your not being able to print
- mouse not working
- keyboard not working.

The skill is proving that it is not the individual components that are at fault but the motherboard. You also need the skill to prove that it is not the motherboard that is at fault. There are no serviceable components on a motherboard. So, if you have clearly identified that it is the motherboard that is faulty, then it must be replaced. There are some companies, such as ADT, that offer board level repairs. However, they are uncommon, and often they serve regions as large as Europe due to demand.

The computer not starting.	Check the power supply and power supply connectors.
The computer is starting but the system is sending a series of beeps via the onboard speaker.	You will have a problem with memory, the BIOS or the keyboard.
Devices such as your modem, network card or soundcard not working as the PCI bus has failed (see pages 316–17).	The motherboard may need replacing.
Your hard drive, CD-ROM or floppy drives are not working as the IDE data bus is not operational (see pages 316–17).	The motherboard may need replacing.
Your video board or monitor is not operational.	Check the card or the monitor.
You cannot use the USB port.	Is USB enabled or is there a fault with the cable? You can insert an extra USB riser card; otherwise, the motherboard may need replacing.
You cannot print.	Is there a fault with the parallel port, printer or parallel cable? If the printer is USB go back one step.
Your mouse is not working.	Other than the mouse, it may be the serial/PS2 connector.
The keyboard is not working.	Other than the keyboard, it may be the PS2 connector.

▲ FIGURE 2.41 *Motherboard fault finding*

GLOSSARY

Modem is shorthand for **mo**dulator **dem**odulator. This describes the technical process involved in converting the digital signal of a computer system to the analogue signal of a telephone line.

NIC and modem

The NIC (network interface card) and modem (Figure 2.42) are used to connect the computer to external systems. The technology used to achieve this is inherently complex and often prone to failure. Common faults tend to be based on the loss of communication between your computer and the remote host.

▲ FIGURE 2.42 *NIC/modem*

Troubleshooting faults with an NIC or modem can be very complex and requires a high level of understanding networking. You are always faced with various potential causes for a modem or a NIC not working and the loss of communication.

You may be able to solve communication problems by doing these checks:

- Is the cable plugged in to the NIC or modem and connected to the wall socket?
- Does the cable that is connected to the NIC/modem work on another system, or in another wall socket?
- Is there a fault with the network/phone system, with your ISP or organisation's networking team?
- Does another NIC/modem of the same type work instead?
- Is TCP/IP or another suitable protocol installed?
- In system properties, is the NIC or modem recognised?
- If TCP/IP is correctly installed, is the network addressing correctly configured settings (automatically detect settings may be appropriate)?

GLOSSARY

TCP/IP (transmission control protocol/internet protocol) is a method used to send data from computer to computer across networks and the Internet.

Practical task

Checking the networking settings on Windows is not difficult. However, it is essential that you do not change the settings on a pre-configured computer. You may prevent it from communicating with a network or, even worse, prevent another computer from being able to communicate with it.

To access the network setting for a computer, right-click on 'My network places' or 'Network neighborhood' (if you are using Windows 98).

Find the local area connection and select Network properties. Then find the TCP/IP settings.

Using Figure 2.43, identify the settings that are labelled in the diagram.

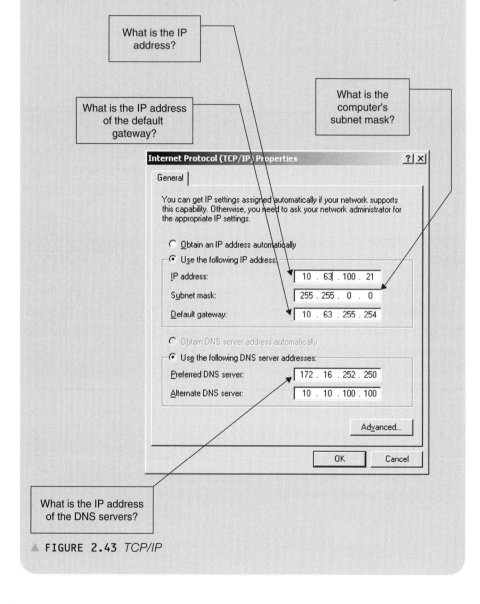

▲ FIGURE 2.43 *TCP/IP*

BIOS, CMOS, CMOS battery and POST audio/visual error codes

The BIOS, CMOS, CMOS battery and POST audio/visual error codes all work together to ensure that the computer system will:

- successfully boot up each time you switch it on
- store all of its settings, so that the next time the computer is rebooted, it will start as before
- inform you if any problems occur during the computer startup process.

The BIOS is typically placed in a ROM chip that comes with the computer (called a ROM BIOS). This ensures that the BIOS will always be available and will not be damaged by hard disk failures. It also makes it possible for a computer to boot itself.

> ## Go out and try!
>
> CMOS is used as part of the BIOS. Using the Internet carry out research to discover where else it is commonly used in computer technology.

The CMOS battery provides a continuous supply of power to the BIOS and the system clock, allowing the computer system to retain information about:

- the current date and time
- any system startup requirements, so that the BIOS can correctly load the correct services when the computer is switched on.

The battery is a unit that is recharged by the motherboard when the computer is operational, but through each 'recharge and use' cycle there is a slight degradation in performance. So, in time, CMOS batteries will decay with use. This problem is common on older computers, and you might occasionally find it occurring on newer computers. The fault will make itself apparent when the computer is switched on:

- The BIOS reports that the CMOS checksum is incorrect, which has been caused by a loss of power to the CMOS.
- The date/time reverts to the system default time. This may be midnight on 1 January 1990.

GLOSSARY

CMOS (complementary metal oxide semi-conductor) is a rewriteable long-term memory that is used to maintain hardware settings on boot up, as well as information for the system clock.

BIOS (basic input-output system) is a specialist chip on a computer motherboard. Among its many roles, it is involved in managing the way a computer boots up.

GLOSSARY

ROM (read only memory) is a memory that can be read many times but may only be written once.

RAM (random access memory) can be written to and read from many times.

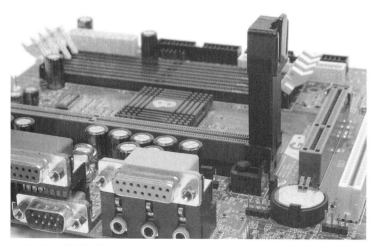

▲ **FIGURE 2.44** *CMOS battery on a motherboard*

If the CMOS battery is the removable watch type, then a suitable replacement can be bought from a high street retailer. On some older motherboards, the CMOS battery is a sealed soldered unit that could only be repaired by:

● replacing the motherboard
● removing the battery and soldering on an equivalent replacement.

Practical task

With the permission of your supervisor or tutor, open the base unit of a computer that is in good working order and has a removable CMOS battery. Ensure that it is not connected to the mains and that you have appropriate anti-static protection.

Remove the battery and attempt to reconnect the computer (to monitor, power, keyboard and mouse). What error message do you see? Will the computer start? Did the BIOS reset? Does the system detect all the components?

An important function that the BIOS carries out is to **boot up** the system. When the PC is first turned on, its main system memory is empty, and it needs to find instructions immediately to tell it what to run to start up the computer. These are found within the BIOS.

During this process, **POST (power on self-test)**, the BIOS will check all essential system components during boot up before handing over control to the processor.

Power supply

The power supply (Figure 2.45) provides the electricity for all the components in the computer system via connectors.

▲ FIGURE 2.45 *Power supply*

There are three types of connector:

1 the main block for the motherboard (called an AT or ATX connector)
2 floppy disk drive connectors
3 hard drive, CD/DVD-ROM connectors.

These connectors provide various systems with a variety of voltages according to the requirements of the component: +/- 3.3 V, +/- 5 V and +/-12 V.

The motherboard power connection for an ATX motherboard is shaped so that it cannot be fitted the wrong way around (this being potentially disastrous for the motherboard).

Only electronics experts should attempt to repair a power supply; it needs to be done by a trained technician. You are likely to encounter two problems with the power supply that you can solve:

● The power may not be correctly connected to a given device, so that the component appears to be faulty, when actually the problem is that it does not have electricity. Turn the power on!
● The cable fuse may have failed. Check why it has fused. Fix the problem and then replace the fuse.

Occasionally, power supplies will fail dramatically and 'blow'. If this happens, your components will cease to work.

Slot covers

On a computer case, the slot covers (Figure 2.46) serve two purposes:

● They protect the inner components from dust and debris.
● They allow you to remove them and add new components to your computer system.

▲ FIGURE 2.46 *Computer slot cover*

The only problem you may have with a slot cover is where it has not been removed and is 'hiding' another component, or the slot is poorly fitting and the card/device inserted is not correctly connected.

CD-ROMs, DVD-ROMs, CD Writers and DVD Writers

For the purposes of fault finding, CD-ROMs, DVD-ROMs, CD-Writers and DVD-Writers behave the same, despite being different technologies (Figure 2.47). The reason for this is simple. The technology sends the same information as far as the motherboard and the operating system are concerned.

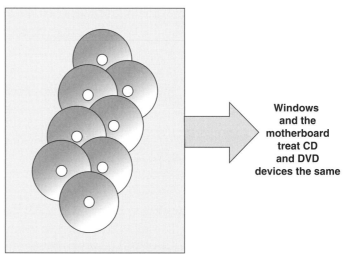

The computer could contain a CD-ROM, DVD-ROM, CD-Writer, DVD-Writer

▲ FIGURE 2.47 *CD/DVD technology*

These are likely faults of using CD/DVD technology:

- The drawer does not eject.
- The drive makes loud noise.
- You are unable to play music CDs.
- You have problems writing CDs and DVDs.
- CD/DVD burning software is not managing to create a CD/DVD.
- You are unable to read a CD or DVD.
- A CD or DVD cannot be auto-detected.
- The media created by your CD/DVD burner is not being recognised by any other system.
- A CD or DVD ejects unexpectedly.

▲ FIGURE 2.48 *CD-ROM*

CD/DVD technology now costs so little that if you have a problem with components it is often more cost-effective to replace the system outright. At the time of going to press, the costs of purchasing are:

- CD-ROM   £10
- DVD-ROM   £16
- CD-Writer/Rewriter   £26
- DVD-Writer/Rewriter   £45

If you have a fault with any of the above systems, it is worth asking yourself these questions:

- Is the CD/DVD media damaged?
- Is the IDE or SCSI cable connected correctly from the motherboard to the CD/DVD unit?
- Is there power from the power supply to the CD/DVD device?
- Does the software correctly detect the CD/DVD device?

- Are you trying to write data at a speed too fast for the quality of the media?
- Are you using the correct type of media? (DVDs have two formats that are not recognised by all devices.)

A little-known issue with CD/DVD devices is a fault with the electrical ground, from the device to the motherboard. This will prevent the whole system starting up.

USB

First introduced in 1998, USB (universal serial bus) is a **plug and play** interface between a computer and add-on devices (such as audio players, joysticks, keyboards, scanners, printers and much more). With USB a new device can be added to your computer without having to add an additional card or, sometimes, even having to turn the computer off. The power of USB is that with the connection of a USB hub to a computer, you can connect up to 128 devices to one line. Some devices take their power straight from the computer's USB line; others use the USB only for communication and have their own power source.

USB supports a maximum data speed of 12 megabits per second, whereas the normal speed for data devices is 1.5 megabits per second. Since being developed, the USB 2 standard is now available with data speeds of up to 480 megabits, and is USB 2 compatible with the older standards.

All current operating systems are USB compatible, so you can use USB technology on Windows '98, ME, 200, 2003, XP', as well as Linux, Solaris and Novell.

▲ FIGURE 2.49 *USB port*

These are the problems you are likely to encounter with USB:

- You may lack sufficient USB ports on the computer system. If so add another USB card or attach a USB hub (this can cost less then £10).
- For some older systems, the operating system may not recognise the drivers for the USB. If so, you need to upgrade the operating system and/or purchase a new system.
- The devices on the USB may be drawing too much power. This happens when printers and scanners, which consume more power, are only powered by the USB. A good printer or scanner needs to be powered by an external power supply for your USB to be able to support other devices.
- The system has recognised the insertion of a new device but does not have appropriate drivers to install the new component. This normally occurs when the device/technology has been manufactured *after* the latest operating system. To solve this, most manufacturers will provide a driver disk, or you can download the driver from their website.

Practical task

What devices can be attached to your computer using USB? Compare the types of devices using USB and decide how their performance is improved by the newer USB standards.

Data cables

Your computer will have a myriad of data cables (Figure 2.50) connected to it internally and externally. On the standard computer system, there are cables that connect:

- the hard drive to the motherboard
- the CD/DVD/ROM or Writer to the motherboard
- the floppy drive
- various USB devices
- CD-audio to the sound card
- external systems such as USB/serial and parallel devices.

Finding faults with cables can be problematic and require a systematic approach to discover what may be wrong (check power, check cable, check device). Most cable faults occur when there is:

- damage to the cable
- damage to the connector.

▲ FIGURE 2.50 *Data cables*

Keyboard

The keyboard (Figure 2.51) is a complex array of switches, with the potential for failure. Problems with the keyboard are likely to be local, involving the operating system and related to the motherboard.

These are faults you are likely to encounter:

- When you press a key, you see on the display the wrong output for the symbol key you pressed.
- Characters appear without your typing.
- You press a key and multiple characters appear.
- Nothing happens!
- Some characters work; others do not.
- The computer beeps every time you press a key.

▲ FIGURE 2.51 *Keyboard*

With a keyboard, you are just as dependent on the operating system as the hardware is. When trying to resolve any faults, ask yourself these questions:

- Is the keyboard connected?
- Are you using the right keyboard? (The United Kingdom has a different keyboard standard from countries such as Germany, France and the United States.)
- Is the correct keyboard driver loaded? (Windows will use US settings by default. This makes life difficult with symbols such as £ $ " and @.)
- Is the keyboard dirty? (The keys may be stuck down; you may need to clean the keyboard.)
- Given the type-matic rate, is the keyboard setting too sensitive?
- If the keyboard keeps beeping every time you press a key, the keyboard buffer is full, which means that there is a greater problem with your operating system. You may need to restart the computer to diagnose the problem.

Practical task

1 Go to Settings/Control Panel, select the keyboard icon, and double-click on it to open the Keyboard Properties dialogue box (Figure 2.52).

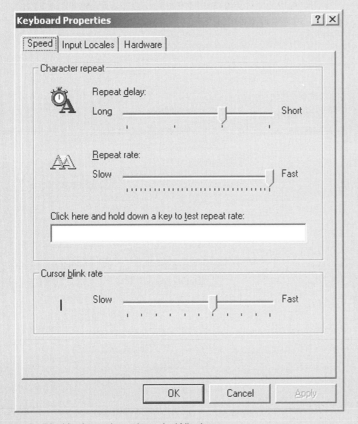

▲ FIGURE 2.52 *Keyboard settings in Windows*

(Continued)

2 Calibrate the speed of the keyboard response time in Windows, change the keyboard type (as some users have specialist keyboards) and configure the locale (country used).

3 Configure the regional settings of the computer (Figure 2.53). (Find these in Settings/Control Panel/Regional settings.)

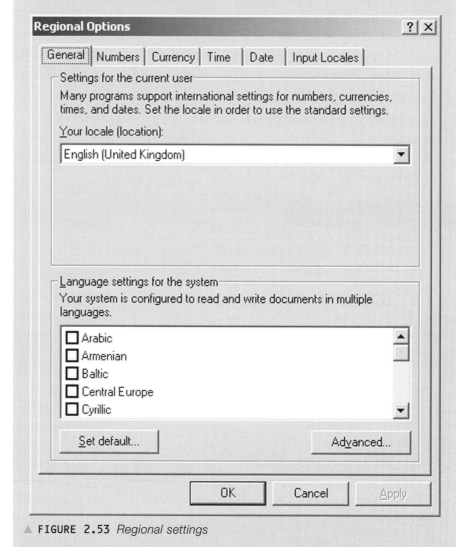

▲ **FIGURE 2.53** *Regional settings*

4 Also set the system to your local region as this will also have an affect on how the keyboard behaves.

Peripherals

Although there is a wide array of peripherals, this section looks only at the most common printers. There are three types of printer technology in commercial use, and you will encounter different issues according to the type.

If you are called out to deal with a **laser printer**, the problems you may encounter include:

- paper jam
- loss of power
- printer overheating
- no image or output
- lines in output
- faint image or output
- corrupt image/output being created.

If you were called out to deal with an **inkjet printer**, the problems you may encounter include:

- paper jam
- ink being spilt or sprayed
- loss of colour or certain colours
- misaligned output
- no output
- stripes in output
- grinding sound.

Line printers are often used for continuous stationery such as invoices, despatch notes and wage slips. They are used commercially, but rarely in the home. If called to deal with a **line printer**, the problems you may encounter include:

- tractor feed not holding the paper
- head jammed
- head lost contact with the ink ribbon.

(a)   (b)

▲ **FIGURE 2.54** *Printers: (a) Laser (b) Inkjet*

Most users depend on the printer and see it as a major investment in computer resources, so it is important to be able to resolve printer problems.

While faults differ according to the printer technology, the solutions can be summarised:

● When you have a paper jam, carefully and systematically remove the paper and any debris from the printer. Open all doors and lift all flaps/covers. Take care not to make contact with the printing mechanism; this can be hot (in the case of a laser printer) or create a mess (as in an inkjet printer). Reload the paper, placing it in the paper tray and ensuring there are no creased or damaged sheets.

● If there is a problem with ink or toner, run the printer through a cleaning cycle. If it is an inkjet printer, use a piece of paper towel to clean the head; with a laser printer, shake the toner cartridge several times according to the manufacturer's instructions; and for a line printer, simply change the ribbon, which comes in a cartridge.

● Most printers are not user serviceable. So, if the printer is making an inappropriate sound, once you have eliminated a paper jam, send it to a suitably qualified professional, whom the manufacturer recommends. If you try to dismantle a printer, you will have difficulty in reassembling it.

● If there is no output, or the output you receive is 'garbled', the likely issues are: no driver, wrong driver, fault with the connector on the PC or printer, or a faulty printer cable. Driver reinstallation is simple, and can be done with the resources provided from the manufacturer's CD or website. Printer cables are not expensive and are easy to replace; most systems now use USB. Faults with connectors are more problematic as they are directly soldered onto the board of the PC.

Practical task

1 Open Windows. Go to Start/Settings/Printer. Click on the Printer menu (Figure 2.55).

▲ FIGURE 2.55 *Printers*

2 Right-click on one of the printers that is installed on your system and select the Properties option.

3 Click on Print Test Page (Figure 2.56) and check the quality of the print out.

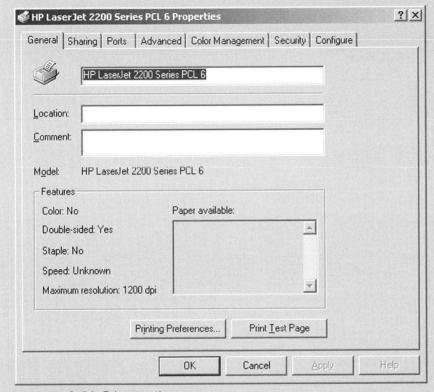

▲ **FIGURE 2.56** *Printer options*

4 If your printer offers you the opportunity to change the printer preferences, click on this option and look at what you may be able to achieve.

A printer is a mechanical device that needs software installed in the host operating system to control it. Each printer has a **unique driver** written specifically for the version of the operating system installed on your computer.

If the wrong driver is installed or the driver has become damaged or deleted, then the printer is likely to:

- display garbled message
- do nothing!

When you install a printer which is older than the operating system, Windows may detect the printer and offer the correct driver. However, if the printer is more advanced than the operating system, you will most likely need to install the printer driver for the new printer.

When you right-click on the Printer/Properties (Figure 2.57), you also have an option that enables you to change the printer driver (Figure 2.58).

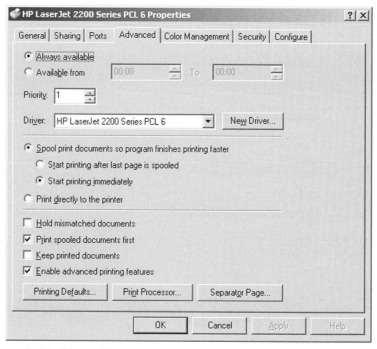

▲ FIGURE 2.57 *Printer driver options*

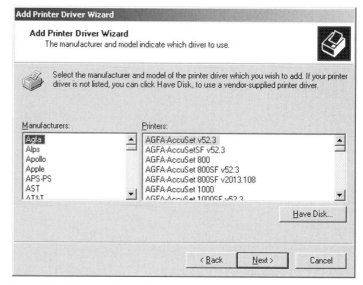

▲ FIGURE 2.58 *Printer driver wizard*

Practical task

1 Using the printer installed on your system, find and click on the Printer Driver option. Using the Hardware/Driver wizard, change the printer driver to one that is unrelated to the printer that you are running.

2 Once complete, attempt to print. Does it work? What is the result?

Liaise with clients to gather relevant information

Gathering information from customers is an essential part of the troubleshooting and fault-finding process. These are the reasons why:

- They may be the cause of the fault!
- They are often the person who spots the fault.
- They may be the last person who operated the system before the fault occurred.
- They witnessed the fault occurring for the first time.
- They are more likely than anyone else to know the computer system involved.

Given that your job depends on the customer being satisfied with your level of service and good manners, the way you communicate with and 'handle' the customer is essential.

▲ FIGURE 2.59 *Computer professional repairing a computer system*

You may have to gather information from the customer over the phone, via email or a written letter/memo. Sometimes, it is from face-to-face discussion. Remember, although you have more technical knowledge than the customer, you must be patient and treat them with respect. After all, the customer you are dealing with may be a senior member of staff in an organisation or company. You need to see yourself as an ambassador for your team and profession, and make sure that you do not patronise the customer, even if it is their fault.

Establish with the customer what the cause of the problem is:

- Establish the kind of environment the computer system operates in. This has an impact on the performance of some systems. You need to find out if:
  - the environment is dusty
  - there is air conditioning
  - conditions are humid
  - the temperatures are very low or too high.
- Help the customer to give you enough information so that you can recognise the symptoms/error codes, thus enabling you to come prepared with the correct replacement components, software or fault-finding resource.
- As much as possible, use non-technical terms to discuss the problem with the customer, whose explanation may be correct, but not accurate. Use their experience to diagnose the issue. 'It makes a groaning sound' could describe the processor fan or a hard drive failure. Such a non-technical description may help you by eliminating time-consuming checks and tests.
- Establish when the problem occurred, what the situation was, what the computer system was being used for and how it was operating prior to the problem.

Check your understanding

1 What would you do if there was a recurring problem in a computer that you couldn't solve?

2 How do you detect that a computer has a memory problem? How might you solve it?

3 What problems are you likely to encounter with components such as CD-ROMs and CD-Writers? What checks would you make in the system to detect these?

4 Given you have customer with a computer problem, how would you go about obtaining information from that customer as part of the troubleshooting process in finding out what the problem is?

5 What problems might you face with printers? How would you solve them?

2.3 Identify repair options and select the most appropriate option

Unit 4 discusses the techniques involved in system repair and installation and supports this section.

Hardware methods of upgrading/improving system performance

You may have to deal with a computer system that no longer performs to expectations, its components are reaching the end of their life expectancy, the software demands higher specification devices, and there is need for more storage, quality or memory. If you are considering a hardware solution:

- you can do a comprehensive troubleshoot to find out whether you need to upgrade/replace hardware to improve system performance
- you could first of all do routine maintenance to establish if you do need to replace the system
- you can look at what hardware resources may need replacing, rather than replace the whole system.

It is essential you look carefully at all the possible methods of upgrading a computer system hardware; many factors are involved. These include identifying the need to:

- replace external devices such as keyboards, mice, monitor or printers to improve quality or usability
- replace the computer system to bring the minimum specification of the system in line with current technology
- replace the operating system to ensure compatibility with common systems and software
- add more memory to improve performance of the existing system
- replace or update specific applications to improve use, quality or relevance
- add a larger hard drive to improve storage and also system performance
- replace the graphics card, which will improve performance as well as quality of output
- replace components for current technological developments (such as adding a wireless card).

This may be based on a technological need, in that the computer system is in need of improvement, or there may be a business need, in that the commercial use of the computer system now exceeds the specification of the computer system. A personal need, where the use of the computer system requires an improvement to the computer system, is when the individual desires the improvement.

Many companies will have suitable procedures on how and when to replace devices when an upgrade has been identified. This will differ for each company you encounter. The following are the most common needs for upgrades:

- The upgrade, if minor, will be carried out immediately as the department requiring it will pay for it.
- The upgrade, if related to a commercial need, will take place immediately.
- If the computer system requires complete replacement, this tends to be done once every three years (or longer).
- If the upgrade is related to a personal need, it will be ranked according to importance.

Each task will have a set of instructions on when this is to be completed, who can authorise it and how it is to be accomplished.

The need for a systematic approach to troubleshooting problems

Take your time to think through the problem to discover what is wrong and how it might be corrected. Ask yourself these questions:

- What is happening?
- What could the fault be caused by?
- What is the faulty component controlled by?
- What is the faulty component connected to?

Figure 2.60 shows the kind of problems you may have to deal with.

- **It won't print** This could be caused by the printer's drivers not being installed, the wrong drivers for the printer being installed, the printer not being switched on, a faulty cable or faulty printer, or it may need ink or paper.
- **It won't boot or keeps beeping** The keyboard may have a button stuck down. There may be a fault with the processor, BIOS or motherboard (see beep codes indicating faults on page 297).

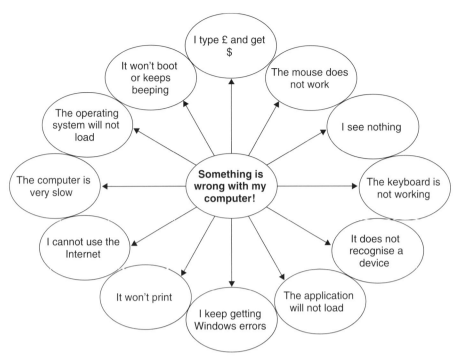

▲ FIGURE 2.60 *Fault finding*

- **You type £ and see $** Have you the wrong regional settings? The default for Windows is the United States, so go into the control panel and set it to UK (English).

- **The mouse does not work** Is it connected? Does it need replacing? Is there a fault with the PS2 serial port? Is Windows detecting it? If it is a wireless mouse, is it fully charged?

- **You see nothing** Have you switched the monitor on? Is the monitor faulty? Is the graphics card faulty? Have you plugged the monitor into the graphics card?

- **The keyboard is not working** Is it plugged in? Have you connected it to the right port (you can mistakenly insert it into the PS2 mouse port)? Does it need replacing?

- **It does not recognise a device** Have you installed the appropriate drivers? Is the device working correctly on another system? Will your version of Windows work with the device? Is it plugged in correctly?

- **The application will not load** Is the link working correctly? Has it been deleted or uninstalled incorrectly? Is there a licensing issue? Is there a conflict with another application? Is there enough memory for the application to run correctly?

- **You keep getting Windows errors** Is there enough hard drive space? Do you have enough memory on your system? Is there a virus? Has something been removed?

- **You cannot use the Internet** Is your network/Internet connection working correctly (you may need to get information from someone else to ascertain this)? Is your operating system's network settings correctly configured? Has anyone removed or changed the cable?
- **The computer is very slow** You may have a hard drive memory or virus issue, or you may be expecting your computer to run too many applications at once.
- **The operating system will not load** You may have an issue with memory or the hard drive. If you can start the operating system in safe mode, then you may be able to resolve the problem. Otherwise, you may need to reinstall the system.

Once you have read Unit 3, you should be able to solve most of the above issues.

Practical task

If your study centre has a PC repair facility, arrange suitable supervision so that you can work on an old computer and complete a series of fault-finding tasks.

1 Look for:

- issues with the PC hardware
- issues with the operating system
- issues with any applications.

2 Ask yourself these questions:

- Does it take a long time to start?
- Are any parts of the system running too slow?
- Are there any issues with the display?
- Are there any issues with the keyboard or mouse?
- Are there any error messages?
- Are there too many applications in startup?
- Are all additional facilities working correctly?

Repair, fault finding and preventative maintenance rely on technical experience and common sense. An experienced engineer can often pinpoint a problem simply because they have encountered it previously.

Through time, you will adopt common systematic techniques in diagnosing faults on any computer system. Figure 2.61 is a flowchart for fault diagnosis on a standard computer system.

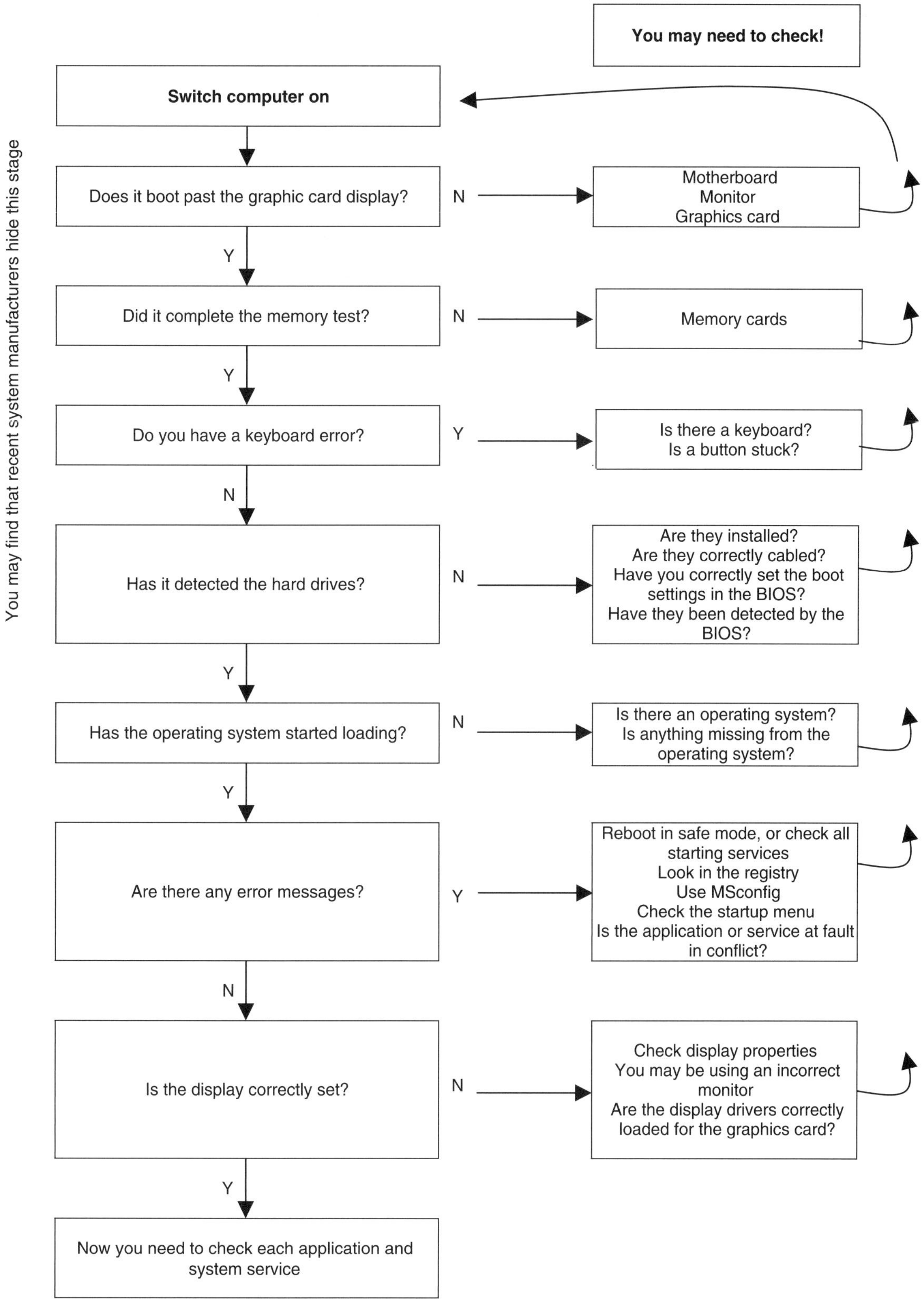

You may need to check!

Switch computer on	
Does it boot past the graphic card display?	N → Motherboard / Monitor / Graphics card
Did it complete the memory test?	N → Memory cards
Do you have a keyboard error?	Y → Is there a keyboard? / Is a button stuck?
Has it detected the hard drives?	N → Are they installed? / Are they correctly cabled? / Have you correctly set the boot settings in the BIOS? / Have they been detected by the BIOS?
Has the operating system started loading?	N → Is there an operating system? / Is anything missing from the operating system?
Are there any error messages?	Y → Reboot in safe mode, or check all starting services / Look in the registry / Use MSconfig / Check the startup menu / Is the application or service at fault in conflict?
Is the display correctly set?	N → Check display properties / You may be using an incorrect monitor / Are the display drivers correctly loaded for the graphics card?
Now you need to check each application and system service	

You may find that recent system manufacturers hide this stage

Notes:
1 No matter how experienced you may become, there are always new and unusual faults that will occur that you cannot prepare for.
2 You may wish to use this chart in section 2.4 (see page 161).

▲ FIGURE 2.61 *Systematic fault diagnosis*

To maintain your skills and develop good diagnostic routines, adopt these tactics:

- Maintain your knowledge of new developments in the computer hardware and software sectors.
- Be prepared to try out new operating systems, components and applications as they appear on the market.
- Keep yourself up to date by reading manuals, textbooks, guides and websites on new products.
- Keep in touch with new developments, including interesting variations on technology and where technologies merge. Keep an open mind and be prepared not to dismiss a manufacturer's attempt to revise technology, as often happens. The variation could become the innovation; for example, optical mice have been available for over fifteen years and have only become commonplace in the last two.
- Ensure that you are also aware of the limitations of the technology. Overloading processors, memory and hard drives have ruined many a good computer and an engineer's reputation.
- Remember that learning does not finish at school or college. Taking courses in technology and maintaining or attaining certification are the marks of a professional in the computer industry.

Go out and try!

Achieving professional certification is the difference between making a career in computing or it being 'just a job'. Leaders in the computer industry, such as Microsoft, Cisco, Novell and CompTIA, all provide a wide range of professional courses that are suitable for an engineer like you.

1 Visit the following websites:

- cisco.netacad.net
- www.comptia.org
- www.microsoft.com/traincert/
- www.novell.com/training/

2 From the information available:

- list the certifications that can be completed and the industry sector that they can help you in
- check if your school or college is offering any of the qualifications – you may find that they are an academy for Cisco, Microsoft or CompTIA.

There are a wide range of troubleshooting tools and techniques at your disposal. Searching the Internet or the shelves of your local computer retailer can be productive. You may expect to find:

- PC hardware diagnostic software
- registry checking and management software
- diagnostic tools to check software.

PC hardware diagnostic software will run a series of comprehensive tests on your system to check whether each component is operating as expected. Normally, you will expect PC hardware diagnostic software to check:

- motherboard, including the microprocessor, any maths co-processor, DMA, IDE, PCI, AGP controllers and the real-time clock
- video alignment and management for the monitor
- video adapter tests, checking the resolution, colour depth and speed
- parallel port tests
- serial port tests
- disk drive tests (drives A and B), checking access and read times
- fixed disk tests (hard drives 1 and 2), checking access and seek times
- main memory tests, completing a variety of tests to check all the memory and access quality.

Registry checking and management software is required, because through time, the Windows registry can become cumbersome and overloaded with 'valueless' information.

A comprehensive introduction to the registry is given in Unit 4 (page 261).

Go out and try!

There are many websites that provide comprehensive information for managing and editing the registry. Go to www.regedit.com and review the different ways you can amend the performance of Windows through regedit.

Diagnostic tools to check software are used for select applications, especially where the application is complex. Some graphical, programming or database systems require maintenance to ensure their continued successful use.

Procedures for replacing components and when to use them

Replacing components is only needed when these problems occur:

- The component is damaged or faulty; this may be replaced under warranty or require the purchase of a similar specification component.
- The device in question is no longer capable of managing the task it has been given because:
  - the hard drive may now be too small
  - the CD/DVD system may be too slow
  - the memory is now too small
  - the printer specification is now better.
- The usage requirements has changed because:
  - the keyboard has to be for someone with an accessibility need
  - the application demands a certain level of resources, especially with the quality of graphics and sound.

Go out and try!

For the latest PC game on the market, look at the specification and list how it may affect one of the computers at your centre of learning. What upgrade may be required?

Factors to consider when evaluating the most appropriate repair and upgrade option

Repair and upgrade solutions may incur more problems, rather than solve the ones you had to deal with.

When deciding the upgrade solution, consider these issues:

- Is the cost of the upgrade required economic? Can the customer afford it? Is it a better investment than a replacement system?
- Is the component replaceable? Is it a technology that has been superseded? If there is a new alternative, will the current system support it?
- Will any new processor work with the slot/voltage specification of the existing motherboard?
- Is the replacement component technically suitable? With some replacement technologies, you have to read the manufacturer's specifications to ensure that it provides what is required.

2.4 Take actions to rectify faults, including referral, and confirm that faults have been rectified

Procedures for rectifying faults

It is important that you use the different systematic fault-finding and troubleshooting techniques to rectify faults (page 115–150).

Standard repair procedures are needed:

- to ensure that tasks are performed to the same standards by all staff
- to reduce the likelihood of error
- to provide a reference guide for staff having to deal with a certain problem for the first time.

Go out and try!

The repair and replacement of each component of a computer system can be described as a sequence of instructions. How would you describe these tasks to someone who is non-technical?

- Upgrading the hard drive
- Replacing the memory
- Installing a new CD/DVD-Rewriter
- Adding a new sound card
- Replacing the display adapter

In Unit 4 (page 293), you will explore in detail the process of testing different systems and laying down an appropriate test. This will enable you to rectify faults in accordance with the manufacturers' and the health and safety guidelines by thorough testing of the system, and to document the faults in a professional way.

Maintaining accurate repair records

Without repair records, you will be unable to keep track of a computer system as well as a user. By maintaining accurate records, you can identify:

- how often a computer fails
- how often problems occur for a specific user
- whether failures are restricted to one customer, site or department
- whether failures are restricted to a certain model of computer system or type of component.

By analysing these records, you or your line management may be able to ascertain:

- whether training is required for a specific user (or users)
- whether there is a need to redefine the hardware specification on purchase of new systems
- whether legal action needs to be taken against a supplier or customer
- whether you need to carefully consider the costs for future support contracts.

2.5 Bring repaired equipment back into service

To repair a computer you may have to remove it from site to carry out the repair yourself or, in special cases, you may have to send it to a manufacturer's/supplier's approved repair centre for the work to be carried out.

In these cases, you have to commission a 'spare' or 'backup' computer so that the user can continue to do their work with the same software as the faulty system.

Go out and try!

Many companies selling PCs use a specific process for handling repairs. Search the web for a range of retailers, or visit local retailers in your region and discover what their usual process for handling repairs is.

Pay close attention to the detail, as this may indicate which companies have the best after-sales support, which can make use of your computer less frustrating.

▲ FIGURE 2.62 *Customer discussing their computer problems with computer advisor*

Commissioning repaired equipment

Once the computer has been repaired, you have to complete a quality assurance process to check whether the computer is working as it should. If it isn't, you need to complete the repair or return it to the manufacturer's/supplier's approved centre for them to complete.

The quality assurance process involves completing a comprehensive test of the computer system; this is an integral part of section 4.3 (page 293).

Go out and try!

Based on the section on testing in Unit 4 (page 293), complete a comprehensive test using the recommended software.

Inform customer that repaired equipment is ready for service

Even though the computer is ready, the customer may not be. They may be very busy, so you need to talk to them about arranging a mutually acceptable time for the reinstallation of their computer system.

As a computer maintenance professional, you may be working with customers who:

- work on the same site
- work at home
- work in other companies
- work during the day
- work shifts
- cannot afford to have their work disturbed.

The completed customer satisfaction form

The customer satisfaction form is an important tool used by line management to ascertain the quality of service the company (as well as you) provides. It is designed to find out how customers feel and to highlight concerns as well as satisfactions.

A good customer survey scores the level of quality, which is based on an odd number that can easily be multiplied/divided. This may be a 1–5 scale (Table 2.2), where 1 is poor and 5 excellent. When the scores are added they may indicate a positive result.

1	2	3	4	5
Poor	Unsatisfactory	Satisfactory	Good	Excellent

TABLE 2.2 *1-5 scale*

For example, in the questionnaire in Figure 2.63, totalling the marks gives an overall result.

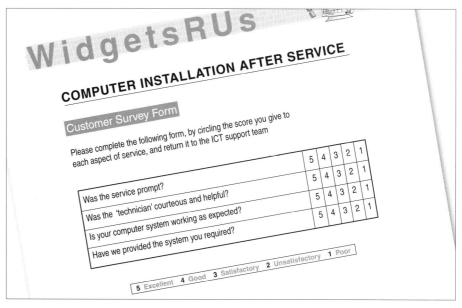

▲ FIGURE 2.63 *Customer survey example*

You can see from the survey that the support technician identified by the customer number may have scored 15 (by adding the columns together), but failed considerably in their 'treatment' of the customer and successful completion of the task. Such a survey would initiate a new visit, possibly by another technician, and an apology by a line manager.

Having collected information from the customer, it needs to be analysed and the results should lead to action points. The forms can identify whether there are any training requirements to be addressed by the company or a need for continued professional development of the employees. The completed customer form is an essential component of the quality assurance process, but it is also a valuable part of the training and customer relations area of the business.

Collection of comments from the customer can be done by paper-based forms, email forms, web-based forms, or even by a telephone conversation where the form is filled in by the telephone receptionist.

Go out and try!

Many websites use customer feedback to measure the quality of their service. This may be via a web-based form or an email. Look at different approaches companies have to extracting suitable feedback from the customer. Ask yourself the following questions:

1 Would I be happy to complete this questionnaire?
2 What do I gain from completing this form?
3 Will my views be acted upon by the company?
4 How can I complain?
5 Is the form easy to complete?
6 Did the form take too long to complete?

2.6 Check the effectiveness of preventative and remedial maintenance procedures

Preventative maintenance is done before anything goes wrong in an attempt to prevent it from going wrong. There will be procedures that need to be followed. These may include monthly checks and cleaning of the computer.

A review should be done to establish how effective these procedures are. If procedures are followed and there is no monitoring or review, then there is no way of knowing if they are having an effect.

Regular monitoring is to ensure that procedures are being done. If decisions are made based on the results of preventative maintenance, but the maintenance is not being done, then the decisions will be unlikely to be in the best interests of the company.

The review will cover aspects such as:

- What is the impact on repair, upgrade and replacement of the components that are part of the preventative maintenance procedures?
- Do the procedures have an impact on prolonging the life of the components?
- Is the time devoted to the preventative maintenance cost-effective or is it cheaper to ignore preventative maintenance and concentrate on remedial maintenance?

It may be that a change in the procedures has a big impact and if so, this needs to be monitored and documented.

Monitor and review the effectiveness of preventative maintenance procedures

You need to do a review of whatever work you carry out. On a computer system, this is important to determine:

- whether the work has been done to the best standards
- whether there may be a recurring fault which requires more detailed analysis of the equipment involved
- whether a department or a user may have a training need, which can be identified through the frequency of their requests
- whether there may be an issue with the technician who needs either training or discipline.

The volume of work in your department may dictate the frequency of checking that takes place. In many organisations, checking the customer feedback takes place monthly, quarterly (every three months) and once a year.

Check your understanding

1 List some of the problems that you may have to troubleshoot in identifying and selecting the most appropriate repair or upgrading options.
2 What factors do you have to consider in evaluating and deciding the most appropriate repair/upgrade option?
3 Why should you follow standard repair procedures and maintain accurate repair records?
4 What procedures should you follow to make sure you have repaired a computer?
5 How should you review and monitor prevention and remedial procedures?

Assignment

This assignment is in six parts.

Part 1

You are to carry out a preventative and remedial maintenance on a computer system.
In your college or place of work, you will work on a computer system for a customer and complete a sequence of essential maintenance activities.

First, you need to identify the purpose behind performing remedial and preventative maintenance.

This needs to be followed by some instructions on how to actually perform preventative and remedial maintenance. This should include details on some actual maintenance that could be performed.

As part of the procedures for remedial and preventative maintenance, you need to write about the following:

- Laser safety procedures – what are they?
- Why do we need to maintain accurate safety records, including MSDS records?
- What different liquid cleansing components exist and what are they used on?
- How should batteries, CRTS toner kits and chemical solvents be disposed of?
- What is ESD and how is it prevented?

Once you have completed the procedures you will need to carry out some preventative maintenance.

This may be to:

- clean the processor fan
- clean the keyboard
- clean the mouse.

You also need to carry out remedial maintenance. To do this, you need to upgrade at least one old component (adding more memory is often the easiest upgrade to install).

Create and keep a record of the preventative maintenance you have completed for the computer system, and include appropriate and remedial action in the record.

Part 2

In this part, you will create a basic guide for a technician to follow. The guide needs to list how to identify common faults that may occur on communication systems and basic repair options.

Faults could include:

- no network signal
- mouse not working
- keys on keyboard not working.

Part 3

Here, you will carry out the following tasks:

- Create and use a data collection form to collect information from customers on what is wrong with their computer.
- Describe in writing how you would confirm the fault.
- Carry out tasks to confirm the fault.
- Describe the procedures that are in place when deciding whether to replace, repair or upgrade a component.
- Describe the factors you considered in selecting the most appropriate repair solution.
- Describe in writing how you will upgrade the computer system and repair the fault.

Part 4

At this stage, you are to show how to detect and rectify faults in a computer system. You will carry out the following tasks:

- Demonstrate how to locate a fault.
- With the help of a tutor/supervisor, resolve the fault.
- Devise a suitable test plan to demonstrate that the fault has been rectified.
- Run the tests and provide evidence that each test has been run.

Part 5

Here, you are to create a customer survey form, based on the one in Figure 2.63, that accurately reflects the environment in your college/workplace. You are then to ask your customer to complete the form.

Remember, you must ensure that a tutor/supervisor approves the customer survey before you use it.

Part 6

From the feedback you receive from the customer survey form, consider the results and, in no more than 500 words, describe what the customer thought of the service you provided and say how you think you can improve the service. You must include both preventative and remedial procedures in your evaluation.

3 Installing Hardware/ Equipment and Systems

INTRODUCTION

In this unit, you will explore the skills involved in installing, repairing and upgrading a computer system, as well as develop an understanding of how the technology works. The main emphasis will be on personal computer systems.

Learning outcomes

In completing this unit, you will achieve these learning outcomes:

- Install the principal components of information and communications technology.
- Carry out testing and address problems when installing hardware, equipment and systems.
- Remove, transport and store equipment.

How the unit will be assessed

This unit is assessed through practical activities by a local assessor and externally moderated. You need to complete the tasks covering all the assessment objectives and to show evidence that the objectives have been achieved. For this, you need to complete OCR forms showing what and how the objectives have been met.

Carry out pre-installation activities

Before installing a computer system, you will need to understand pre-installation activities:

- The safety considerations for location, access and positioning of item
- Surveying the site, taking into account the power supplies, networking cables and components such as switch and telephone lines
- The suitability of hardware
- Checking packaging before opening and keeping a record of the contents
- Precautions needed, such as anti-static handling
- The potential for harm to users or installers due to carrying or use of equipment
- The mains supply provision, networking requirements, telephone for help line
- Ensuring that the computer will meet task needs by working in the environment
- Cabling and connector requirements, network links, cabling terminators (D, Centronics, RJ45), ports to be used (serial, parallel, USB)

Safety considerations for location, access and positioning of item

The placing of computer equipment can have a harmful effect on the user, or cause a major inconvenience in the use of the computer system.

When installing a computer system, ask yourself these questions:

- Are the monitor, mouse and keyboard accessible?
- Is there too much glare on the monitor?
- Can the monitor be seen by all of those who need to?
- Is the layout ergonomic?

Making sure you have easy access to the computer and enough space to use the keyboard and mouse, are crucial to being able to use the computer efficiently. To prevent problems such as RSI, joint and back strains, the monitor and keyboard need to be at the appropriate height and distance. The seating also needs to be appropriate in comfort and support, and there must be reasonable desk space.

GLOSSARY

Ergonomic is the applied science of equipment design and layout to improve our comfort through use.

Ergonomics encourages you to position a computer to suit the user. You can make sure, by checking it out yourself once the seating and equipment are in place.

The factors you need to consider when installing a computer at someone's desk are identified in Figure 3.1.

Ensure that the user can comfortably view the monitor.

Ensure that the user can sit comfortably and has appropriate back support.

Ensure that the keyboard/mouse is in a position that makes it comfortable for the user.

▲ FIGURE 3.1 *The correct position for working at a computer*

You need to make sure a monitor is positioned so there is no glare on the screen. This means placing it to avoid interference from natural or artificial light. This makes it easier for the user to read and see what is on the screen and helps avoid eye strain.

Where monitors are accessed by more than one person at a time, they need to be positioned where there is enough room for people to view it. So, when installing computer equipment you need to find out how many people will be using it and where it should ideally be positioned.

Computer equipment needs to be positioned so that it is not a danger to users. A monitor or base unit, for example, needs to be securely balanced and not likely to fall over and the support for the system, such as an office desk, needs to be strong enough to support the weight.

Survey site, considering power supplies, networking cables and components such as switch and telephone lines

Computers need power (electricity) and so need to be positioned within reach of a power outlet.

When fitting a computer and connecting it to a power supply:

- do not leave trailing wires, as this will pose a trip hazard
- do not overload a single socket, as this is an electrical and fire hazard.

If the computer has a modem/network connection, it must be within easy reach of the power connection sockets. When installing communication cables, consider:

- the absence of interference from external electrical sources, such as photocopiers, lighting, motors, etc.
- the distance travelled by the cable.

Suitability of hardware

The hardware you install needs to be compatible. You can check this against the information on the packaging before you open it:

- Is the device's connector compatible with your system? (It's no good having firewire if you do not have a firewire port.)
- Is the hardware's configuration compatible with the technology your system is using (bus speeds, etc.)?
- Is there a minimum processor requirement?
- Is there a minimum operating system requirement?
- Is there a minimum memory requirement?
- Is there a demand on hard drive resources?
- Does the system need any other specialist components for the one you are installing in order to work?

If an organisation acquires a large quantity of incorrect and incompatible equipment, this may cause:

- serious delays
- financial loss through time or the possession of equipment that is unneeded
- embarrassment.

When ordering, specifying or receiving and installing equipment, it is essential that you check that:

- the processor is compatible with the motherboard, through connector type, voltage, and clock speed

GLOSSARY

Bus is a communication channel used for data.

- the power supply for the same unit is compatible with the motherboard
- the organisation's electricity supply is compatible with the technology being used
- the firmware for the BIOS or other components is capable of supporting the existing technology
- the device interfaces are compatible with the system bus available, for example having an AGP card is useless when the motherboard only has PCI slots
- the external interfaces are compatible with externally connecting devices.

While unlikely, you may need to check the compatibility of the BIOS. The BIOS has an inbuilt computer program (often referred to as firmware) designed to manage a range of technologies available at the time the system was built and it will manage a limited range of upgrades.

In rare cases, a new system may need a hard drive upgrade within a short time. The hard drive may then be at a capacity beyond the recognition of the BIOS. To enable the BIOS to 'handle' the new equipment, you need to go to the manufacturer's website to download the software to flash (upgrade the firmware) the BIOS.

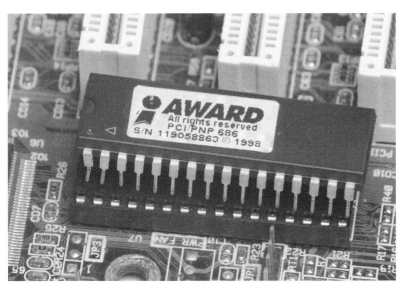

▲ FIGURE 3.2 *BIOS*

If everything is compatible, does the system have enough serial interfaces? Are they the right type for the devices that are used? For example, if your system has two USB interfaces, and you have a USB mouse, keyboard, scanner and printer, you have a 'sockets to plugs' issue that can only be resolved by purchasing a USB hub. While this may sound simple, imagine what will happen if this is translated to a company that has just acquired 100 such systems. The surplus cost will cause serious financial issues which can be career limiting.

Component	Specification	Cost	Manufacturer
ATX case	Must cost no more than £20		
Motherboard	Must support an AMD processor and have onboard, AGP, modem, sound and network card		
Processor	With an AMD Athlon or Duron (or whatever the current equivalent product is) at the lowest possible speed		
Memory	Must be at least 512 MB and be compatible with the motherboard		
DVD-ROM	Obtain the lowest cost device		
CD-Writer	Obtain the lowest cost device		
Floppy disk drive	Must cost less than £6		
Hard disk drive	Must be IDE and cost less than £60 (What is the largest capacity you can obtain?)		
Monitor	Must be a 17-inch CRT and cost less than £80		
Speakers or headphones	Must cost no more than £5		
Mouse	Must be a standard ball mouse and have a scrolling wheel and cost less than £2		
Keyboard	Standard 105 key and cost less than £4		
	TOTAL		

▲ TABLE 3.1 *Computer components shopping list*

The finance director of your company, WidgetsRUs, in an attempt to save costs, has purchased a wide range of computer systems and components that were offered at a heavily discounted price because they were 'end of line' stock.

When the equipment is delivered, you discover that the technology is incompatible with existing systems and that the contract signed by the finance director for purchase prevents you from returning the equipment.

The problem has reached senior management and they are reviewing the career of the finance director. You have been asked to compose a short report (no more than 500 words) to assist their decision, answering these questions.

- What checks did you make to ensure that the serial, USB, parallel and sound connectors were compatible?
- What checks did you make to ensure that the hard drive connectors were compatible?
- How did you know the current version of the firmware for the BIOS?
- How did you check the compatibility of the power supply?

NOTE!

You may wish to use images or diagrams in your report.

Reasons for checking packaging before opening and keeping a record

Any damage to the packaging of goods in transit to a customer raises the possibility that the contents of the package may also be damaged. In such cases, the goods should be carefully checked. If the goods are a computer or a component of a computer, you should carefully check the internal component for damage and send it back if there is anything wrong. If the damage is superficial (e.g. on the exterior of a monitor or computer case) you should try to negotiate a discount.

Go out and try!

1 Examine the packaging of any computer hardware that you recently received and still have. What sort of packaging is used?

2 Consider each of these packaging options.

- Solid polystyrene baffle
- Polystyrene chips or beans
- Air bags
- Bubble wrap
- Shredded paper
- Recycled cardboard baffle

Which do you consider best for each component of your computer system?

▲ FIGURE 3.3 *Various component boxes*

On taking delivery of equipment, check the packaging before you sign the delivery receipt. When you unpack the equipment, check it for obvious damage. If there is damage, do not install or use the equipment.

You should not use any equipment that is damaged. However, given that damage to computer equipment may be microscopic, and therefore cannot be seen, you may only detect such damage when you use the resource.

The motherboard is one component on which such minute faults may occur, for example:

● when the motherboard is dropped
● when the surface is bent through stress by someone trying to force the motherboard into a box or a computer
● when the intricate surface tracks are scratched
● when the motherboard becomes too warm (as in the height of summer in a place that has no air conditioning) and heat expansion causes damage
● when the motherboard has been exposed to extreme cold (as in international transit) and contraction has caused damage.

Given such problems, you must contact the supplier or the manufacturer to demand a replacement, which you are entitled to under UK law, of exactly the same specification. This may involve the supplier/manufacturer shipping a new part, and your shipping back the faulty component.

Of course, any issues of goods being damaged in transit, could mean:

- **delays in the installation** of the system, which in turn leads to missed deadlines for which your employer may be financially liable
- **customer dissatisfaction**, which may lead to legal action, loss of future business, or worse, loss of reputation among other customers
- the installation of a temporary solution while the replacement is being sent, which will incur indirect and **increased support costs**, making the work less profitable.

In the case of damage, you need to record and report what has happened. You may have to write a comprehensive report on the damage and provide a verbal description of the problem so that this can be copied to a supervisor or manager who will handle the matter. You could also photograph the damage as evidence.

You should record and report any damage:

- to minimise any chance of the problem recurring, in that the organisation or, hopefully, the supplier learns from the experience
- to keep an audit trail of issues allows any project supervisors to clearly identify what may have caused problems
- to enable the financial managers to check they are not charged twice for any component and solidus and/or that they have received the discount negotiated for the inconvenience caused.

If there is a problem with the design of the packaging, or even the component, then the original supplier or manufacturer can be informed so that they can rectify the issue and possibly modify the design.

CASE STUDY - Checking a report

WidgetsRUs has recently acquired new premises in Bramingham, a suburb of Luton, where your employer PC Incorporated has won the contract to install 150 computers on site that will support a variety of commercial functions.

As team leader, you are responsible for the installation of the computers on delivery at WidgetsRUs, along with three others.

On the day that the delivery is expected, you are phoned by the manufacturer who informs you that only 90 of the 150 computers are ready; the others will be delivered three days late but with a 10% discount on cost.

The 90 computers arrive on time but the packaging of the base units and monitors have been damaged.

Write a short report of no more than 1000 words that explains:

- what you need to tell your line manager
- how you are going to report this problem of delay in some of the computers to the customer and how you are going to resolve any potential customer dissatisfaction
- the issues involved in the delivery of 60 computers being delayed
- the issues involved by the visible external damage (and the possibility of unseen damage and the consequences of this)
- the costs that may be incurred by these problems.

Once you have completed the report, list in a separate document:

- how you would check for broken security seals
- what checks you would make for any damaged packaging
- what a tilt/shock indicator would show.

Precautions such as anti-static handling

How you protect computer devices depends on how sensitive or robust they are. What you need to protect them from includes shock and anti-static, from whomever handles the equipment.

Printed circuit boards (motherboards, memory and any additional cards) are very fragile and must only be handled at the edges. They should be transported in an anti-static bag in a protective cardboard carton (Figure 3.4).

▲ FIGURE 3.4 *Motherboard with anti-static bag*

Disk drives and **CD/DVD/ROM/RW** drives must also be protected with an anti-static bag (Figure 3.5). In addition, because they have small motor assemblies and sensitive read/write mechanisms, they must be transported in a foam casing to absorb any impact, even a minor one.

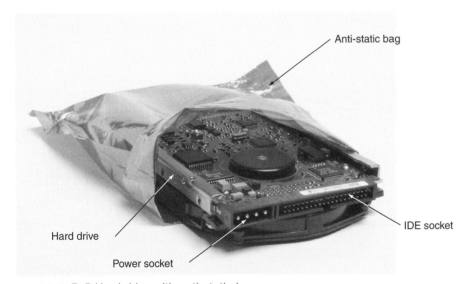

Anti-static bag

Hard drive

Power socket

IDE socket

▲ FIGURE 3.5 *Hard drive with anti-static bag*

The **CPU** must be transported in an anti-static bag and in a plastic form to protect the pins that connect the CPU to the motherboard.

▲ FIGURE 3.6 *CPU and plastic form*

The potential for harm to users or installers due to carrying or use of equipment

To avoid injury, you must make sure you lift an item correctly and seek help when required.

Unit 2 (page 99) covers the consequences of poor manual handling, both involving the correct lifting and the incorrect lifting of heavy or awkward equipment.

Mains supply provision, networking requirements, telephone for help line

The installation of a network computer in an organisation will require:

* the installation of a mains supply with a suitable fuse rating to cope with the load of all the computers and monitors, as well as printers
* the installation of LAN and WAN technology and cabling to ensure communication with the corporate network and the Internet
* the installation of phone lines, for modem connections or communication with other departments and support services.

Ensuring that the computer will meet task needs by working in the environment

The kind of environment in which computers are installed makes a difference as to how well they function.

GLOSSARY

LAN (local area network) is a network that connects computers in an organisation such as a school, college or place of work.

WAN (wide area network) is a network that connects many computer sites within an organisation. The Internet is a super-WAN.

Avoid installing computers:

- where it is **too dusty** – fine dust can compromise a computer system
- where it is **too hot** – heat will damage the processing capability of the computer as well as affect the storage media
- where it is **too cold** – any moisture that forms on the computer circuitry due to the low temperatures will immediately damage the system when the temperature rises
- where it is **too magnetic** – high voltage equipment, such as electricity generators, will affect the entire computer system.

If the conditions are extreme, you may have to recommend improvements. Otherwise, the computer system may not operate effectively.

Network links, cabling terminators (D, Centronics, RJ45), ports to be used (serial, parallel, USB)

The cables required for running a computer system can be damaged by excessive force in connecting them to the system. So, make sure that, for example, plug A will fit comfortably into slot A without having to force it in. If the connector does not fit, gently check the connection and look at any pins for possible damage. Occasionally, a manufacturer mistakenly provides the wrong cable or one already damaged.

On the rear of your computer (Figure 3.8), you will notice a variety of connectors:

- the **DB9** 9-pin connector (Figure 3.7), used for serial devices (mouse, connections to network management devices, etc.)

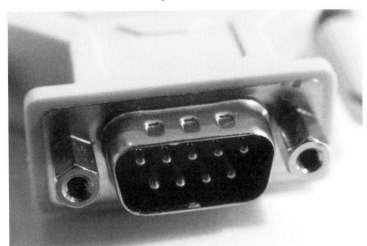

▲ FIGURE **3.7** *A DB9 9-pin connector*

- the **DB25**, a 25-pin connector, found on older computer systems, used to connect to external modems and other communications devices (and sometimes referred to as a RS232-C or EIA/TIA232-C)

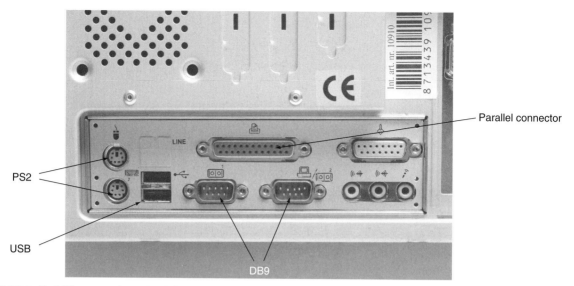

PS2

USB

Parallel connector

DB9

▲ FIGURE 3.8 *The rear view of a PC showing various connectors*

● the **PS/2 connector** used for the keyboard and mouse (different connections can be used for the same devices)

● the **USB connector** (Figure 3.9) used to connect network devices, printers, mice, keyboards and many more

▲ FIGURE 3.9 *USB connector*

● a **parallel connector** (Figure 3.10), once called a **Centronic** connector (after the name of the manufacturer), designed for the high data rates used for printers.

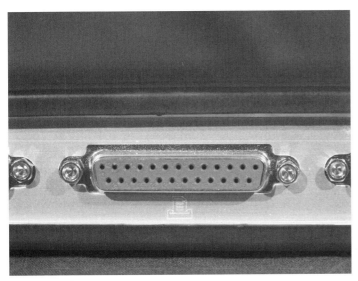
▲ FIGURE 3.10 *A printer port*

Carry out installation activities

Understanding how the components of a computer system operate and interact will improve your ability to solve problems when working as a professional. The systems described in this section were the ones current in 2005.

The computer is the **base unit**; the monitor, keyboard and mouse are **external devices** which enable you to use and interact with the computer system. The standard case of a computer is called an ATX form factor. These connectors on the rear of the base unit enable you to connect various devices of the system:

- **Power** This connects to a normal 240 V mains; you can also have a parasite cable which provides power for the monitor.
- **Fan** This cools the power supply.
- **Keyboard** and **mouse ports** The PS2 standard directly connects these to the system.
- **USB (universal serial bus) ports** You may find additional connectors on the front of some computer cases.
- **Printer** and **serial ports** These are used to connect various devices that can send and receive data to and from the computer system.
- **Monitor interface** Depending on the motherboard, you may have an inbuilt video system or an additional board to manage the signal being sent to the monitor.
- **Sound** and **game ports** These are connectors for your speakers and joystick/wheel if you need them.

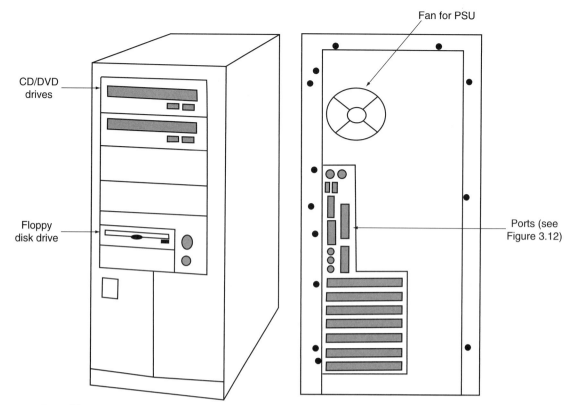

▲ FIGURE 3.11 *The externals of a computer*

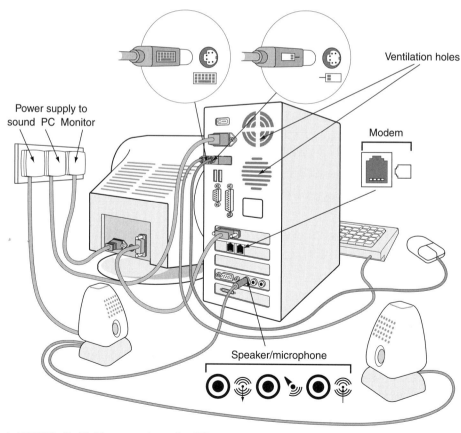

▲ FIGURE 3.12 *The rear view of a PC*

When you open a computer you will find:

- a **power supply**, which serves power to the motherboard, drives and other devices you may have connected inside your computer

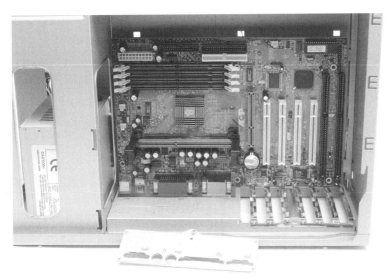

▲ FIGURE 3.13 *Inside a computer*

- **memory slots** for the cards that provide the system's main memory
- **drive bays** and device connectors for **CD/DVD**, **hard drive** and **floppy drive** systems, which provide the backing store
- the **motherboard** with **onboard chips**, **BIOS** and **battery**
- the **processor** connected to a **cooling fan**.

All **motherboards** will have a variety of expansion slots, which provide connections to various additional boards, video, USB, keyboard, mouse, serial and printer connectors.

Several activities need to be carried out during the installation of a computer system:

- The completion of records shows that you have received all the contents of the computer package, such as:
  - hardware
  - software
  - mains lead
  - components
  - cables
  - manuals.
- Remove all transportation materials. Some printers have many moving parts that have to be protected in transit. Most of the protective material comes in the form of tapes, table and small plastic baffles. The manufacturer will provide a guide to the removal of such protection. If you forget to remove any of it, the printer may not print.

- Check that the correct item has been sent. Some devices have many versions, so you need to be sure you have the right one. If you have the wrong one, it could seriously affect performance and use.
- Check the voltage setting and link to the mains supply. A 230–240 V setting is normal in the UK, so if the computer's power supply is set to 110 V, it will need checking and switching before connecting to the power supply.
- Ensure that the computer will link to the main system, which may be the network infrastructure.
- For some printers, you may need to carry out the self-test process on startup.
- Check for any visible damage.
- Ensure that all printed circuit boards, memory, other chips, drives, etc. are handled carefully.
- Ensure that any cooling needs, including processor fan, ventilation and air conditioning, are correctly installed and are operational.
- Check cables using a cable tester or simply swap the cable with a known working replacement.
- Report to the supplier or a line supervisor if an item is missing.

Installing a PC from the box

To install a pre-built computer system you will need:

- a monitor
- a keyboard
- a mouse
- power cables
- a processor base unit
- speakers and/or sound cables.

You will need to test the system, as explained in Unit 4 (pages 293–305).

If you receive the computer boxed, you will need to remove all the packaging, polystyrene baffles and any bags. The safe way is to open the top of the box and turn it upside down, so that the computer or monitor slides out.

You should keep the packaging until the computer is installed in case it has to be returned. Then you should dispose of the packaging in an ecological manner.

NOTE!

For testing purposes you may be asked only to install two applications/ components. In this text, you will be shown how to set up a complete system.

Using the guidance on pages 170–5 you assemble the computer (Figure 3.14) in this way:

- Seat the base unit in an appropriate location. If it is a tower unit, normally, position this on the floor. If it is a desktop unit, ensure that there is adequate space for the keyboard and comfort for viewing the monitor. The base unit must be close enough to network ports and within easy reach of a mains outlet. The rear of the base unit must have adequate ventilation space so that the system can be kept as cool as possible.
- The monitor must be at eye level height for the comfort of the user, and connected to the mains as well as to the base unit. If the monitor is a CRT system, the back must not be covered; this will cause the monitor to overheat.
- Connect the keyboard and mouse, checking that they are within easy reach of the user. Don't forget that the user may be left-handed. Make sure the user is comfortable. Ask them to sit at the computer to check how comfortable they are.

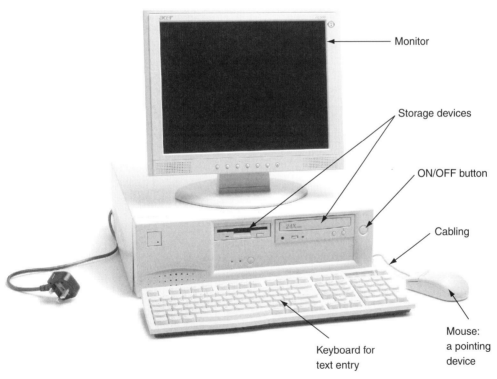

Monitor

Storage devices

ON/OFF button

Cabling

Keyboard for text entry

Mouse: a pointing device

▲ FIGURE 3.14 *A PC*

- Configure the operating system. You may need to:
  - calibrate the mouse
  - set the keyboard speed
  - adjust the screen resolution/colour depth
  - set locale
  - install any applications that the user requires
  - configure any additional user features (disability settings, etc.)
  - apply organisation's security policies, user login, etc.

Installing a component into a computer system

A computer is costly, so you need to take care and give yourself enough time to install it correctly.

Installing computer systems is generally the same; you will need standard tools (see page 117). Once you have the tools and you have the components, now you can upgrade the system.

Installation of a CD/DVD device

The installation of a CD-ROM, DVD-ROM, CD-Rewriter and DVD-Rewriter is exactly the same. The one consideration you will have to make is based on the operating system. Systems later than Windows 2000 have suitable device drivers to allow your system to manage CD and DVD rewriters, whereas earlier systems may require the specific installation of software provided by the manufacturer.

There are five steps to installing a CD/DVD device:

1 Remove device from packaging.
2 Open computer case.
3 Install the device.
4 Close computer case.
5 Check installation is successful.

Step 1 Remove device from packaging

Before you start, check you have all the parts and that the CD/DVD device looks in good order. For this task, you will also need a set of four screws to install the CD/DVD device. Some manufacturers do not supply these, so you may have to obtain them from a technician colleague, who should have them as part of normal equipment for PC support.

If the CD/DVD device is damaged, you need to return it to the supplier. You also need to check that there is a jumper connected to the back of the CD/DVD device as this may be needed in a later step.

▲ FIGURE 3.15 *CD/DVD device*

Step 2 Open computer case

Before touching the computer case (Figure 3.16):

- disconnect the computer from the mains and any other devices
- ensure that you are wearing your electrostatic wrist band and that you are connected to the earth.

▲ FIGURE 3.16 *Computer case*

Once this is done, open the case, but be careful as there will be sharp parts.

Inside the case, there are bays (slots) into which you fit the CD/DVD device (Figure 3.17). You may have to remove a front plate from the outer computer case as well as a metal plate from the inner case assembly.

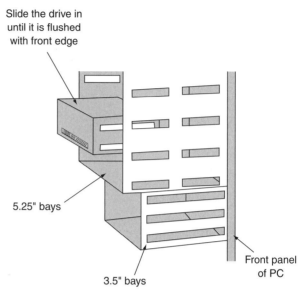

Slide the drive in until it is flushed with front edge

5.25" bays

3.5" bays

Front panel of PC

▲ FIGURE 3.17 *Storage devices and their bays*

Step 3 Install the device

Install the CD/DVD device into any of the bays which are available. When installed, use the screws to secure the CD/DVD device.

Now, connect the CD/DVD device to the system. First, you can connect one of the spare power connectors from the power supply.

To connect the IDE cable (Figure 3.18), you need to decide where to plug it in.

- Will I connect it to the spare IDE slot on the motherboard, if one is available? If this is the case, based on the sticker/legend on the CD/DVD device you will have to set the jumper to 'master' (or 'cable select' in some systems) and use an extra IDE cable.
- Will I connect the CD/DVD drive to an existing cable, if there is a spare connector? If this is the case, you are connecting the CD/DVD device to a cable that probably has a hard drive in residence. You must set the jumper to slave and the CD must be on the middle connector, while the hard drive, which is jumpered to master, will be at the end.

GLOSSARY

IDE (integrated drive electronics) is a hardware standard for the ribbon cable used to connect hard drives and CD/DVD drives to the motherboard.

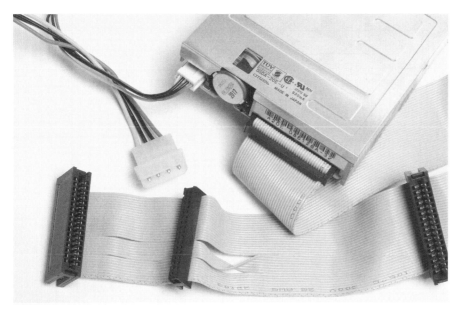

▲ FIGURE 3.18 *An IDE cable*

Step 4 Close the computer case

Now that the CD/DVD device is connected you must ensure that the cabling inside the computer case is tidy. Once you have done this, replace the lid on the computer. Make sure you haven't left anything out. Any spare parts means that you have not completed the job appropriately.

Step 5 Check installation is successful

In the case of a successful installation, when you start the computer it should automatically detect the CD/DVD device and the operating system will be ready to use it.

If the system does not detect the new CD/DVD device, you will have to check certain things:

- Is the CD/DVD device faulty? Before considering this, you should have checked out all the possibilities for the problem.
- Have you connected the device correctly inside the case? Go back to step 3 and check that you have completed this accurately. Are all connectors seated properly?
- Do you need to go into the BIOS and ensure that it detects the drive? Some older systems may require that you restart the computer, press F2 or Del and enter the BIOS configuration utility (Figure 3.19); all systems have a facility to enable you to detect any additional devices. If this works, save the settings and restart the system.

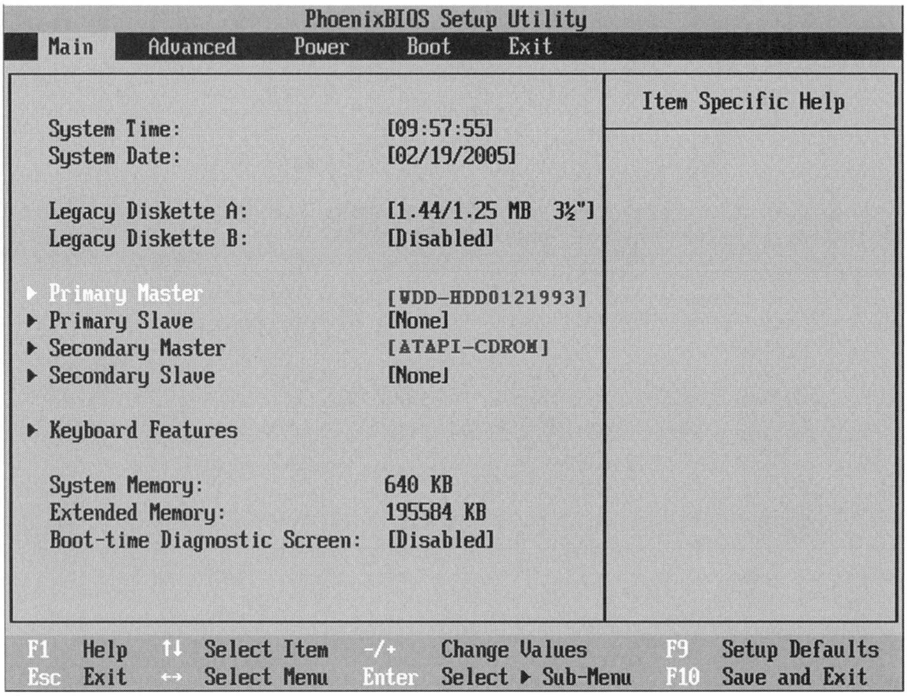
PhoenixBIOS Setup Utility
Main Advanced Power Boot Exit
Item Specific Help
System Time: [09:57:55]
System Date: [02/19/2005]
Legacy Diskette A: [1.44/1.25 MB 3½"]
Legacy Diskette B: [Disabled]
Primary Master [WDD-HDD0121993]
Primary Slave [None]
Secondary Master [ATAPI-CDROM]
Secondary Slave [None]
Keyboard Features
System Memory: 640 KB
Extended Memory: 195584 KB
Boot-time Diagnostic Screen: [Disabled]
F1 Help ↑↓ Select Item -/+ Change Values F9 Setup Defaults
Esc Exit ↔ Select Menu Enter Select ▶ Sub-Menu F10 Save and Exit

▲ FIGURE 3.19 *BIOS setup utility*

Hopefully, the CD/DVD device will work!

Installation of a printer

Operating systems, such as Windows XP, automatically install your printer, if it is a recognisable model.

If the operating system does not detect your printer, because of the age of the operating system, or because the printer is a new and unique model, the process is relatively straightforward and carried out in four simple steps.

1. Plug in the printer.
2. Start the printer wizard.
3. Follow the printer wizard.
4. Test the printer.

Step 1 Plug in the printer

A printer can be directly connected to your system via a USB or parallel interface. Do not forget to switch the printer on, otherwise Windows will not be able to communicate with it.

GLOSSARY

USB (universal serial bus) is an interface which allows you to connect multiple devices on a high-speed data connection.

Parallel is an older data standard, which allows data to be sent in a sideways parallel manner (instead of serial which is a bit-by-bit sequence).

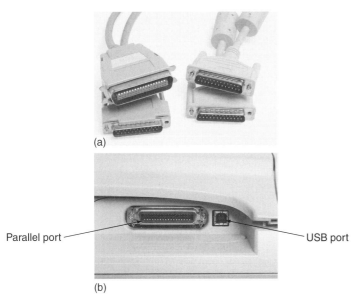

▲ FIGURE 3.20 *(a) Parallel connectors (b) USB and parallel ports*

Step 2 Start the printer wizard

The printer wizard (Figure 3.21) can be found through
Start/Settings/Printers and Faxes. You may already have printers installed
on your system.

▲ FIGURE 3.21 *Printer wizard*

You may have a printer which will be detected by Windows XP. Newer
plug and play printers will also cooperate with the Windows automated
installation process (Figure 3.22).

▲ FIGURE 3.22 *Printer automated installation*

Step 3 Follow the printer wizard

Following the printer wizard (Figure 3.23) is a straightforward process; follow it as much as you need to. Once it has completed a search for the printer, it will advise you that the next stage is manual installation (Figure 3.24).

▲ FIGURE 3.23 *Setting local or network printer*

▲ FIGURE 3.24 *Manual installation of printer*

The wizard will check what type of connector you are using (Figure 3.25) and then provide you with a list of devices to choose from (Figure 3.26).

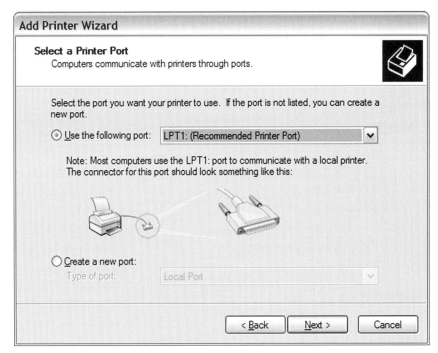

▲ FIGURE 3.25 *Selecting a printer port*

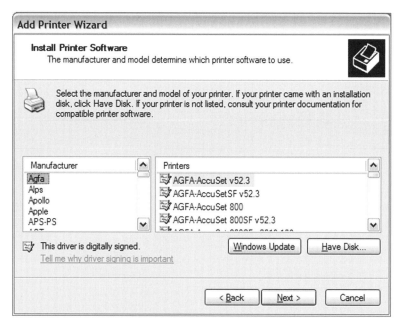

▲ FIGURE **3.26** *Install printer software*

At this point, the decision is yours.

● You could search though the list of manufacturers to see if Windows has a driver but the plug and play did not work, which is unlikely.
● Or you could go online to the Windows update, to see if there is information on the printer, which was manufactured since the creation of the Windows XP operating system.
● Acquiring a disk for installing the printer software (Figure 3.27) and using the manufacturer's own drivers is the recommended solution.

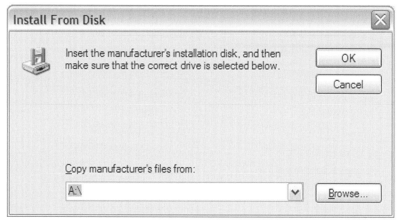

▲ FIGURE **3.27** *Install drive*

Having installed the printer successfully, if you have a network, you may be asked if you wish to share your printer (Figure 3.28) with other computer users who may need to use your printer while your computer is switched on.

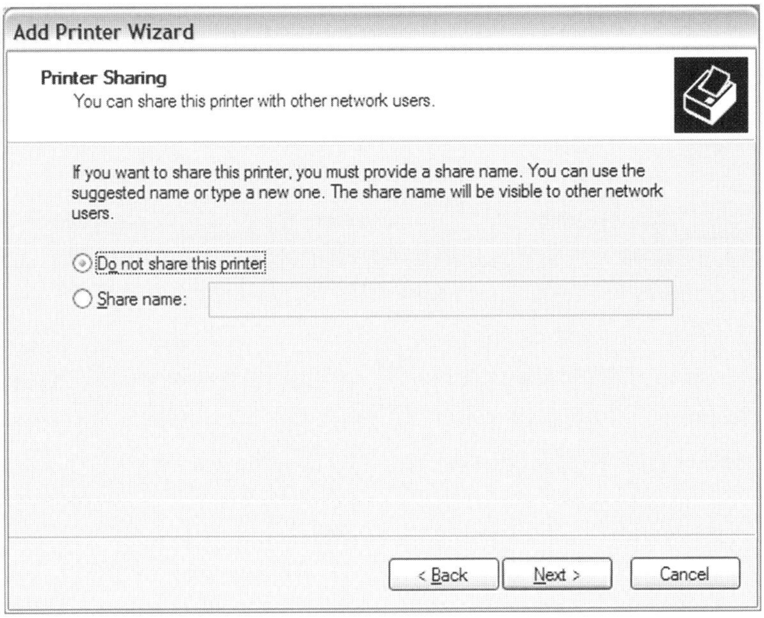

▲ FIGURE 3.28 *Printer sharing*

Step 4 Test the printer

The wizard is now ready to send a test page to the printer (Figure 3.29).

▲ FIGURE 3.29 *Print a test page*

If this doesn't work, you may have to start again at step 1 and repeat the installation process. Be aware, you may have a faulty printer, which can only be established according to manufacturer's guidelines or by checking with a similar model which works.

Carry out post-installation activities

On completing the installation, you will need to complete a series of tasks:

- Tidy away packaging and store for later use in transit or possible return if the equipment is faulty. This is not feasible for most organisations as the space required is too great.
- Ensure that the user is happy with the new equipment.
- Double-check the cabling, ensure that the system specification and software requirements are correct, and that any password(s) required are enabled as appropriate.

With upgrading a computer or simply installing it for the customer, you need to keep an accurate record of the installation process.

- It is a useful reference if the computer system develops any faults in the future. This record can be used to prove (or disprove) the cause.
- As a documentation a supervisor/manager can refer to if you have encountered an issue for which you need assistance.

A normal record will contain:

- each of the steps in installation
- the hardware and software installed
- any issues encountered and solutions rendered
- any settings implemented for the user
- all software installed
- any configuration of the hardware or the operating system.

Check your understanding

1 What factors must you consider when positioning a computer system?

2 List what you have to check before installing hardware.

3 When taking delivery of computer equipment, what should you do before unpacking the equipment?

4 Name five computer connectors and explain what they are used for.

5 List the standard tools you need to install/upgrade a computer system.

6 What checks would you carry out to make sure the installation of a computer system was successful?

3.2 Load and configure the system software

So far you have read about what technology is available in the computer system but learnt nothing about the system that holds it together and provides the connection between you, the user, and the technology.

The system type depends on the technology and the purpose.

- Windows is a **disk operating system**, whose primary purpose is file and device management.
- **Real-time operating systems** are used for defence and control-based systems.
- **Network operating systems** provide a wide range of services to many other computers or users across a network.
- **Cluster operating systems** concentrate on sharing processing power.
- **Multi-user operating systems** focus on many users sharing the processing power of one resource.
- **Dedicated operating systems** are used for personal digital assistants, DVD players, etc.

The operating systems and versions that are currently available include:

- Windows XP for home or professional use
- Windows 2000 and 2003 server products
- Windows CE for personal digital assistants
- Novell Netware server product family
- Linux (there are many variations, each with its own advantages)
- Unix for multi-user systems
- Sun Microsystems, Solaris 9
- Mac OS X, for the Apple platform
- QNX for dedicated real-time systems
- Free-BSD

There are other systems that can be added to the list.

Install two items of software/driver either from media or the Internet

In the previous section, you explored the complexities of installing and configuring an operating system. But, have you ever installed an application or a game, only to find that your computer was incapable of running the software? Applications and games vary in complexity and the resources that they require. Checking the system resources is essential, as you or your employer may invest considerable quantities of money to find that:

● the money is wasted
● existing computers need to be upgraded at some expense
● new computers need to be purchased at a considerable expense.

Therefore, it is important that, before an application is installed or purchased, you check the availability of resources recommended in the software installation instructions. These can be found from various sources, such as:

● the side of the box or disk case
● the manufacturer's website
● promotional literature provided by the manufacturer
● by contacting the company or liaising with an appropriate representative.

For most systems, you need to carry out some checks:

● What is the speed of the CD/DVD-ROM, especially if the application uses resources from this media during operation? (A slow CD-ROM can affect the performance of a game.)

- How much RAM is required to run the application? Be aware that this is normally described as the minimum requirement and does not take into account that you may need to run other applications at the same time. An excellent rule of thumb is that you need to have twice as much RAM as that recommended by any application.
- The speed and capacity of the processor is paramount. It is unlikely that you can run the application on a processor that is slower than the specification recommended by the manufacturer. Some applications demand extra processor resources, especially if the application relies on the processor carrying out mathematic functions. For example, *Flight Simulator* by Microsoft is heavily dependent on the maths capability of any processor.
- How much storage is available on your hard drive? Even in these times of extensive hard drive space, you need to be mindful of the capacity of the application. Through time, you are likely to absorb hard drive space.
- The licence will restrict what you can do with the software. You may find that you have limited the desired use of the application (see pages 236–43).

Practical task

Search on the Internet and identify what the system requirements are for:

- the current version of Microsoft *Office*®
- the latest version of Microsoft *Flight Simulator*®
- the number one ranking game in your local games retailer.

It is important that you backup and virus check the system prior to the installation, as well as when you have completed installation. No application from any manufacturer can be guaranteed as virus or trojan-free, and it is considered wise to ensure the integrity of your system (see pages 254–5).

There are many applications that you can install. To develop comprehensive skills you will need to install:

- a device driver for a printer
- a web installable application
- a comprehensive office suite
- a utility or resource.

Each of these need to be done by reading the manufacturer's installation plans or instructions. You can also create your own.

Based on a computer game that you have or like, create a simple plan listing all the stages involved in installing software. This could be presented as a diagram.

The principles behind installing a **device driver for a printer** as a service (a resource for an application) are the same as when you have to install or repair hardware (and operating systems).

Go out and try!

Windows uses drivers for many systems. Look carefully through the system settings in your Control Panel and list any drivers used for:

- graphics card
- monitor
- printer
- keyboard
- mouse
- digital camera or scanner.

Web installable applications are a recent development. The software vendor does not want you to have the software, so you cannot be tempted to resell or pirate their hard work.

Applications that are installed from the vendor across the web tend to be:

- small applications such as games or utilities
- add-on components to an existing application that you have purchased
- patches and system updates where the application requires modification.

Go out and try!

Visit www.flash.com and www.shockwave.com. If your computer's web browser is not up to date with the latest plug-in, they will offer to install the resource for you.

Microsoft distributes its web browser, *Internet Explorer*, by this method, as they need to revise and update the application as new web attacks occur. To obtain this application you need to visit www.microsoft.com and search in downloads for **Internet Explorer 6 service packs**.

When you select the download option on the right-hand side of the screen, you will be able to download and run an installer application that is only about 450 K in size. On starting the installer, you will have to accept the EULA (Figure 3.30). You may wish to choose to customise the browser on installation (Figure 3.31).

▲ FIGURE 3.30 *Internet Explorer 6 service packs*

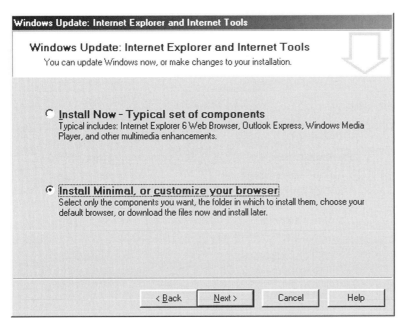

▲ FIGURE 3.31 *Install upgrade*

Internet Explorer provides a wide range of components that can be included or excluded (Figure 3.32). If you click the Advanced button, you can download the entire application for installation on another computer (common on some secure systems).

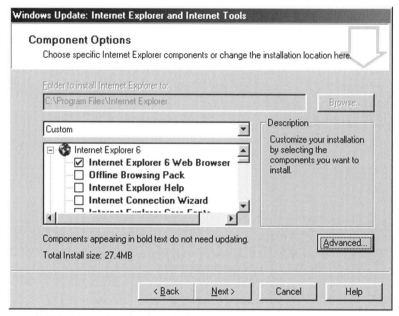

▲ **FIGURE 3.32** *Customise the installation*

Internet Explorer will download (Figure 3.33) and install like any other application.

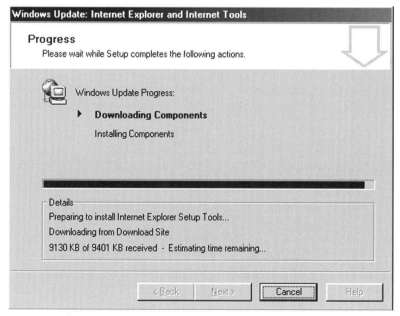

▲ **FIGURE 3.33** *Progress details*

Go out and try!

Go to www.real.com as well as www.shockwave.com. Each of these sites provide web downloadable applications (real audio player and web tangent). Install either of these applications as applicable and either listen to the web radio or play the web games on the shockwave website.

Microsoft *Office*® is a very popular and comprehensive office suite, containing:

- word processor
- database
- presentation software
- spreadsheet
- email application
- utilities.

Go out and try!

Microsoft *Office*® is not alone as an office application. Carry out research into others on:

- openoffice.org
- Star office.

Installing Microsoft applications is very straightforward. Once you have obtained the installation CD and the licensed serial number, make sure that you have a computer that will successfully install your version of *Office*®. For this example, you will install *Office XP*®. You need at least:

- 400 MB of hard drive space (if everything is installed)
- 400 MHz processor
- 128 MB of RAM.

In the installation process, you may wish to change the **default file locations** to another hard drive or a network drive; this will change all the references in the Windows registry (the system database). While valid, you may find that some features of the application will not work, or additional software will not recognise your application.

Once the CD has loaded and started, you will be faced with the licence screen. You must enter your details (or those of the user) and the product serial number. (*Note*: The example provided in Figure 3.34 is invalid and you must use one provided with a licensed CD.)

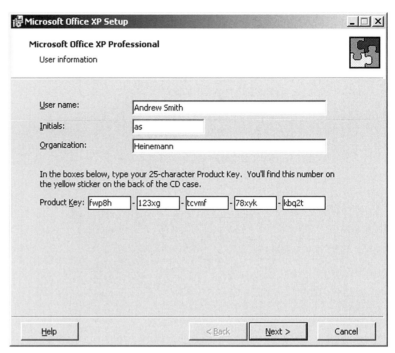

▲ FIGURE 3.34 *Enter details on licence screen*

If the product serial number is valid, you will be taken to the EULA (Figure 3.35), which you must tick to proceed.

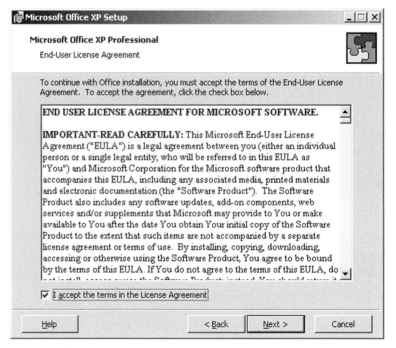

▲ FIGURE 3.35 *Tick and proceed*

Choose the Custom installation option (Figure 3.36).

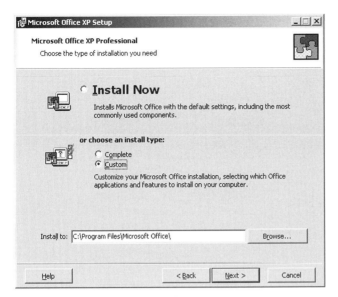

▲ FIGURE **3.36** *Decide on type of installation*

Now you will be presented with a choice (Figure 3.37). Select the type of application(s) you wish to install. It is important to remember that some users do not need every feature that Microsoft *Office*® has to offer.

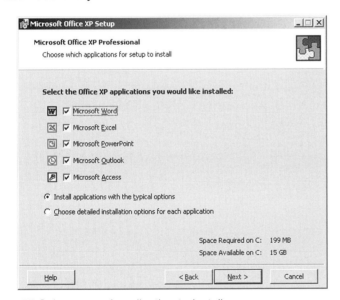

▲ FIGURE **3.37** *Select type of application to install*

Select the 'Choose detailed installation' option.

A menu is offered, so you can 'drill down' the options and elect to add or remove specialised components.

Practical task

Using Figure 3.38 find the Office Assistant (Figure 3.39) and select the option to prevent installation.

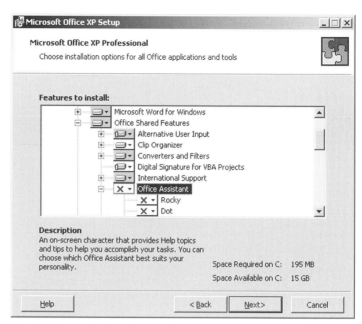

▲ FIGURE 3.38 *Choose installation option*

▲ FIGURE 3.39 *Office Assistant*

Once you click Next, the application will install itself (Figure 3.40). Depending on the speed of your system and CD-ROM drive, this could take up to ten minutes (Figure 3.41).

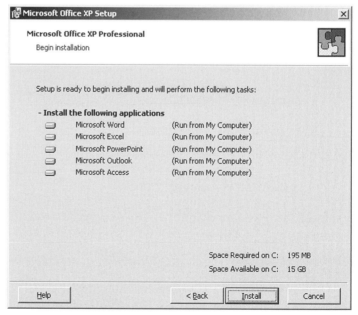

▲ FIGURE 3.40 *Begin installation*

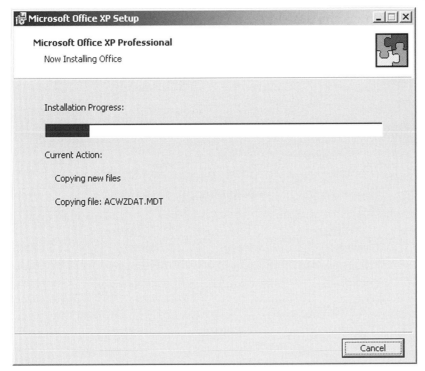

▲ FIGURE 3.41 *Application being installed*

Now that you have installed Microsoft *Office*®, you (or the user) will be able to use it.

It is important that you check the system functions after installation of software. You may find that:

● the software conflicts with another application, in that the installation has overwritten some system files or re-associated files where you normally used another application to run a file type
● the computer is unable to successfully operate the application due to the lack of memory or processor capability.

Go out and try!

There are many freely available very good MP3 players. The three that are commonly used are:

● Windows media player
● Winamp
● Real Player.

Each will try to associate the MP3 file format with their player.

Therefore, install each one (one at a time) and attempt to play an MP3. You will notice that the last application installed will be the one that plays the MP3, while the others are still installed on the computer.

Remember, companies are limited by various licences, which if violated can result in legal action by the manufacturer.

It is unlikely that you will have problems with the installation of an application. However, if you have a problem, it is important that you make a record of this. Your experience may:

● provide evidence of a greater problem with the software or hardware system in use at your workplace
● support action that will be taken by your employer to obtain a refund or support from the manufacturer/supplier
● assist the manufacturer of the software (or the hardware) in rectifying the issue.

Once you have installed an application, it can be modified. This feature is normally available with complex applications such as Microsoft *Office*®.

You may wish to:

● add or remove a component
● repair an installation
● remove the application.

With Microsoft *Office XP*®, you can reuse the installation CD to carry out all these actions. Adding or removing software is the same as specialist installation of components of an application (Figure 3.42).

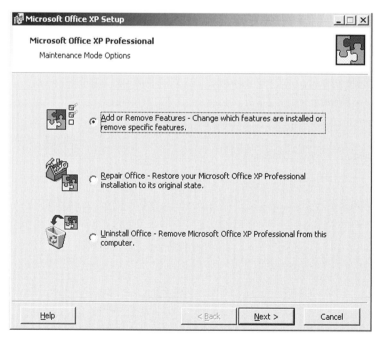

▲ FIGURE 3.42 *Add or remove software*

Repairing *Office*® means that you can completely reinstall the application or allow the software to run a diagnostic for you (Figure 4.43).

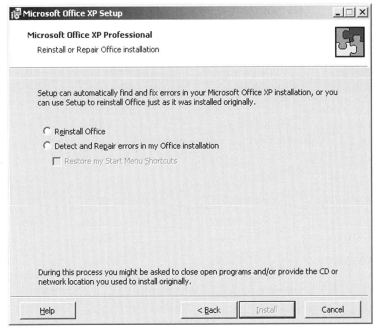

▲ FIGURE 3.43 *Reinstall and run diagnostic*

Uninstall will remove the software from the computer. This means that all relevant files and folders, applications libraries and registry entries will be removed.

Testing an application is no different from testing the installation of hardware or an operating system. It is important in that you look at how the application performs under extremes, as well as with 'normal' work.

Practical task

Create a test plan for the comprehensive testing of your Microsoft *Office XP*® installation.

Look in detail at:

- the size of the *Word* document and the amount of images/drawings it can support
- the range of complexity of spreadsheet and formulae
- the size and complexity of database.

If you want to produce an active test, remember that you can copy and paste information to extend the size of application files.

Problems with applications not working properly after installation can be resolved:

- by correctly shutting down and restarting the operating system; the application may need the operating system to load specialist components on startup
- using the task manager in the operating system to close software applications
- if the application 'freezes', simply closing and restarting it
- restoring the application to 'factory set' defaults
- using system utilities such as the system monitor to check if there is an issue with system performance.

Using the operating system to restart an application is different, depending on the version of operating system you use. Windows XP and 2000 are the same, and Windows 98 is the same as its predecessor Windows 95.

In Windows XP or 2000, press Ctrl, Alt and Del simultaneously; a window will appear called the 'Windows Task Manager' (Figure 3.44). This provides you with a degree of control of the underlying operating system and the applications that it is running.

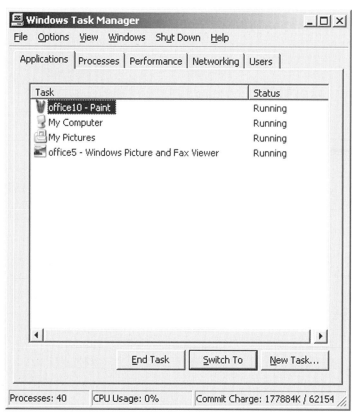

▲ FIGURE 3.44 *Windows Task Manager*

The Windows Task Manager allows you to see:

- applications that are running
- processes (independent activities, which may be utility programs) that are being run by Windows
- current processor and memory performance
- networking throughput (the amount of data the network card or modem is handling)
- who is logged into your computer.

As shown in Figure 3.44, you can prompt Windows to terminate an application using the End Task option. This will prematurely terminate the application and you will lose any unsaved work.

You can also start a new task as in the Start menu/Run option, except you can start tasks that can be added to the processes tab.

If your system is running many processes at any given time, these are the elements that ensure that Windows is able to provide you with the resources that you expect. Each time you start an application or install a utility you may start another process, which can degrade the memory and processor performance of your computer. Figure 3.45 shows how having many users increases the number of processes that will be operational.

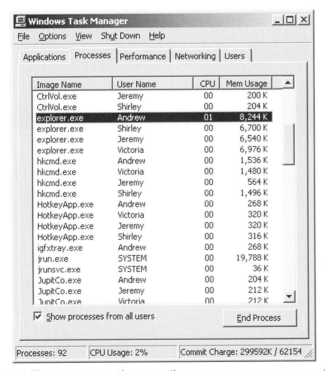

▲ FIGURE 3.45 *The more users there are the more processes are used*

Explorer is an integral system process, which provides control for all the file and desktop management.

Go out and try!

1 On the computer you are using, stop the Explorer process, using the End Process button. You will get a warning message (Figure 3.46), but press 'Yes'.

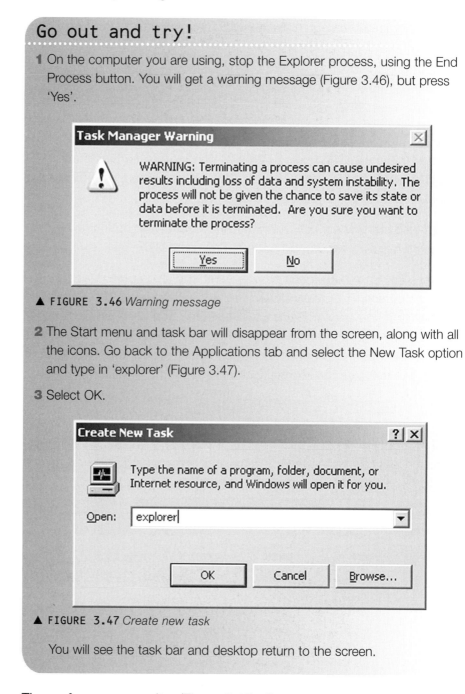

▲ FIGURE 3.46 *Warning message*

2 The Start menu and task bar will disappear from the screen, along with all the icons. Go back to the Applications tab and select the New Task option and type in 'explorer' (Figure 3.47).

3 Select OK.

▲ FIGURE 3.47 *Create new task*

You will see the task bar and desktop return to the screen.

The performance monitor (Figure 3.48) allows you to look at how the system is coping with the load that it is being given. This is particularly useful if you have a computer that is struggling with an application (or applications).

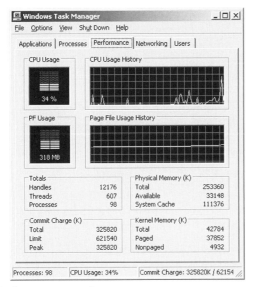

▲ FIGURE 3.48 *Performance monitor*

The performance monitor provides you with information on:

- how the processor is being used at this moment and over the last five seconds
- page file usage (this is memory management, by the use of virtual memory which is an area on the hard drive)
- how much memory is used and is available
- how many tasks the processor and operating system is managing.

While not a requirement of your studies, looking at how the network connection is performing (Figure 3.49) can provide an indication of the reason behind possible problems with an application.

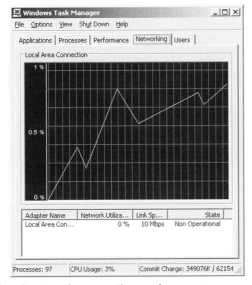

▲ FIGURE 3.49 *Check network connection performance*

A busy network connection could be an indication of:

- a slow server that is providing the application or data, which needs to be reported to the network administrator
- a trojan, virus or network denial of service attack that is affecting the performance of the computer and may need you to install a firewall or anti-virus software (see page 254).

The final tab (Figure 3.50) gives an indication of who is logged into the computer. The more users that are connected, the more processes that are being used by the processor and memory. If your login gives administrative rights, you can warn, disconnect or logoff another user.

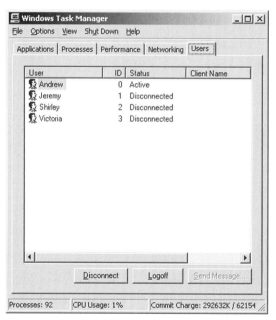

▲ FIGURE 3.50 *You can logoff users*

Using uninstall, adding, removing components, and using the application's own ability to repair itself, are an important part of the daily management of a computer system. It is important that, once this is completed, you report to either the user or management the outcome of the repair procedures that you have carried out. This is important because:

- the result may affect the customer
- there may need to be an analysis of why the problem originally occurred
- your organisation may need to look at the problem if this is a recurring issue.

This is best done by producing a report of any repairs that are carried out, along with any tests that you may have carried out on the software.

In managing the installation of any application from any source, it is essential that you **record all changes/settings made and prepare a report on the installation**. There are reasons for doing this:

- If the software is removed, you may wish to return the system to its normal settings. Therefore, there is a need for accurate records to enable a restore.
- You may need to use the information for troubleshooting, e.g. in the case of conflict with another application or system component.
- To suit your local system needs, you may decide to change default file locations of an application and need to inform any user/technician in the future.
- To suit the system or user (in the case of accessibility), you may decide to change input device settings.

Check your understanding

1 List some of the more common operating systems.

2 How would check that the operating system meets the needs of a customer, before you install or purchase it?

3 How do you test an application if you have a problem with it? What action would you take to attempt to solve the problem?

4 What is the function of the performance monitor? What sort of information can you obtain from it?

5 If you have a busy network connection, what is this indicating?

3.3 Carry out post-installation functional testing

Testing any system is an essential part of the quality control process. A customer expects to receive a computer that has been tested and is working to their expectations.

Carry out full testing of hardware

Unit 4 deals extensively with the processes involved in systems testing. In this unit, you explore the use of an operating system and other utilities, to test for:

- **registry integrity**, using CHKREG
- **viruses**, using a suitable anti-virus application
- **disk performance**, using benchmarking and disk management software
- **system performance**, using benchmarking software.

Registry integrity

This can be tested via many tools which can be downloaded from the Internet. With Windows XP, you may use CHKREG, which can be downloaded from the Microsoft website. The registry is a complex database, which is updated by various applications, system processes, as well as viruses and trojans. Checking the registry may improve system performance as well as delete 'keys' (entries) which are erroneous.

Viruses

Using a suitable anti-virus application, you can attempt to ensure that your computer is 'risk-free'. AVG is a free application which can be downloaded from the Grisoft website (www.free.grisoft.com). To ensure that your system is virus free, you must ensure that the anti-virus software you use:

- updates its virus database daily
- checks your drives daily (after the virus database has been updated).

Relying on the automatic features of the anti-virus software is not safe. You have to develop good habits and check:

- anything you have downloaded from the Internet
- any free CDs or DVDs received from friends.

Disk performance

This can be tested using benchmarking and disk management software. Tools such as the fresh devices benchmarking software allow you to check the performance of your system as well as your disk drives. Windows XP has a tool in Control Panel/Administrative Tools/Computer Management which will monitor the performance of all your storage devices, as well as check the 'tidiness' of your drives, by running a defragmentation tool (Figure 3.51).

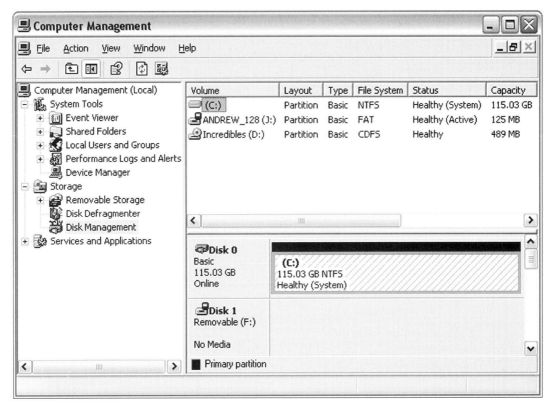

▲ FIGURE 3.51 *Disk fragmentation*

System performance

Using benchmarking software can help you to run regular checks to monitor the health of the system. There are a wide range of tools available via the Internet. It is important that, whatever tool you use, it must check for:

● CPU performance
● hard disk performance
● video system information
● motherboard and system bus information
● peripheral performance
● network performance.

User acceptance comes when the system is in use. Many users, while not technical, will know if the system is not performing to normal expectations. Once you have tested any system, it is reasonable to agree an acceptance period, during which the user may raise any issues and you, or your organisation, are on call to support and rectify any issues.

Select the methods of registering products and complete all documentation to a professional standard

It is important that you complete the appropriate **software registration card** (Figure 3.52) or corporate documentation and submit this information to the software manufacturer or your supervisor.

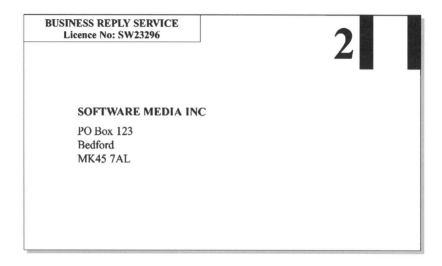

BUSINESS REPLY SERVICE
Licence No: SW23296

2

SOFTWARE MEDIA INC

PO Box 123
Bedford
MK45 7AL

Thank you for buying this application. To ensure that we can provide comprehensive warranty support, please complete this card and return it to Software Media Inc. (No stamp required if posted within the UK.)

Title   Name

Job title

Company

Address

                                         Postcode

Country

Email

Date of purchase/installation

▲ FIGURE 3.52 *Software registration card*

In many cases, you can register **online** by visiting the manufacturer's website, phone a **registration free phone hotline**, or send your organisational information to a specialist **email address**.

Some manufacturers will prevent you from being able to use their software until you provide them with your personal information. They will then issue you with the application serial number or email you a piece of software that will unlock the application or operating system.

Design a form that keeps a record of all instances of Microsoft *Office*®
installed at your centre. On this form, ensure that you include:

- date installed
- version of application
- serial number or identity of computer upon which software is installed
- location of computer.

Registration may take place as part of the testing process, and may have
an impact on the warranty of the hardware if not completed.

3.4 Address routine problems

In your professional career, you will encounter many routine problems
that occur with different computer systems. This section identifies the
most common ones and what you may be able to do to solve them.

Identify routine problems

The routine problems include:

- the need for a bug fix for the device driver with the version of
  operating system
- the operating system needs a patch
- insufficient disk space
- out of memory
- incorrect version of driver
- no apparent network connection
- earlier/later version of file installed
- cable may be faulty
- incorrect ends to cables
- device fails to show any sign of life
- device starts POST but hangs
- existing software fails to run correctly.

The need for a bug fix for the device driver with the version of operating system

Changes in operating systems occur frequently, involving the development of a completely new operating system or an updated version.

The complexity of an operating system increases the chances of 'things going wrong'. Many operating system creators do announce the changes to the hardware community in advance, but this may not be enough time for the manufacturer to create an appropriate solution to a potential problem.

When an issue with most 'good' manufacturers is recognised, a product will release a 'bug fix' as soon as feasibly possible.

Go out and try!

Visit www.hp.com (Hewlett Packard). On the front page is the support and drivers link. Check through the extensive resources and make use of the 'alerts' option to ensure that you are aware of any product issues and bug fixes as soon as they occur.

The operating system needs a patch

Computer hackers search for vulnerabilities in operating systems and exploit them. To counter this software manufacturers have to continuously 'update' the operating system.

This applies to the best known systems, such as Windows, Linux, Novell, as well as others. Since Windows 2000 was launched, Microsoft has used a technology called 'automatic update'. You can find this on Windows XP, by selecting the option in the Control Panel.

Once started, Windows will load any new updates; these updates or 'hotfixes' are designed to improve the operating system. Occasionally, an operating system will need to undergo a complete revision. This is known as a service pack. Recently, Microsoft issued a major service pack for their operating system.

When you are carrying out a new installation of an operating system from CD, you need to know whether the service packs will be available. Visit v5.windowsupdate.microsoft.com, and check that this new installation has all the current 'fixes'.

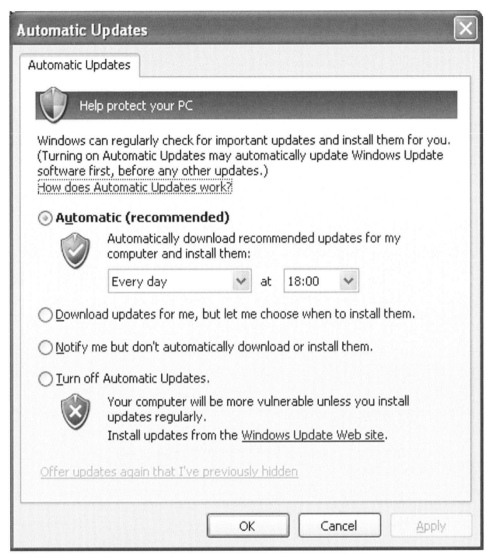

▲ FIGURE 3.53 *Disk automatic updates*

Insufficient disk space

Insufficient disk space is normally caused by:

- the user having too much data on the hard drive
- the user having too many applications on the system
- the hard drive being too small for the task intended.

The issues of too much data or too many applications can be resolved simply. Often the best solution is to use the uninstall tool for each application, and to ensure that the data is compressed and possibly backed up onto a CD or DVD.

If the hard drive is too small, adding a new hard drive is straightforward, as long as you consider:

- the need to put the new hard drive as a slave on the spare IDE (or serial ATA) line
- the possible installation of the operating system and all applications on the new hard drive
- the need to backup all of the data onto a removable medium (which may be a CD or DVD)
- the need to copy all data to the new hard drive.

Sometimes, the problem is caused by disk fragmentation.

Dealing with out-of-memory issues

A computer to run successfully makes many demands on its memory. During normal operation, there are various demands on a computer's memory (Figure 3.54):

- The operating system uses at least 25 per cent of the available memory.
- If you have an onboard graphics card, it will use memory proportional to the quality of the graphics required.
- Any applications running use memory for each application running, as well as memory for the 'item' you are working on. Obviously, a large *Word* document takes up more memory than a smaller *Word* document.
- The operating system will have many services running, and each will demand some of the memory.

GLOSSARY

Service is a system-based utility that is constantly running in the background, while your computer's operating system is managing your system. There are many services such as Internet Explorer and anti-virus software. You can view all the services by pressing Ctrl–Alt–Del and selecting the Processes tab on the Task Manager.

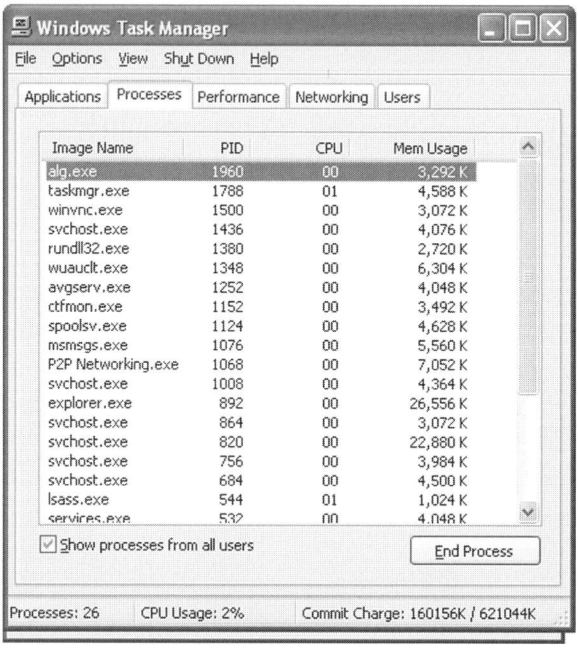

▲ FIGURE 3.54 *Processes task manager*

Memory can be improved by:

- ensuring that you are not running too many applications
- increasing the virtual memory (Figure 3.55) used by your computer
- replacing the existing memory with larger size memory cards.

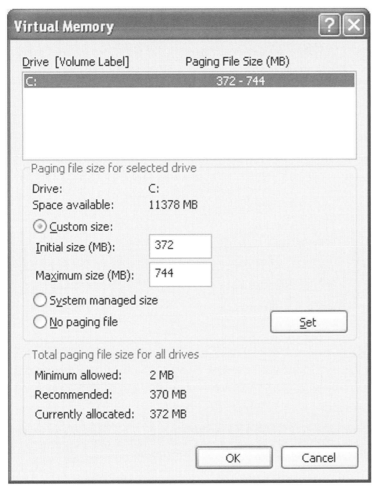

▲ FIGURE 3.55 *Virtual memory*

Incorrect version of driver

Software and hardware manufacturers cannot guarantee to provide the correct driver version for any system.

In Windows XP, Microsoft offers a tool for searching the Internet for the latest drivers (Figure 3.56) that may be appropriate for your system. All manufacturers ensure that the latest driver is available via the Internet, so this tool lets you find the version you require.

▲ FIGURE 3.56 *Connect to Windows update*

No apparent network connection

You may not be able to solve the problem of lack of communication with a network if the fault is within the local or remote system. To establish whether this is a problem you can or cannot deal with, you may need to liaise with an appropriate network support specialist.

If there is no support available, you may be able to check by confirming that the cable is connected to the network card at the rear of your computer, as well as plugged into the wall socket. This can be confirmed by a green/orange light, which may flicker occasionally. If there is no light, there is no communication. This means:

● there may be a fault on your cable, which could be replaced
● there may be a fault on your network card, which could be swapped
● the fault is outside your control.

Alternatively, you could use the DOS command PING 127.0.0.1 (Figure 3.57); this is called testing the loopback.

● If there is a reply, then the local network card is operating as expected.
● If there is no reply, you need to seek help to check the computer's TCP/IP settings (Figure 3.58).
● If there is no reply, there may be a fault with the network card, or it may not be installed correctly.

GLOSSARY

TCP/IP (transmission control protocol/internet protocol) is an inter-computer communication method used across the Internet.

PING is a utility used to check if two devices across a network can communicate with each other. It also measures how long the communication takes.

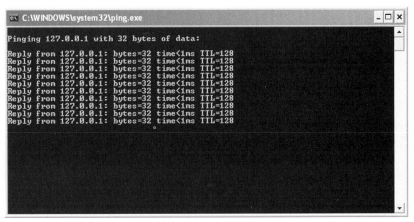

▲ FIGURE 3.57 *PING*

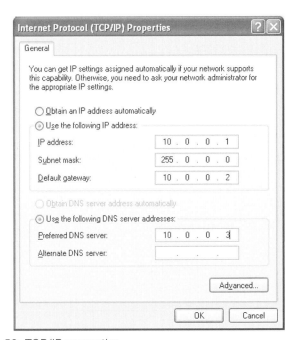

▲ FIGURE 3.58 *TCP/IP properties*

Earlier/later version of file installed

All operating systems, applications and drivers are version driven. If the wrong version of an essential component is installed, often by accident when another application is installed or removed, an existing application may cease to work. The easiest solution is to reinstall the removed application or reinstall the application at fault to override the version issue.

Cable may be faulty

There are two ways to test if a cable is faulty:

● Use a specialist tester, which may cost a small fortune.
● Swap the cable with another one from a working system, to identify if the fault is cable related.

The latter solution is cheaper and therefore preferable.

Sometimes, the fault with the cable may not be the system involved or the cable itself. Cables are vulnerable to external electrical interference from devices such as microwave ovens or power cables.

Incorrect ends to cables

While most cables are standardised, you may have to change the type of connector at the end of a cable. Sometimes, the connectors at both ends are female or male.

Companies such as Belkin, Black Box and Maplins offer a range of connector adapters, which are professionally referred to as 'gender benders'. The gender bender will change the male type connector to female, and likewise for female to male.

Go out and try!

Visit www.maplins.co.uk and carry out a search for 'gender benders'.

Device fails to show any sign of life

There are several reasons why a device shows no sign of life:

- There is no power reaching the device.
- There is no data reaching the device.
- Someone forgot to switch it on.
- The device may actually be faulty.
- The incorrect drivers are installed.
- You are using the wrong application or operating system.
- The device may need some routine maintenance.

Device starts POST but hangs

This occurs when the device starts on a self-test process but hangs midway. You can read about how POST operates for each system in this unit and in Unit 2 (page 138).

When the device stops, you need to find out what it was supposed to be doing according to the manufacturer's guidance. This will indicate where the fault lies. With BIOS-based POST, or printers, the process is straightforward. Go to the manufacturer's website, and you will find comprehensive information on the problem.

Existing software fails to run correctly

Faced with this problem, you may have to remove the component or software that has recently been installed, or reinstall the software that is a problem. The problem is often caused by the new application loading newer or older drivers or system extensions which are incompatible with the existing application.

3.5 Remove different types of equipment and follow procedures for transporting and storing equipment

This section explores the essential subject of moving computer equipment. The transport of a computer system, including base units, CRT monitors and larger printers, can be problematic and you may be responsible for making sure the equipment is moved safely.

Identify health and safety issues, including preparing a list of any hazardous items within the equipment

Before you move any equipment, you have to do several things:

- Complete a risk assessment of the physical task and ascertain how the computers may need to be lifted and moved, along with any other physical hazards that may be encountered on route. Obstacles such as stairs, in the absence of lifts, are a suitable risk. You may have to consider the use of trolleys or other lifting equipment, if you are moving many computers; a hydraulic trolley is useful and reduces the effort.

- Ensure that your risk assessment complies with the Health and Safety Executive's own assessment policies, as well as your own company's practices. Ensure that the loads are manageable and that others are not put at risk from the work you are carrying out. You may have to check this with a local health and safety office or on the Health and Safety Executive website.

- Carry out research to identify the currently recognised hazards in hardware devices. This could include:
  - the carcinogenic (cancer causing) properties of printer toner so you need to ensure that none is spilt and, if it is, then you need to know how to remove it safely

- the drop hazards associated with CRT monitors, where the implosion and broken glass, as well as phosphorous coating, all contribute towards creating hazards
- the sharp edges on some computer cases when opened can cause deep and potentially infected wounds.
- You must keep an accurate record (called an inventory or audit log) of what equipment has been moved and to what location, to ensure that no equipment is lost and, in the case of hazardous substances (printer toner), that the location of them is recorded.

Select and use appropriate means of removal

Computer equipment usually needs to be moved because:

- it has become obsolete and is no longer required
- it is being moved to another location
- it is being replaced by new technology.

You and your colleagues may remove the equipment, with suitable lifting equipment, or it may be carried out by a removal company which specialises in computer transportation or computer technology disposal.

There are many computer disposal companies who will remove your company's computers and accept full liability for doing this. Some of them will recondition the computers and sell them on. Others will distribute them to charitable causes here, in the UK, as well as internationally.

For removing printer toner and CRT monitors, you must call in professionals who will dispose of these according to the law. They must never be disposed of as if they were part of normal waste, because of the potential dangers they present (see page 110).

Select suitable transport methods and storage locations

You must be aware of the following when transporting computer equipment:

- Handling equipment may be specially configured computer or hydraulic trolleys (Figure 3.59).
- Manual handling training (covered in Unit 2) involves the careful lifting of computer equipment while keeping your back straight.

- All computers need to be kept in dry conditions prior to installation. If the equipment has been in cold, damp or humid conditions, it must be left at an ambient (normal) temperature for at least four hours before you switch it on, just in case condensation has settled on any electrical circuit. If you turn on the computer too soon, the condensation on the circuitry could cause a short circuit and therefore a fire.
- The need to safeguard the equipment against theft.
- To avoid the computer equipment being affected by electromagnetic or electrostatic fields, do not store it too close to power rooms or electrical generators. Many large companies make the mistake of storing computer equipment in the basement, which is where many of the electrical systems are located!

▲ FIGURE 3.59 *Transporting computer equipment*

3.6 Conform with regulations affecting the disposal of ICT packaging

In this environmentally conscious age, the disposal of ICT product packaging is of paramount importance – to protect the environment and to support the recycling process.

Identify safety issues when disposing of ICT packaging

Any ICT-related waste has to be held in appropriate facilities until it is disposed of. The kind of waste you may have to manage includes:

- cardboard, which is a potential fire hazard
- polystyrene, foam and PVC packaging, which are environmental hazards
- toner cartridges, which are a hazard to humans
- old computer hardware, which is a general environmental hazard.

Many local authorities and private companies will assist in the disposal of the various waste items. Many toner companies will sell you new toner at a discounted price, if you return your used cartridges.

Many organisations, such as school/college or company, may employ a professional who acts as the dangerous goods safety adviser. They will determine the health and safety issues for your organisation and may be aware of any issues regarding ICT-packaging disposal.

The circuitry and metal in a computer system is recyclable if the technology cannot be reconditioned to be used again; the copper, gold and steel (from most cases) can be recovered.

Select and use appropriate methods for disposing of ICT packaging

In the UK, there are many 'statutes' which affect the management, transport and disposal of ICT packaging:

- The **Environmental Protection Act 1990** covers all regulations relating to products that may damage the environment.
- The **Carriage of Dangerous Goods (Classification, Packaging and Labelling) and Use of Transportable Pressure Receptacles Regulations 1996** is a complex legislation and refers to the

transportation of CRT monitors as these are classed as pressure receptacles. If damaged or involved in an impact, these may implode, which is as dangerous as an explosive encased in shrapnel.

- The **Carriage of Dangerous Goods by Road Regulations 1996** covers how all dangerous equipment is to be safely transported.
- The **Special Waste Regulations 1996** relates to any products that are toxic, very toxic, harmful, corrosive, irritant or carcinogenic. This includes laser printer toner.
- The **Producer Responsibility Obligations (Packaging Waste) Regulations 1997** controls the disposal of packaging.
- The **EC Landfill Directive 1999** exists to ensure that all waste that now enters landfill sites is biodegradable and will have no long-term effect on the environment.
- The **EU Directive on Waste Electrical and Electronic Equipment (WEEE)** manages the safe disposal of any computer or electronic equipment.
- The **European Waste Catalogue,** as directly quoted from the Environment Agency, is 'a classification system for waste materials. It categorises wastes based on a combination of what they are and the process or activity which produced them.'
- The **Waste Directive (91/156/EEC)** amends the original **Framework Directive on Waste** issued by The Council of European Communities in July 1975 (75/442/EEC). It is the overarching legislation on waste disposal.

Go out and try!

Visit websites such as http://www.letsrecycle.com/ and http://www.environmentagency.gov.uk/ to discover more about environmental protection legislation.

Check your understanding

1 What do you need to check to determine whether the computer system is performing as it should?

2 List some of the routine problems you are likely to come across in a computer system.

3 What is a patch? What would you do if a system needs one?

4 Explain what virtual memory is. Why it is needed?

5 What sort of checks would you do if the network connection doesn't seem to be working?

6 Bearing in mind the importance of health and safety in using computer equipment, what steps would you take to minimise/eliminate risks posed by hazards?

Part 1

Using the information on the steps to take in building and installing a computer system, create a checklist that will provide you with an accurate record of the process involved, covering pre-installation, installation and post-installation. Make sure that the checklist is comprehensive and covers every task in detail. Once this is complete, use the checklist on two installations.

Part 2

With the agreement of your tutor, you are to plan the installation of:

- an agreed operating system
- an agreed application.

To achieve this you must:

- produce a report on all pre-installation activities performed
- produce a report on the installation of the operating system, including screen grabs where possible, recording any changes/settings made
- produce a report on the installation of the application software, recording any changes/settings made
- produce a report on all post-installation activities.

This must be carried out and observed by your tutor, and an appropriate document produced and signed as evidence.

Part 3

Here you are to create a test plan that comprehensively addresses the needs of:

- post-installation testing of hardware
- different methods of product registration.

Part 4

While completing your installation(s), create and maintain a log of any routine computer problems that may occur. Document the problems as well as the solutions.

Part 5

Produce a report containing:

- the identification and explanation of the importance of health and safety issues
- the identification and explanation of appropriate means of removal of old equipment
- the identification and explanation of suitable transport methods and storage locations for ICT equipment
- a description of safety issues to be considered when disposing of ICT packaging and regulations to be conformed with
- a description of different methods by which ICT can be appropriately disposed of.

4 Installing and Maintaining Applications and Systems Testing

INTRODUCTION

This unit deals with two separate skills involved with ICT systems support: the installation and maintenance of a variety of common applications, and the purpose and importance of systems testing.

Learning opportunities

In completing this unit, you will achieve these learning outcomes:

- Understand the legal regulations and issues affecting the registration, installation and use of software.
- Install a variety of applications.
- Identify and remedy common application installation faults.
- Uninstall installed software safely and be able to resolve any issues.
- Carry out systems testing and analyse outcomes.

How this unit will be assessed

This unit is assessed through practical activities set by your local assessor and externally moderated. You need to complete tasks covering all the assessment objectives and to show evidence that the objectives have been achieved. For this, you will complete OCR forms showing where and how the objectives have been met.

> Carry out preparations in advance of installation, including confirming registration of software, assessing health and safety issues and confirming user requirements

This section covers a wide range of issues:

- The types of licence schemes available for the application you may install
- The different methods of software registration
- The types of payment expected from the software manufacturer
- The number of systems that can legally use the application
- The licence terms and conditions

As well as developing your understanding of the range of applications available, you should be aware of user requirements and issues regarding health and safety.

Software licensing

GLOSSARY

To have a **licence** is to have official or legal permission to do or own a specified thing. (*Source*: www.dictionary.com)

In the case of software, it is easy to duplicate the work of others, accidentally or deliberately. However, because the law of copyright applies to software, if you reproduce, copy or duplicate any part of the software you have committed a crime.

Anyone caught infringing the copyright law can be prosecuted and, if found guilty, subject to:

- considerable fine
- paying the costs of the software licences 'misused'
- paying the legal costs of the 'victim'
- having the equipment deemed to have been used in the infringement of the copyright repossessed.

Software worth £250, if copied illegally, could cost £10,000 in legal liabilities.

Most software manufacturers work closely with FAST (Federation Against Software Theft) to ensure that software theft is kept to a minimum. If you are considering using 'pirated' software, remember that most applications when installed send a specially formulated message to a web server managed by the manufacturer of the software. This tells them that their software has been 'pirated' and by whom. The manufacturer can take legal action against anyone who pirates their software.

Go out and try!

Visit www.fast.org.uk and www.copyrightservice.co.uk. Find information on the following:

- When did copyright law start to apply to computer programs?
- What else does copyright cover?
- How can you register your copyright?
- What does FAST believe are the common types of piracy?

Unlike book and published material, there are no concessions for acquiring copies of parts of software. You can use someone else's written material if you attribute ownership. However, using parts of someone's software can raise the same legal problems as if you had copied the whole system.

You can only legally copy software for backup purposes. For example, when you purchase a new application or system, you can take a copy of the software's installation disk(s) and place the original(s) in a fireproof safe. This is accepted good practice.

So that different companies and private individuals can access their software, most software manufacturers provide a wide range of licence agreements. However, not all companies offer licence agreements. For many, the purpose of producing software is to earn money and make a profit.

Table 4.1 lists licence agreements in common use. As each agreement is a legal concept, you may find that there are others in existence.

Go out and try!

Visit www.pugh.co.uk and compile a list of all the different software licensing agreements available.

CASE STUDY - Software Licensing

Jacob Smith manages the software audit for the Luton branch of WidgetsRUs. He discovers that the company is losing money as it is only acquiring single-user licences for a well-known office product.

Write a short report of no more than 500 words on what may be the better software licensing alternatives.

Licence type	Explanation
Individual	For the user or computer only. Duplication of software on to any other computer system can invalidate the licence and incur potential legal action.
Concurrent	Where a user may have many computers but use only one at a time, in the case of home, office and laptop. A concurrent licence will add to the cost of the software.
Site/Campus	For the offices of one specific organisation. This may be a regional or national branch or the site of your school/college.
Corporate	For the entire organisation, including all sites.
Freeware	There are many definitions for this type of licence. Common etiquette implies that this software is free to use. However you cannot distribute it or sell copies of it without making some financial concession to the owner.
Shareware	Shareware is like freeware, but the expectation is that, if you like the software, use it regularly or intend to use it for commercial gain, you have to pay a fee to the creator. The differences between freeware and shareware are grey, as the creator decides the terms.
Open source	The code for the software is freely available for you to edit, compile and recommend improvements. Commercial gain is based on an agreement between yourself and the original creator(s).
Educational	Reduced software licensing for schools, colleges and universities, as well as some applicable charities. The purpose is often to encourage the proliferation of the software.
Student	For the student, often an older version or a reduced cost, where you get the software only, with no manuals or support.

▲ TABLE 4.1 *Licence agreements*

Registration

When you purchase software, you might be expected to register with the manufacturer. The purpose of registration is to:

- ensure that you are apprised of any updates or faults with the software
- protect you from the software manufacturer's specially trained team of legal experts, if there is a 'false' claim against you for copyright violation
- allow the software manufacturer to record how many 'licensed' copies you have
- provide the basis for any customer support agreement and product guarantee.

GLOSSARY

A **guarantee** is:

1 A promise or an assurance, especially one given in writing, that attests to the quality or durability of a product or service.

2 A pledge that something will be performed in a specified manner.

(*Source*: www.dictionary.com)

There are many forms of registration and some companies will allow you to use more than one. You can register:

- by phone
- via email
- by using a postcard
- online
- by software via web-based server
- by licence key
- by dongle.

Registering the software by phone is possibly the least reliable method, often companies use this method to establish a customer/supplier relationship with you and to obtain useful marketing information.

Most software has a serial number; often the phone call will involve the recording of this serial number as a copyright protection system.

Registering by email can be done anonymously, but it is not difficult to submit a fraudulent email. Many companies are aware of this and will send you a reply with a link to their website. When activated, this will display a form that will capture your customer details before they send you an activation code.

A postcard is used for games as a method of ensuring that you have a product guarantee. This is still used by some companies, but its effectiveness is less than desirable. See Figure 4.1 for an example of the sort of postcard that may be included with software you may purchase and install.

Thank you for buying this application. To ensure that we can provide comprehensive warranty support, please complete this card and return it to Software Media Inc. (No stamp required if posted within the UK.)

Title   Name

Job title

Company

Address

                                  Postcode

Country

Email

Date of purchase/installation

▲ FIGURE 4.1 *Postcard*

Many software manufacturers now favour online registration (Figure 4.2). It saves on labour costs and enables them to keep track of licences throughout the world. The manufacturer can also obtain valuable information about a company.

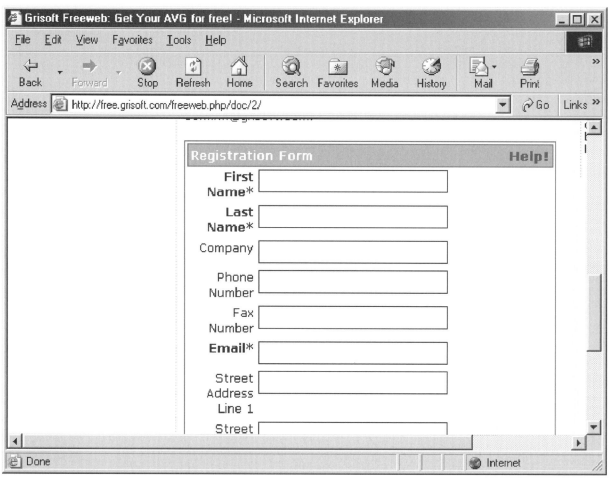

▲ FIGURE 4.2 *A web-based registration form*

A well-managed and designed system will ensure that you cannot use the software until you have received a valid code from the server.

Go out and try!

AVG is a free anti-virus application created by Grisoft. To use this software you must register online before you can obtain, via email, the activation code. Visit www.free.grisoft.com to register for and download this software.

Some software will automatically attempt to connect to a web-based server. Once this connection has been established, you will be issued with a serial number and asked for personal details. Some individuals may experience problems with this method if, when the software attempts to use a port, it is blocked by the firewall.

A licence key may be supplied on the CD/DVD, inside the packaging or via other means. Without the licence key, you will not be able to install the software. Licence keys are often mathematical formulae based on an identity unique to the application.

A dongle is a small piece of hardware that has to be added to your computer before the software will work. It contains a small circuit with an activation code or command routine. Dongles may be attached:

- to spare serial ports
- between the parallel port and printer
- to a spare USB port
- between the PS/2 port and the keyboard
- in a PCI card on the motherboard.

Go out and try!

Using a search engine (such as Google), do a search on dongles. Compare the results with the previous activity and ascertain what is the most common type of dongle in use.

Payment

Many contracts are not legally binding until payment has been made. This means that the licence is not valid until payment has been received and accepted. Most software manufacturers will not release software until you have made the purchase. This can be a problem for large campus agreements, which may be valued in the tens or hundreds of thousands of pounds. Problems occur when the individual responsible for software licensing has neglected to:

- make the annual payment
- update the agreement to cover all the different uses of the software.

Any lapse in payment, or neglecting to keep the manufacturer informed how you may be using their software, allows them to take legal action against you.

Use

There is often confusion with software licensing. 'I have it on my computer at home and on my laptop, but I can't use both at once!' is a much heard complaint. Actually, this is a case of having installed two copies or instances of the software. For two instances, you have to have two licences. But you might have only purchased one.

You must ensure that you have the correct licence agreement to allow you the freedom you require, as stated. At a corporate level, copyright theft is a serious issue.

Some manufacturers and nations will impose conditions regarding software use: where it can be used and for what it can be used.

Licence conditions

'The devil is in the detail' is often quoted by legal professionals. Don't get caught out, read the small print (Figure 4.3). Don't just click on the 'I Agree' button. Be sure what you have agreed to.

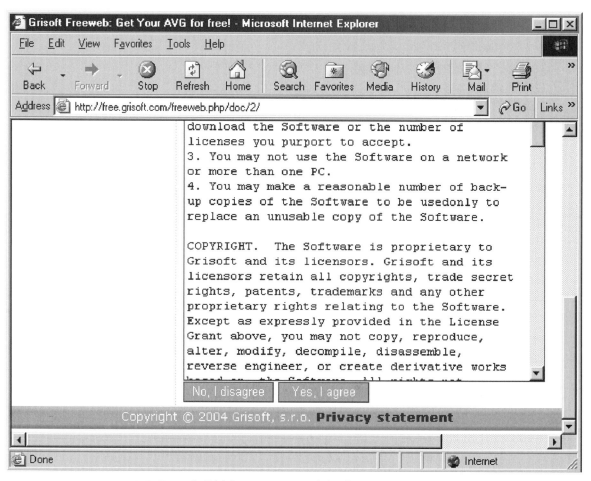

▲ FIGURE 4.3 *Make sure you read the licence details before you agree to the conditions*

Some companies prohibit the sale of their software to certain countries where piracy is rife. Other licence conditions which impose restrictions on use may include:

- the types of applications created with the software
- the use of the software
- the companies that cannot use the software
- prohibitions by national governments
- age restrictions.

Go out and try!

Look for the licence conditions for software you own or use. Ask yourself these questions:

- Have I broken any of the conditions?
- Do I understand the terms I have agreed to?
- Is there anything I have agreed to that I should be concerned about?

Range of applications

Computers have the ability to process large quantities of information and complete a wide range of calculations at any given time. So, they are often used in numerical and scientific modelling, for example in doing research or planning large-scale traffic systems.

There are many common types of software:

- Operating systems
- Application software
- Utilities such as CODEC
- Drivers and link libraries
- Servers
- Programming and applications development

An **operating system** manages the resources on your computer, and enables you to access it. There are at least six types of operating system in common use:

- A **workstation-based** operating system manages your personal computer. Examples include all versions of Windows, the various systems for Apple computers and Linux.
- A **server-based** operating system offers resources across distributed network systems. Popular examples include Windows NT/2000/2003, Linux, Unix and Novell Netware.
- **Multi-user** operating systems enable more than one person to access shared time on large-scale computer systems, e.g. Windows 2000/2003 and Unix.

- A **real time** system is created to produce codes on chips for specialist systems.
- In a **cluster-based** operating system processing is distributed among many computers (called a Beowulf). Google is an example of a cluster in use.
- A **minimal** operating system is used for PDAs (personal digital assistants).

There are many examples of **application software**:

- Office-based word processing, spreadsheet data and financial manipulation and database
- Publishing
- Website management and design
- Image manipulation
- Graphical and design
- Multimedia and interactive
- Animation and 3D
- Architectural and engineering design

Database systems are a variation on applications, where the sole purpose is to manage and manipulate large quantities of data. Most database systems operate on a large scale and are designed to be used by many users at any given moment.

Unlike applications, a **utility** is a program that carries out a specific task but is not used in the creation of a product. On your computer, you will find many utilities. They enable you to:

- check and repair your hard drive
- manage the computer's memory
- use a calculator
- watch videos.

For example, a CODEC (coder decoder) is used to interpret the files used for various media systems, so your computer can play/view MP3, MPEG, AVI, Wav files.

Drivers and **link libraries** control all the devices and connections between the operating system and application software. For example, printing a page requires a print driver (Figure 4.4). Such drivers, required for a unique hardware component, are still licensed software.

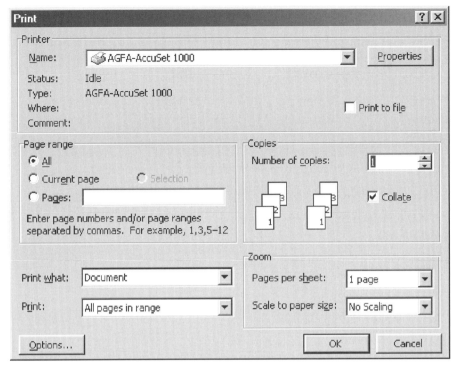

▲ FIGURE 4.4 *A printer driver*

Servers are the mainstay of many systems, providing application resources for everyday use, such as:

- a file server, containing copies of all your work
- a web server for information or e-commerce
- a mail server for communication.

Programming and applications development is carried out by a variety of computer professionals in the pursuit of creating applications, **applets**, utilities and operating systems.

Programming is carried out using a variety of 'languages', such as:

- Visual Basic
- C++, C#
- Java.

Go out and try!

Use a search engine (such as Google) to discover what other programming languages are available. What are they used for?

Health and safety

The workplace is governed by the **Health and Safety at Work Act 1974**. All employees are responsible for their own personal health and safety, as well as that of everyone else working around them. Anyone who breaks the law can be prosecuted and may be imprisoned if the offence is serious.

The Act combines several other acts of law, and is supported by a wide array of legislation to ensure that employees can work safely. As a computer maintenance professional, this law will apply to you.

Under the Health and Safety at Work Act, you have four main responsibilities:

- to work safely
- to cooperate with your employer in any work safety systems
- to report any hazardous conditions
- not to interfere with safety systems for any reason.

You also have other legal responsibilities:

- to be aware of fire procedures and evacuation
- to carry out accident reporting procedures
- to be aware of any special safety features in your workplace (this may be especially important if you work for a manufacturing organisation)
- to know what action needs to be taken in an emergency.

Practical task

In the UK and Europe, health and safety legislation has a major impact on daily work life. Review the list of health and safety responsibilities that apply to your workplace or place of study. Identify those which have an impact on what you do. Explain why.

When you install computer applications, you have to make sure that the work you complete is safe. In the case of the safety of users, you have to:

- ensure that the computer is replaced, and is safe to use
- ensure that the keyboard/monitor is in a comfortable position
- ensure the brightness of the display, the colours used, the size of font required are set to the user's own physical needs.

See pages 170–1 for a more detailed description of health and safety issues when installing equipment.

User requirements

Applications and operating systems are configurable to ensure that they meet a specific user's requirements. For this you need to:

- configure the system with most features locked down to prevent unauthorised access
- set accessibility options so that individuals with physical, visual or hearing disabilities can use the system or application
- tailor the application so that it produces resources according to corporate requirements (e.g. setting the standard font, size, line spacing, auto-saves, etc.)
- set the region applicable to the user wherever in the world they are located.

Practical task

Configuring user requirements is a task most computer professionals carry out. Using your computer, change the appearance of the operating system so that it will be suitable for someone with eyesight problems:

1 Find the Control Panel, in the Setting menu (Figure 4.5).

▲ FIGURE 4.5 *Control panel*

(Continued)

2 Select the Accessibility Options (Figure 4.6).

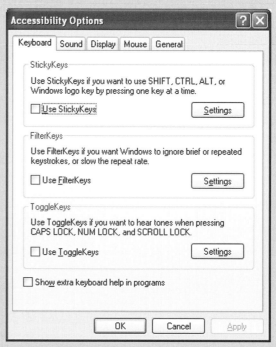

▲ FIGURE 4.6 *Accessibility option*

3 While high contrast is 'objectionable' to those whose sight is normal, it is a great asset to many who are sight impaired. Select the Display Options and select High Contrast (Figures 4.7, 4.8).

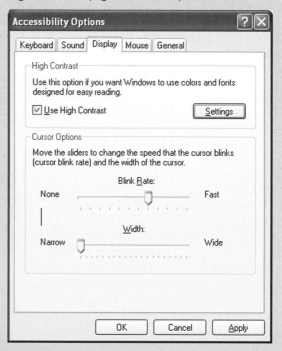

▲ FIGURE 4.7 *Display options*

(Continued)

▲ FIGURE 4.8 *High contrast*

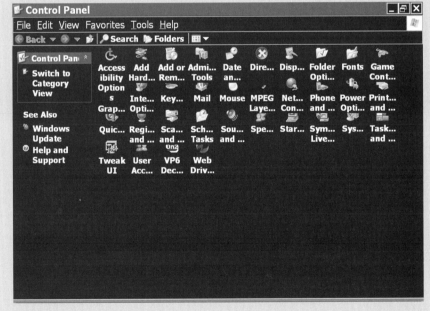

▲ FIGURE 4.9 *High contrast in action*

Install software

Software is installed in three steps:

- preparation and pre-installation
- installation
- post-installation troubleshooting if required.

Pre-installation

Before you can install any software you must:

- complete reasonable checks to ensure the system(s) used for installation meets or exceeds the manufacturer's minimum requirements
- ascertain whether you need to make a fresh install or install over an existing one
- establish that the media holding the software before installation is suitable, as well as that the media holding the installed application is capable
- identify the best location for upgrade if required
- establish the most suitable installation procedure for the application.

It is critical that you complete a wide range of reasonable checks to ensure the system(s) used for installation meets or exceeds the manufacturer's minimum requirements. It is essential that you ask yourself these questions:

- Is the processor specification of the system capable of managing the application or operating system?
- Is there enough memory to allow the application or operating system to operate successfully and produce the work as required by the user?
- Is there enough hard drive space to store the installed software/operating system, as well as enough resources for any created resources?
- Do you need any additional devices on the computer system?
- Is the specification of the graphics adapter capable of handling the resources required, especially for graphics, animation and games applications?
- Is Internet access available if required?

A manufacturer may give a minimum specification, but this is often the lowest requirement. The profession advises against this low specification; for your system to operate effectively with all the demands you may place on it, you should ensure that the software is installed on a higher specification system, if at all possible.

Go out and try!

1 Look at the software (including PC games) you have and identify the minimum specification set by each manufacturer.

2 Go to www.microsoft.com/windowxp/home/upgrading and look for the minimum hardware specifications for the Windows XP Home Edition operating system.

It is very important to ascertain whether you need to implement a fresh install or whether you can install over an existing copy of the application. You would normally conduct a fresh install:

- when the operating system has been installed for the first time and you wish to install the application to complement the needs of the user
- on the purchase/acquisition of a new computer
- when a user requires the software for the first time on an existing system
- if the operating system has been reinstalled and you need to ensure that the system is returned to the state previously enjoyed by the user.

Reinstalling software or operating systems is normal when you have acquired a manufacturer's upgrade but it may also be a sign that issues have previously occurred with the system. You will normally reinstall software when:

- the initial installation was corrupted or damaged in any way
- there was an issue/error in the original installation process
- the user (or you for that matter) has accidentally deleted essential files
- some files or application/operating system components have been corrupted or damaged due to a faulty hard drive
- some files or application/operating system components have been corrupted or damaged due to virus, worm or trojan issues.

If you have to reinstall an application, ensure that all the original files are removed before installation takes place (see 'Uninstalling software' on page 274). For the reinstallation of an operating system, it is prudent to remove the original operating system directory. You might choose to drastically reformat the hard drive, but you could delete many user documents doing this.

GLOSSARY

Virus: A code hidden in another program designed to cause damage or inconvenience.

Worm: A program that can move itself around a network (or the Internet), often with a harmful payload, designed to cause damage or inconvenience.

Trojan: This is a computer program used to access someone else's system through deceit and which allows the sender to obtain access to that system at a later date. A common example is Sub7 which can be hidden in a fun screen saver. Once loaded Sub7 will allow the sender to take complete control of the targeted computer.

By establishing that the media holding the software before installation is suitable and that the media holding the installed application is capable, you can avoid considerable consternation.

- Check whether the computer will be able to accept the CD type. Some CD-ROM drives struggled with the 800 MB format, as did some recordable media types.
- Make sure the computer will be able to accept the DVD type. There are two types of DVD format, + and –, which can be read by different DVD players and readers.
- Confirm that the computer on which you are installing the software or operating system has enough storage space on the hard drive.

Sometimes, the upgrade requires storage resources that are not available in the original software location. So, you might need to identify the best location for the upgrade. This may be another hard drive or a remote network drive.

Establishing the most suitable installation procedure for the application is good when it works. However, some applications/operating systems have specific procedures set out in an accompanying manual. It is likely that you will need to:

- check the software package for contents and read the manual
- virus check the media
- backup valuable data
- ensure that you have implemented the user's requirements for the application
- identify common problems and how to resolve them.

Go out and try!

You might have to establish the minimum installation requirements for all the software and operating systems in use by your company. Carry out extensive research on manufacturers' websites to establish the minimum specification for:

- Windows 2000
- Windows 2003
- Macromedia Flash MX 2004
- the latest version of Adobe *Photoshop*
- Microsoft Office XP
- the latest version of *AutoCAD*
- the latest version of *Doom*.

Installation process

Installing software may seem straightforward: you follow the dialogue boxes and select the options available, watch the progress bar, and 'hey presto', it's installed. However, installing software for an employer or a customer can be fraught with issues if not done correctly.

To ensure that you have completed the task of installation in a professional manner you must:

- check the software packaging and review the contents
- read the manual
- virus check all software installation media
- ensure that you have created a backup of valuable data
- ensure that you have implemented the user's requirements
- identify any common problems.

Checking the contents is essential. You need to make sure that the following is included.

- A copy of the licence agreement, to ensure that you are working within the terms of the agreement and therefore not installing the software illegally
- A serial number or licence key if required, otherwise installing the software will be a wasted process
- A copy of the guarantee, so that you may have recourse to a claim against the manufacturer if the software does not work or causes damage
- A copy of the terms and conditions, specifying how you can use the software
- The manual, to read, understand and digest the finer qualities of how to use the application
- The media for installation, checking to see if it is damaged, or to ascertain if any discs are missing
- The hardware or cables that are required

You should have access to a manufacturer's manual for installing software. This may be available as:

- a book or leaflet describing the software
- a CD containing extensive resources
- an online help included in the applications, as in Figure 4.10
- a link to a website provided by the manufacturer.

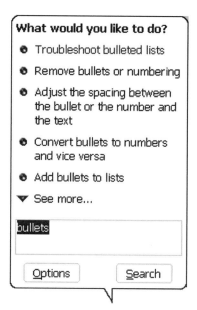

What would you like to do?

- Troubleshoot bulleted lists
- Remove bullets or numbering
- Adjust the spacing between the bullet or the number and the text
- Convert bullets to numbers and vice versa
- Add bullets to lists
▼ See more...

bullets

| Options | Search |

▲ FIGURE 4.10 *Online help*

Go out and try!

Finding manuals for some software can be challenging, but achievable when one knows how.

Visit www.microsft.com and find supportive information on:

- Flight Simulator 2000
- Windows XP
- Visio.

Don't assume that there is no need to virus check the media on which the software has been provided. No matter how reputable the software, it is possible for it to be infected by a virus during production.

Also, given that software piracy is increasingly sophisticated, there is a greater chance of purchasing software that contains a risk.

So, check all media before you install it. This must be accomplished with a robust anti-virus application. Every computer must have suitable **anti-virus** software and every organisation must have a procedure to deal with viruses and the protection of the computer system.

Go out and try!

In Unit 3 (page 218), you installed and managed an anti-virus application. Now use those skills to develop and use the virus scanner to check some of your software installation media.

Before starting an installation, you must back up valuable data. There is just a risk, though an unlikely one, that installation may corrupt the storage medium, which, in turn, will cause the loss of essential files. Remember, most of your customers need their computers for their jobs/livelihoods. For them, the loss of data can mean the loss of income or business. For your company, it may mean a claim of compensation.

Go out and try!

Based on the backup skills you have developed in Units 2 and 3, create a backup of your My Documents folder.

When installing software, it may not be simply a matter of allowing the application to complete a default installation. You may have to implement the user's requirements for the application. This may mean you have to:

- store the software in a separate location on a fileserver or separate hard drive
- configure an application to reflect the user's needs
- ensure that additional features are installed.

You may wish to install a utility called VNC (virtual network computing). This is used as a remote access system for help desk professionals. It is designed so that you can remotely control someone else's computer. These are the steps to follow in installing it.

Step 1 Download and register

Go to www.realvnc.com and click on the 'download it now' link on the left-hand side (Figures 4.11 and 4.12).

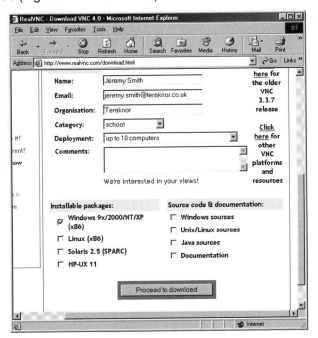

▲ FIGURE 4.11 *To download and register*

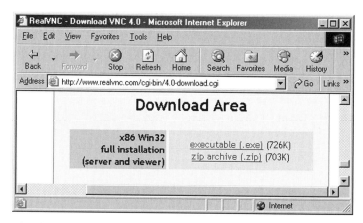

▲ FIGURE 4.12 *Download*

Step 2 Check the manual

As the software is free from the Internet, you need to read the manual on the website; on the left-hand side, there is a link for documentation.

VNC is a server that resides as a service on your computer. The server can be accessed with a client called the 'viewer from any computer' on the same system.

Step 3 Check the legal agreements

VNC is distributed under a GNU public licence (GPL) which can be found at http://www.gnu.org/copyleft/gpl.html . This is a public 'freeware' licence that allows you to copy and distribute the software, but not to sell it.

Step 4 Virus check the media

You must check the software for a virus. Using AVG (Figures 4.13 and 4.14), or another suitable anti-virus application, scan the file before using it (AVG has a 'Scan selected area' test feature).

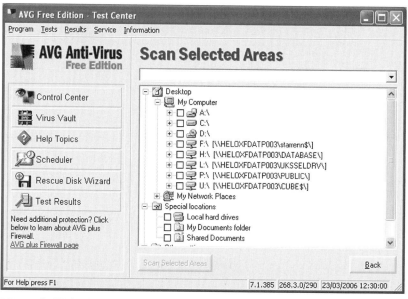

▲ FIGURE 4.13 *An AVG custom test*

▲ FIGURE 4.14 *Completion of test*

Step 5 Install the software in a unique location

Most applications allow you to install software in any location; the VNC
utility is no different. Following Figure 4.15, set the location to
'C:\IPRO_VNC'.

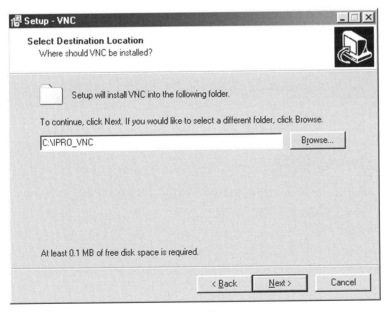

▲ FIGURE 4.15 *Selecting location of installation*

Step 6 Change settings to reflect user's needs

VNC comes in two parts: you may be required to install the server only
on one computer, as the viewer will allow the user (if in possession of the
password) to access other users' computers.

If this is your first installation, it is best to leave both boxes (shown in Figure 4.16) checked. It is worth following through the installation as you can configure icons and programme files groups that this application belongs to. Follow this and the application will be fully installed.

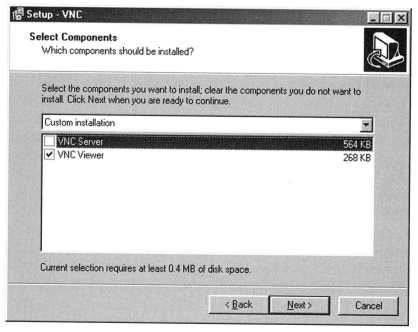

▲ FIGURE 4.16 *Configuring installation*

Step 7 Configure the software

Now that you have installed VNC, it will automatically open and present you with the VNC server properties (Figure 4.17).

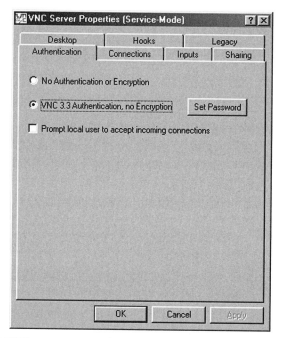

▲ FIGURE 4.17 *VNC server properties*

It is important to set the password so that anyone attempting to access your computer's desktop can only do so if they have the valid password. For this exercise, set the password as 'password'.

Take a look at the Connections tab; this has very useful network security options.

Step 8 Check it is working

To check the software is working, open the VNC viewer from program files (Figure 4.18). You will have to enter the IP address of the computer you wish to connect to as well as the password; you will then have a connection. (If there is no other computer, use 127.0.0.1, which is a loopback connection to the computer you are using.)

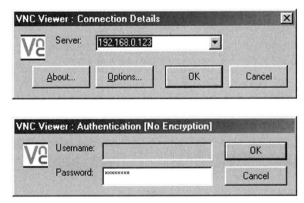

▲ FIGURE 4.18 VNC viewer login

You will see the screen shown in Figure 4.19 and can remotely control the computer you have linked with.

▲ FIGURE 4.19 VNC session

> **NOTE!**
> Completing this practical task meets observation criteria 1B. This is an observed activity, though you may wish to obtain screen grabs of the process, which you will need to date, time and sign.

If the installation is not successful, you will have to identify the problem. These are some of the common problems you may meet:

- Failure to read media
- Individual files not loading
- Registration key(s) failing
- Application not running
- Other applications no longer running correctly
- Failure of an application or system component to load/run
- Issues when you change the software from the default settings
- Failure to communicate with devices (screen driver failures, screen display is incorrect, fails to print)

The failure to read media could be caused by:

- an issue with the network connection to the resource that contains the installation files
- physical damage such as a scratch on the CD/DVD-ROM
- the CD/DVD-ROM needing to be cleaned
- the files on the hard drive memory stick having been corrupted
- there being a technical problem with the hard drive or DVD/CD-ROM drive.

For the media issues, having a backup copy of the installation files is the solution. Hardware and network faults require a level of technical troubleshooting which you should have gained from studying Units 1 and 3.

The problem of individual files not loading can be limited to a small set of causes:

- The file was missing from the installation folder.
- The file has been corrupted.
- The file has read access denied.

To resolve the first two conditions, you may need to recopy the installation files, or check the storage media for faults using tools such as scandisk. If the file has read access denied, you may need to:

● right-click on the file to check permissions
● identify who else may be using the file.

As explained in Unit 3 (page 218), the Windows registry (Figure 4.20) is a database that contains a detailed description of the resources required for the hardware and software system. When an application is installed, it needs to register itself with the operating system. The registration key(s) fails when the application does not succeed in updating the registry or there is a fault in the registry.

▲ FIGURE 4.20 *The registry*

Often, restarting the computer and reinstalling the application will resolve the issue if it persists. This is what you can do:

● With Windows XP, rollback to a previous instance using system restore.
● Download CHKREG from Microsoft, to conduct a registry repair.
● Inform the software manufacturer that there is an issue with the software or seek advice from their support desk.

'The application will not run!' is a common problem. There is no one answer, and you have to troubleshoot the problem at the computer or over the phone. You must ask the right questions to establish what the issue might be:

● Is there anything you have done that is different from the installation instructions?
● Does the system on which you are installing the software conform to the manufacturer's recommendations?
● If you have had similar issues in the past, what has been done to rectify this?
● Have you read the manual? If so, what does it say you have to do?
● Some applications require you to restart the computer before first use. Have you done this?

If other applications no longer run correctly or a system component fails to load or run, you have installed an application that has:

- overwritten essential files from the previous application
- a hardware, software or operating system conflict between the two applications.

It may simply be a memory issue, and you are unable to run both applications at the same time. This can be remedied by only running one application at any given time or purchasing more memory (if possible) for the system.

Issues can often occur when you change the software from the default settings. This is often due to the nature of the additional setting not necessarily being compatible with the system, the resources available, or simply, you have changed the wrong setting.

For the uninitiated, changing the Windows operating system from the defaults is immediately problematic; you could be asking the computer to attempt tasks that it is not designed for. Whenever you change any setting on any application:

- ensure that you only make one change at any one time
- keep a record of each change you have made and why you did it.

With some installations, the failure to communicate with devices becomes apparent.

- The screen driver fails because the extent of the graphics required is greater than the screen or the graphics card can manage. This is often the case with older computers and newer games, as the demand on graphical resources is high.
- The screen display is incorrect, as in some applications. Again, those that are graphically oriented require higher resolutions. An excellent example is Macromedia's Flash MX 2004, which needs a high resolution and is difficult to use at 1024 x 768 (Figure 4.21).
- Your computer may fail to print if the application has loaded any specific print drivers. Some scanner applications link to the printer to provide a 'virtual' photocopier; Adobe *Acrobat Creator*® has a virtual driver to create the PDF (portable data file) format.

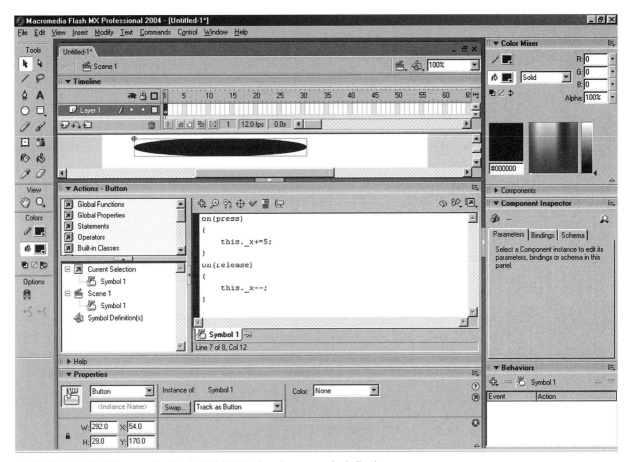

▲ FIGURE 4.21 *Micromedia Flash MX 2004 showing crowded display*

Identify and address problems

Having a 'broken' application to hand is not safe and may cause your computer, or that of your customer, serious problems. This section deals with an application that is intentionally damaged by your centre and which you will repair. This should have no impact on a computer.

In this section, you will have the opportunity to look at these issues:

- Replacing source files
- Obtaining individual files quickly
- Accuracy when entering data
- Why you have to reboot the system
- The need to test all applications on the system following new installation
- How to restore defaults
- When to conduct a complete reinstall
- Using the undisclosed system restart or task manager to shut down application

Replacing source files

Replacing source files can be a dangerous task and will be carried out on AVG, the free anti-virus system from Grisoft. You will carry out the following practical task, to remove essential DLLs, run the program to cause an error and then replace the DLLs to establish that the program is working correctly again.

Practical task

Here you will replace source files.

1 Create a temporary folder and call it 'AVG_DLLs'.

2 Open the folder C:\Program Files\grisoft\AVG Free (Figure 4.22).

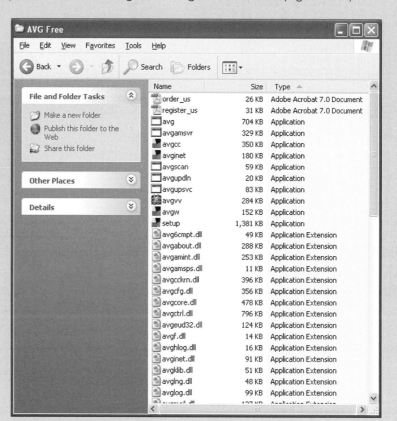

▲ FIGURE 4.22 *C:\Program Files\grisoft\AVG Free*

3 Shut down the AVG control centre. You will find this in the bottom right-hand corner of your desktop, in the system tray.
As in Figure 4.23, right-click and select the Quit AVG Control Center option.

(Continued)

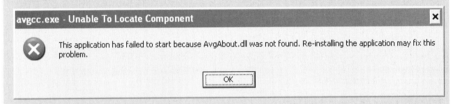

Launch AVG Control Center
Quit AVG Control Center
Launch AVG Test Center

AVG Free - Online Services
Check for Updates

▲ FIGURE 4.23 *Quit AVG control centre*

4 Now that the anti virus software is out of action, you can do some damage! Copy the DLL file avgabout.dll to the folder you created, AVG_DLLs.

5 Select the file avgabout.dll in C:\Program Files\grisoft\AVG Free and delete it!

6 Now try to run the AVG control centre from the start menu; you should get the error as seen in Figure 4.24.

avgcc.exe - Unable To Locate Component ✕

This application has failed to start because AvgAbout.dll was not found. Re-installing the application may fix this problem.

[OK]

▲ FIGURE 4.24 *AVG runtime error*

7 Replacing the source file is very simple; all you have to do is to copy the file from AVG_DLLs to C:\Program Files\grisoft\AVG Free

8 Restart the AVG control centre; it should now operate successfully.

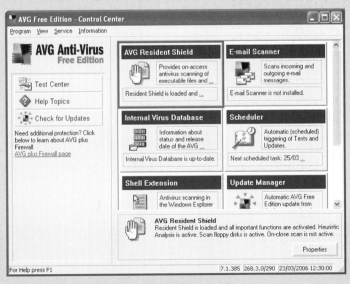

▲ FIGURE 4.25 *AVG control centre working again*

Obtaining individual files quickly

Microsoft developed a system to let you repair installed applications quickly if they use MSI files.

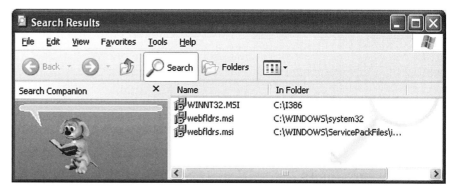

▲ FIGURE 4.26 *MSI files for Windows XP*

With these files, if you have an application that is damaged, you can right-click on the file and then install, repair or uninstall the files contained within the file which should be part of the application (Figures 4.27 and 4.28).

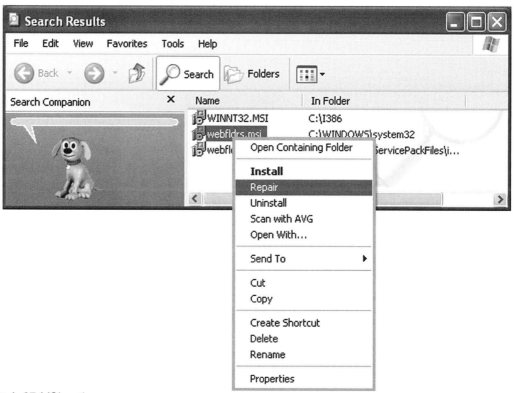

▲ FIGURE 4.27 *MSI options*

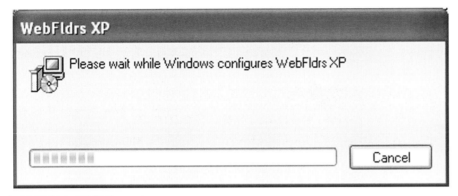

▲ FIGURE 4.28 *MSI repair*

Accuracy when entering data

Often, the installation of the applications and operating systems require you, the professional, to enter a considerable quantity of information, to ensure that the application/operating system is installed to the requirements of the user. You need to set up a user name and password, and to let you access all aspects of the computer, this needs to be at administrator level (Figure 4.29).

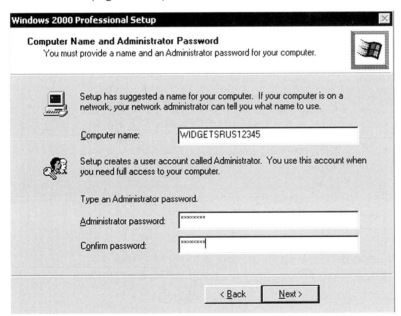

▲ FIGURE 4.29 *Entering data during an installation*

Why you have to reboot the system

There are two types of applications with respect to the impact they have during installation:

- those that have no impact on the underlying system, or have no need to integrate with the underlying system
- others which have an impact on the underlying system or rely on the underlying system to operate.

Since the advent of the Windows registry with Windows 95 and NT4, there has been a strong tie between applications and the operating system. (In Windows 3.1, the registry was a series of .INI files.) The link between the registry and the applications has improved, but some applications require drivers and other files to be loaded by the operating system prior to the application being started. Therefore, the only solution is to reboot (Figure 4.30) the operating system, so that the required drivers can be loaded. This tends to happen more with applications that manage hardware, or require specialised operating system resources.

▲ FIGURE 4.30 *Reboot*

Rebooting the system is also often associated with the failure of the operating system. This must only be done when no other option is available. Rebooting while the operating system and applications are running may cause irreversible damage to essential files. You can complete a warm reboot, by pressing Ctrl-Alt-Del simultaneously. If that fails, press the reset button or off/on switch.

The need to test all applications on the system following new installation

When you install an application, ask yourself these questions:

- How do you know it is working?
- Are there any faults that you may not be aware of?
- Have all the components loaded successfully?
- Is it doing what you expected?

What are the benefits of creating a fault logsheet for the computer systems you may work on? What information might you include on a log sheet? Discuss this with others in your group and devise a design for a fault log sheet that meets all your requirements.

How to restore defaults

When software no longer works the way we wish, or the changes to it are no longer appropriate for the task at hand, or there is a new user, you might need to return the software to its original state. Restoring software back to its defaults can be done systematically, if you have kept an accurate record of all the changes you have made. However, in case you do not have this information, you can restore the factory settings defaults on some applications.

The example in Figure 4.31 is from Macromedia's Flash MX 2004. In the Preferences tab are settings for the editor that operates the inbuilt ActionScript™ programming language. No matter what settings are changed, you can return to the original settings simply by pressing the Reset to Defaults button.

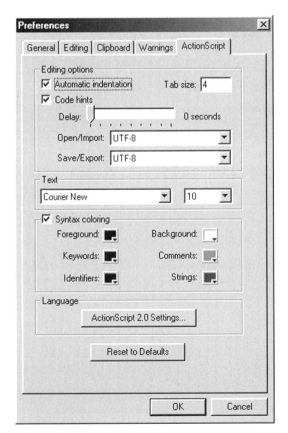

▲ FIGURE 4.31 *Restore defaulter*

When to conduct a complete reinstall

For many reasons, an application could be damaged beyond repair. You can try certain things:

- You can attempt to reinstall it from the MSI file(s)
- You can attempt to copy the files back into the directory from a backup
- You can attempt to copy files from another computer with a similar installation

However, it may still not work. In the next section (page 274) you will look at the process of uninstalling an application. It is advisable to attempt to do this before reinstalling the application; otherwise, you may create further problems with the Windows registry.

Once you have uninstalled an application, then you can go back to the original media and reinstall.

Using the undisclosed system restart or task manager to shut down an application

Applications do not always work according to plan; they will hang and freeze, for example. This could be an operating system problem, fault in the application, or lack of memory.

Try pressing Ctrl-Alt-Del. This will invoke the Task Manager (Figure 4.32).

▲ FIGURE 4.32 *Task Manager*

Sometimes, windows will freeze when an application has issues, and you cannot open any other application or window. This means that you have a problem with Internet *Explorer*. *Explorer* is an essential part of the file, application and desktop management system. To resolve this, you can restart *Explorer* 'on the fly'.

Click on the Processes tab (Figure 4.33).

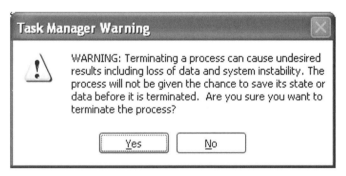

▲ FIGURE 4.33 *Processes tab*

Then select *Explorer* and press the End Process button, where you will be presented with a warning dialogue (Figure 4.34).

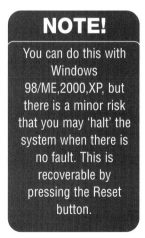

▲ FIGURE 4.34 *Task manager warning*

> **NOTE!**
> You can do this with Windows 98/ME,2000,XP, but there is a minor risk that you may 'halt' the system when there is no fault. This is recoverable by pressing the Reset button.

Now select File/Run and type 'explorer' in the Create New Task dialogue box (Figure 4.35). *Explorer* should now restart and the system should restore itself.

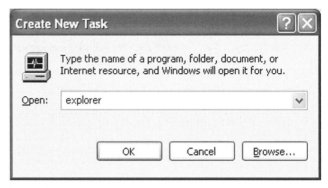

▲ FIGURE 4.35 *Create new task*

The Task Manager can be used to terminate all applications and many processes; the danger is the damage that may be caused. A process is a defined service that is running on behalf of Windows to manage a component of the operating system. Termination, without checking what the process does, may cause considerable problems, with resulting data or operating system damage.

An additional tool provided by Microsoft for recent versions of Windows is for systems that fail. These can be accessed remotely, with the professional using the 'TSKILL' command. Knowing the PID (Processes ID) (Figure 4.36) allows the professional to issue the command to terminate a process remotely (Figure 4.37).

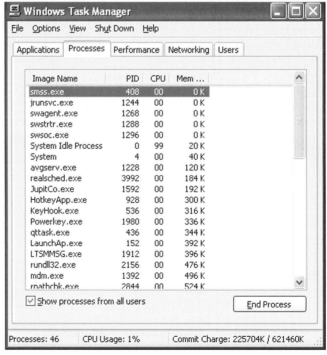

▲ FIGURE 4.36 *Processes ID*

```
C:\WINDOWS\System32\cmd.exe                               _ □ ×
Microsoft Windows XP [Version 5.1.2600]
(C) Copyright 1985-2001 Microsoft Corp.

C:\Documents and Settings\Andrew>tskill
Invalid parameter(s)
Ends a process.

TSKILL processid | processname [/SERVER:servername] [/ID:sessionid | /A] [/V]

   processid          Process ID for the process to be terminated.
   processname        Process name to be terminated.
   /SERVER:servername Server containing processID (default is current).
                      /ID or /A must be specified when using processname
                      and /SERVER
   /ID:sessionid      End process running under the specified session.
   /A                 End process running under ALL sessions.
   /V                 Display information about actions being performed.


C:\Documents and Settings\Andrew>tskill 1744

C:\Documents and Settings\Andrew>
```

▲ FIGURE 4.37 *TSKILL*

Think about what would happen to your computer if you allowed someone irresponsible to have the remote access to your system and they knew the TSKILL command.

Check your understanding

1 What must you do to reproduce software from another source? What are the consequences of not doing this?

2 How would you register software you have purchased?

3 Name six different types of application software.

4 What are utilities? What do they enable you to do?

5 What checks should you make before you install software?

6 Why would you need to reinstall software? What do you need to do before doing it?

7 If the software installation is not successful, what problems might have prevented this?

4.2 Uninstalling software

Identify and describe reasons for uninstalling software

Knowing how to successfully uninstall software is just as important as knowing how to install software. If you fail to uninstall software correctly, the operating system is left with wasteful overheads with files, registry entries and device drivers. Uninstalling software successfully involves knowing:

- how to justify the decision to uninstall software
- what the implications of registration are
- how to carry out any backup of data and the reasons for keeping some data
- how to use the operating system to remove the application
- how to use the 'remove application' feature or a supplied uninstall component
- how to overcome problems caused by just deleting directories
- how to carefully search through the registry
- how to use the Windows system to restore utility
- how to carry out system testing to ensure successful elimination of any previous faults.

For this unit, you have to provide evidence that you can uninstall two software applications successfully.

Justify the decision to uninstall software

Some users, and especially computer professionals, enjoy keeping as many applications as possible. Unfortunately, this causes a wide range of issues, some for your computer and others for the organisations you may work for:

- The retained installation of an application that is not used might prevent another colleague using it, because there are not enough licences.
- The retained application might slow down the boot process of the computer, because drivers have to be loaded into memory for the application, when they are not required.
- The retained application occupies a considerable quantity of hard drive space on an already full system, and this might cause virtual memory and fragmentation issues.

- The application has been superseded by another, or a later version.
- The company no longer holds a licence for the application.
- There is a recognised fault with the application.
- The computer is going to another employee who does not need it, or cannot use it.
- There is no longer any support for the application in question.

Practical task

Look at the computer you have at home and consider the following question: What software could I remove because I no longer need it or use it?

- Why would this be an issue?
- Why could this be a benefit?

The implications of registration

Before continuing, review the section on page 238–41.

With software licensing being an important consideration in the installation of all software, the need to record the removal of software is of the same importance as the recording of all computers that contain a certain licensed application.

This allows applications to be reinstalled on other computers, thus ensuring that your company is within its licence agreement on the quantity of installations. Some software manufacturers impose on companies the need to maintain auditable records of all computers that contain their software, and they or their representatives may check that this is the case.

Many companies, without prompting, carry out their own internal software audit, to check that you have kept accurate records. This does not stop at their checking the paperwork; they will either randomly visit selected computers to ensure compliance or have software mechanisms that will report on what software is on which computer.

Go out and try!

1 Visit http://www.sassafras.com/, a well-known creator of 'auditing' software.
   - How does the software work?
   - How does it help the software-auditing task?

2 Now, using a search engine (such as Google), conduct a search on 'Software Audits'. What is the general consensus of advice in this area?

Carry out any backup of data and the reasons for keeping some data

In this section you will explore why it is important to create a backup of essential system data before you uninstall an application.

When you (or the operating system/application utility) remove an application, a wide range of files, directories and registry entries are removed. This has an inherent potential for disaster:

- User files may be included in some of the directories.
- The removal of some files may cause a system instability or failure.
- The removal of some registry entries may cause a system instability or failure.

Therefore, the backup, if you choose to complete one before uninstalling, should include:

- any user files not associated with the application being removed
- a copy of the application folders in case a full or partial restore should be undertaken
- a copy of the registry prior to the application removal.

The user files held on a system are entirely dependent on the user's personal behaviour and the privileges they have been granted. Most corporate networks stipulate that all employees keep work on one of their many managed servers. As these are backed up every night, they afford a reasonable level of security, as far as disaster recovery is concerned. If a user has stored valuable data on a local hard drive, ask them; it is most likely they will tell you, especially when you inform them that they may lose it otherwise. Often users are unsure where their data is kept; this is not ignorance, most users are simply not technically minded.

If you are using Windows, you will often find the user's data in:

- C:\my documents\ if they are using Windows 98, or
- C:\documents and settings\[users name or login ID] if they are using 2000/XP.

If you intend to copy the folders that store the applications, good luck! While many applications store their 'programs' in one common place in Windows, this is not always the case, especially for older applications or resources that come from some other companies.

Like most tasks in computing, a little detective work is required. You have to search the contents of the hard drive. To save time, you may find applications in C:\Program Files, in a named folder on the root of C:\, and, rarely, in C:\Windows or C:\Windows\system32.

GLOSSARY

Root is a term used to describe the top of the hard drive directory structure (cunningly called a tree).

The Windows registry is a complex database, where a great deal of damage can be inflicted if it is not treated with the appropriate respect.

For Windows 98, and all other versions of Windows, open regedit, using the Run dialogue box (Figure 4.38).

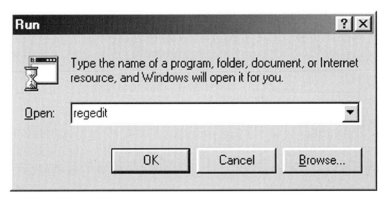

▲ FIGURE **4.38** *Starting regedit*

In regedit, select File, and then export and name the file backup DD_MM_YYYY, where the DD_MM_YYYY represents the day, month and year of the backup (Figure 4.39).

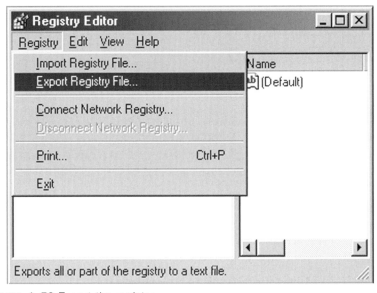

▲ FIGURE **4.39** *Export the registry*

At any time there is an issue with the registry due to an application being removed, you can import the saved registry file and overwrite the new settings with the previous values.

Use the operating system to remove the application

At one time, knowing the directory the application existed in, as in systems like MS-DOS, was all that was required. Now, applications weave themselves into the operating system, in such a way that no one, except the original team of software developers, has any idea of what resources the application actual uses.

An application tends to have certain features:

- The core application files are in a programme directory, stored in 'C:\programme files', but this is not always the case.
- A wide range of registry keys are recorded in the Windows registry.
- Its own DLLs are in C:\windows\system32.
- It shares other DLLs with other applications or the operating system.
- In some cases, other program directories are hidden in the main C:\windows folder.

Therefore, it is essential that you use the resources provided by the operating system or the software application to remove the application. Doing it yourself could damage the operating system.

In this section, you will learn to:

- use the 'remove application' feature or a supplied uninstall component
- overcome problems caused by just deleting directories
- use the Windows system to restore utility.

Use of the 'remove application' feature or a supplied uninstall component

There are two safe methods to remove applications that are provided by Microsoft as part of their operating system and by manufacturers as part of their software features.

The Windows Add/Remove programs feature comes as part of the control panel (Figure 4.40).

GLOSSARY

MS-DOS (Microsoft disk operating system) was an early text-based operating system which preceded Windows. MS-DOS technically ceased to exist at version 6.22, with Windows 3.1, but hardened techno-nerds are aware that MS-DOS persisted as the base for Windows 95 and 98. DOS no longer exists, as it has been replaced by a full graphical operating system with access to a command line interface to access the older MS-DOS commands.

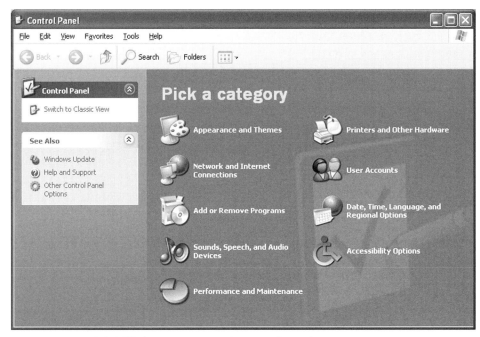

▲ FIGURE 4.40 *Add/Remove programs in control panel*

When you have selected the Add/Remove Programs feature, it may take at least two minutes to check the registry for all the applications installed that can be removed (Figure 4.41).

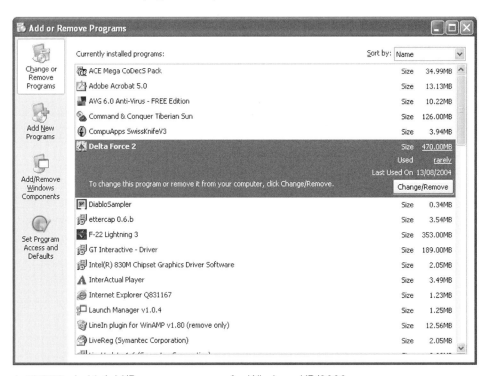

▲ FIGURE 4.41 *Add/Remove programs for Windows XP/2000*

In Windows 98, you will see a completely different window (Figure 4.42).

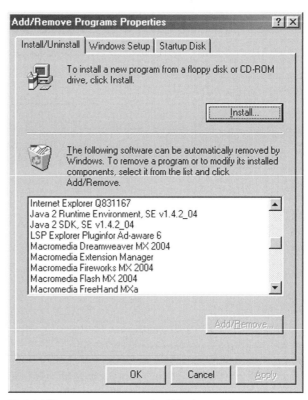

▲ FIGURE 4.42 *Add/Remove programs for Windows 98*

As can be seen from Figure 4.41, the Windows Add/Remove Programs feature can be used to:

- change or remove applications
- add new programs
- remove Windows components
- set program access.

As you click on each application, you will see:

- how often the application has been used
- when it was last used
- the total size of all files stored on the hard drive, relating to the application.

Go out and try!

If you have Windows XP or 2000 on your computer, look through and check each application that is installed via the Add/Remove programs feature. Consider how system resources may be saved if you removed applications that are 'rarely' used.

To remove an application, click on the Change/Remove button. In Figure 4.43 and Figure 4.44, Delta Force 2 is being removed from the system as the game has now been superseded. This removes the application, its files, directories, DLLs and registry entries.

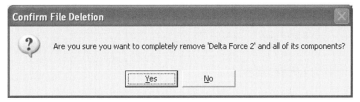

▲ FIGURE 4.43 *Removal of an application*

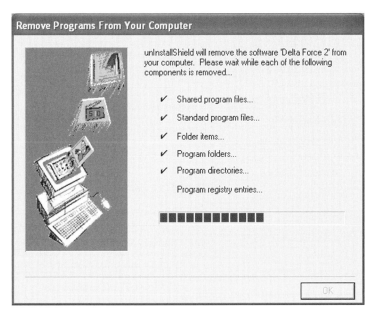

▲ FIGURE 4.44 *Application removal dialogue box*

The Microsoft Add New Programs (Figure 4.45) is a seldom-used feature. Application installation is often best done through the CD/DVD/Download provided by the software manufacturer. However, Add New Programs is a 'helpful' tool for users to manage the installation of applications and to ensure that their version of Windows is current through the Windows update feature. The Windows update feature is explored in greater detail in Unit 3 (page 222).

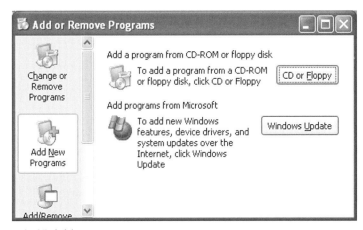

▲ FIGURE 4.45 *Add new programs*

The add or remove Windows components is a throwback to earlier versions of Windows; there is very little difference. When you have selected this option, it will take a moment to scan the registry, before displaying the components wizard (Figure 4.46).

▲ FIGURE 4.46 *Windows components wizard*

Here you are able to work your way through each option and decide if you wish to add or remove a component by clicking on the checkbox. If the checkbox is greyed, Windows is indicating that there is a subordinate window with other options.

If you have selected any of the options, click on Next and Windows will install or remove (uninstall) the component for you (Figure 4.47).

▲ FIGURE 4.47 *Configuring components*

Although unrelated to the process of installing or removing components or applications, the Add/Remove Programs window has an additional option: allowing you to set program access and defaults. This is a powerful tool for administrators, allowing them to manage the access to various applications and, where there is a choice, independently setting the default application (Figure 4.48).

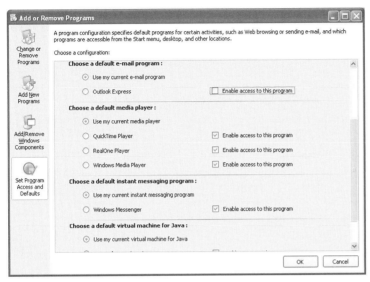

▲ FIGURE 4.48 *Set program access and defaults*

To uninstall an application, use the application's own uninstall feature. Often, this feature is part of the program menu for the application in question (Figure 4.49).

▲ FIGURE 4.49 *Uninstall*

Depending on the 'makeup' of the uninstaller, it will ask if you are sure this is what you wish to do, before you click the Uninstall button (Figure 4.50).

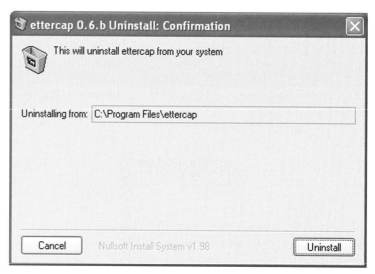

▲ FIGURE 4.50 *Uninstall confirmation*

Then, when the process is complete, close the dialogue box (Figure 4.51).

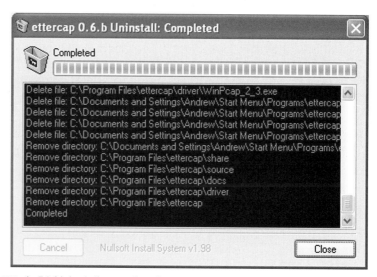

▲ FIGURE 4.51 *Uninstall completed*

Overcoming problems caused by the deletion of directories

Do not remove the application directory without following the correct uninstall process. Otherwise, this may:

● cause Windows to crash
● invoke errors at startup
● force the Windows registry to have redundant entries
● allow Windows to load drivers that are not required.

If you have done this, there are certain ways of correcting the problem:

- If available, reinstall the directory from a backup.
- Completely reinstall the application, so that you can then uninstall it correctly. Although this may seem illogical, it works.
- Check that the file(s) are in the recycle bin, ready for recovery.
- Use an application that will undelete the directory.

The recycle bin (Figure 4.52) is a 'user friendly' resource that has been available since Windows 95. This was designed to supersede Microsoft's own undelete application.

▲ FIGURE 4.52 *Recycle bin icon*

When you delete any folder or files it will be placed in the recycle bin (Figure 4.53). If you select the 'Restore all items' option, Windows will replace the deleted folders/files in the location from which they were removed.

▲ FIGURE 4.53 *Recycle bin contents*

If you right-click on the recycle bin, you can empty it (but only if you are sure that is what you want) as well as configure its properties (Figure 4.54).

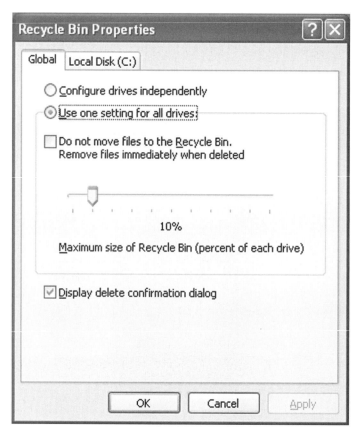

▲ FIGURE 4.54 *Recycle bin properties*

You can force the recycle bin to reject all files and ensure that they are permanently deleted. If you don't want to reject all files, you can set the recycle bin to be at most 10 per cent of your hard drive. With the average hard drive being at 60 GB, you will have a recycle bin at 6 GB. This is suitable for holding most 'full' applications after accidental deletion.

Go out and try!

Look at the recycle bin settings on your computer. Is there anything that you may wish to do, to improve the settings?

You can use an undelete utility to recover a directory or a file. What many people do not realise is that when you delete a file, it is not erased; only the file system reference to the file is deleted. This means that the file will continue to exist until it is written over at a later date.

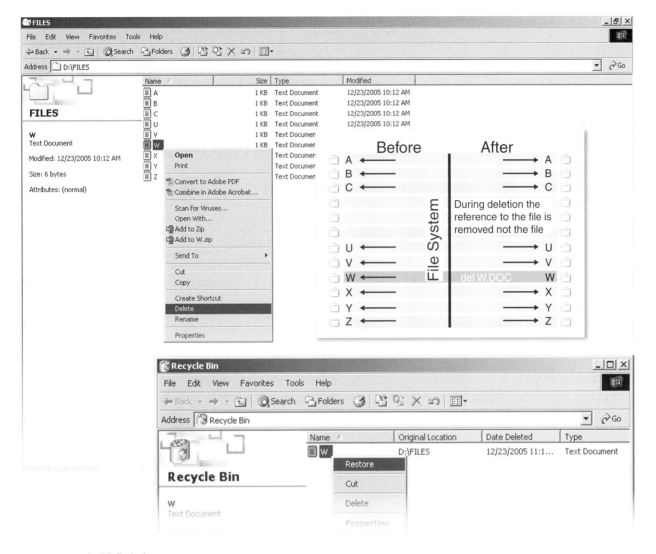

▲ FIGURE 4.55 *Deletion process*

Go out and try!

1 Companies like ExecSoft provide utilities that will search the system for any selected files. Visit and download an undelete utility from http://www1.execsoft.com/delutil_i.exe (*Note:* It only works on Windows 2000/NT and XP.)

2 Once installed, open the Deleted File Analysis utility and complete a search of your local hard drive. To test the software, copy an unimportant file, then delete the copy and use the utility to find the deleted file. Select the file(s) in question and press the Undelete button.

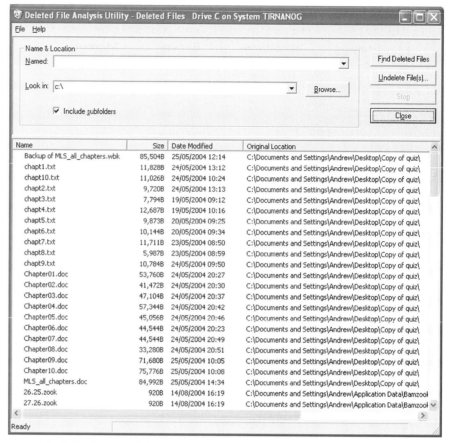

▲ **FIGURE 4.56** *Successful search for a deleted directory*

Use of the Windows system to restore utility

A new feature of the Windows XP product family, the System Restore, can be found in Programs/Accessories/System Tools. It enables you to create a restore point, thus allowing you to:

● install applications
● add utilities
● update drivers
● change settings.

Windows XP automatically creates a restore point every time you make a change (called a checkpoint). Information on this feature can be found in Control Panel/System Properties/System Restore tab.

You can switch off the system restore feature as well as adjust the amount of hard drive space dedicated to maintain restore points and checkpoints (Figure 4.57).

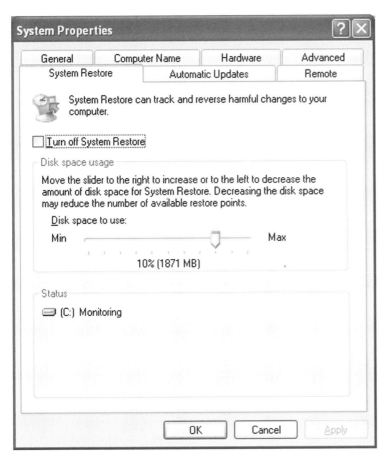

▲ FIGURE 4.57 *System restore/system properties*

Creating a restore point is a simple process, something you may wish to do the next time you add or remove an application (Figure 4.58).

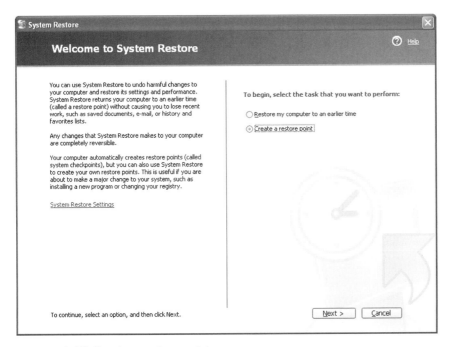

▲ FIGURE 4.58 *Create a restore point*

Follow the instructions on the System Restore wizard and name your restore point as appropriate (Figure 4.59).

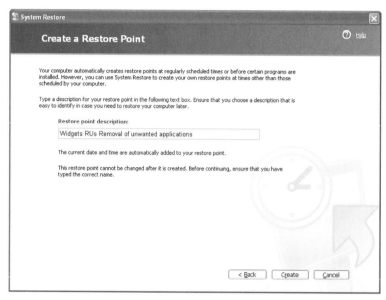

▲ FIGURE 4.59 *Naming a restore point*

Once you have clicked on Create, you may have to wait at least two minutes, while Windows creates the appropriate snapshot (Figure 4.60).

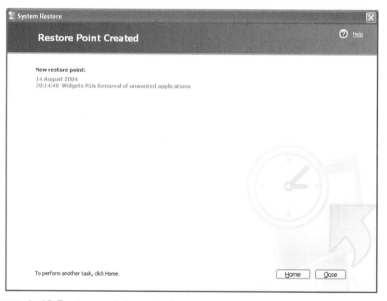

▲ FIGURE 4.60 *Restore point created*

If you have to restore from an earlier position, the application did not install or management decided that the user can keep the application after all, you can restart the System Restore wizard and select the 'Restore my computer to an earlier time' option (Figure 4.61).

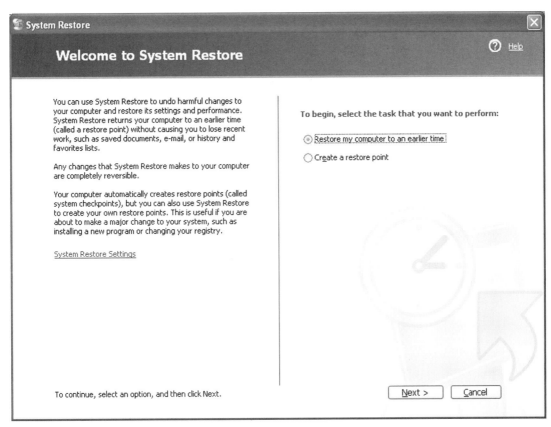

▲ FIGURE 4.61 *Restore my computer to an earlier time*

You can select a variety of restore positions (the checkpoints highlighted in the calendar) or search for the named restore point you have created (Figure 4.62).

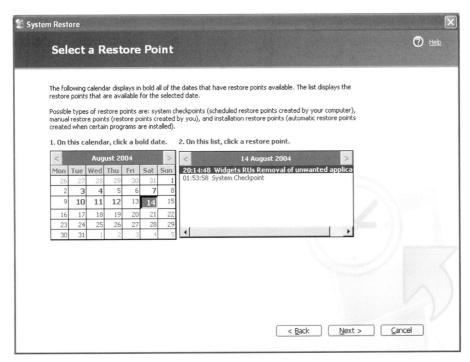

▲ FIGURE 4.62 *Select a restore point*

Once you have selected the restore point (Figure 4.63), Windows will restart your computer and return your system to its previous state.

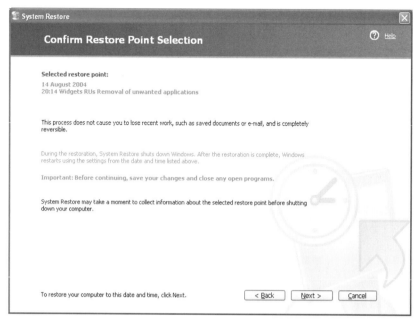

▲ FIGURE 4.63 *Confirm restore point*

Go out and try!

Using a computer with Windows XP, create a restore point. What would be the benefits of having a weekly or daily restore point available?

Carry out system testing to ensure successful elimination of any previous faults

In section 4.3, you have the opportunity to explore in detail the need for systems testing and the appropriate technique you will choose to follow. It is important that your testing methodology is thorough, as you will have no wish to revisit the same computer with the same problem.

Check your understanding

1   How would you justify uninstalling software?
2   What are the features of an application?
3   How do you use the Windows system to restore utility?
4   What problems can be created if you fail to backup essential system data before you uninstall an application?
5   How do you use the remote application feature?

4.3 Apply common types of test procedures and analyse results

In computer systems support you need to carry out regular testing to ensure that the computer technology is working 'normally'. When a computer problem needs to be resolved, the repair, and therefore testing, requires a systematic approach. Otherwise, you may make the problem worse.

A systematic approach involves:

- the preparation of test plans
- the selection and application of test procedures
- the selection and application of hardware tests
- identification of common faults
- logging and analysing results.

Prepare test plans

When you are faced with a computer system fault, you must plan how you are going to solve the problem. Planning how you are going to tackle a problem will save extra work in the long term. A good plan ensures that you have considered all the possibilities beforehand. The advantages are:

- you do not waste your time on a pointless pursuit
- you begin to appreciate the problem in hand, and ensure that you have the:
  - tools
  - spare hardware
  - software
  - diagnostic tools if required.

You will need to consider how long it will take to complete the test and which steps you may need to take in completing it. Some tests, especially those involving hard drives, are time-consuming and wasteful if you have to wait for them to finish. With a well thought out test, you can use the 'waiting' time to work on another problem, or time the activity to start over a lunch break, or when you are about to leave for the night.

Many computer system faults (or **run-time errors**) are 'commonplace'. They have been encountered previously (page 117–50) and the solutions are well documented. It is likely that your college, employer or hardware/software manufacturer has predefined plans/procedures in place.

There is no perfect test plan; different organisations will have different approaches. However, it is likely that your test plan will contain:

- details of the problem
- tools required
- health and safety considerations
- hardware and software resources required
- suggested time to take on problem
- a timeline of tasks
- details of the customer
- information provided by customer that may be essential to understanding the problem (or tasks to avoid, such as formatting the hard drive, because it has essential data).

When you have completed the test, you should also record the outcomes, i.e. the results of the test.

Test procedures

There are four types of test procedures for a computer system:

- A routine test to check if the computer system is working as expected
- A test procedure for a recognised problem
- Test procedures for undiagnosed hardware faults
- Test procedures for undiagnosed software faults

There are many different types of system problem and each may need a procedure:

- Power supply fault
- BIOS error
- RAM fault
- Hard disk failure and problem
- CD-ROM misread
- Floppy disk error
- Keyboard fault
- Mouse problem
- Application crash
- Operating system failure
- Crashing after hardware or software upgrade
- IRQ conflict
- Printer consumable problem
- Printer failure and other peripheral problems

On pages 295–305 you have the opportunity to learn about the common types of faults which may occur. However, you may be faced with the need to know how to find a likely area of fault by **elimination** (see Figure 2.61, page 157).

Select and apply hardware tests

Before you start testing a computer, consider these points:

- The failure of a hardware component can affect applications. This is true for printers, mice, digital cameras, Internet video cams, hard drives, flash drives and the battery on your laptop.
- Installing a new application or deleting an old one can affect the performance of a computer system, especially when it is done incorrectly.

One test procedure is to ask the user/customer questions:

- Have you or someone else installed anything on this computer?
- Has anything out of the ordinary been happening on the computer recently?
- Have you downloaded anything from the Internet?
- Have you changed any hardware (this may be the keyboard, mouse or printer)?

This may provide you with considerable insight into what the actual problem may be.

Common types of faults

You are going to encounter many faults in your professional experience as a computer systems support expert, some expected and some not expected. This section looks at a range of faults that you may have to deal with.

Power supply faults

Power supply faults are the most dangerous and must be managed with some caution in your professional capacity. Do not open the power supply. You should not attempt to repair it. Trying to do so will put yourself and others using the computer at risk.

> **WARNING!**
> At your level of knowledge and skill opening the power supply is dangerous and you are unlikely to be qualified to fix any of the components.

Power supplies are switch mode, which means that they can offer voltages of 12 V and 5 V. A damaged power supply can affect the entire computer system, damaging all components.

The commonest fault occurs when someone switches the power input from 230 V to 110 V (Figure 4.64). As UK mains supply is 230–240 V, this will 'blow' the power supply. Replacing the power supply is a low cost task (£5 to £20). This is the easiest and safest solution.

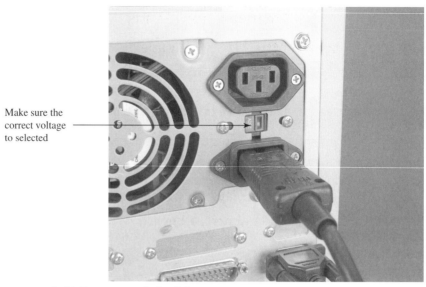

Make sure the correct voltage to selected

▲ FIGURE 4.64 *Power supply for PC*

You have to distinguish between a BIOS error message and a fault with the BIOS (Figure 4.65). Each manufacturer's BIOS has a differing set of 'codes' according to their specifications. This means that when your computer starts up, the BIOS, which checks your system, detects an error and it will inform you. They are referred to as 'beep' codes, given to the sound sent to the inbuilt speaker (Table 4.2).

▲ FIGURE 4.65 *BIOS*

American megatrends	
Number of beeps	**Issue**
1	Fault with system memory
2	Parity checking (fault checking) failure
3	Base memory issue
4	System timer failure
5	Processor failure
6	Keyboard controller
7	Mode failure
8	Display memory error
9	BIOS error
10	CMOS fault
11	Processor cache memory error
Continuous	Memory or video issue
Award/Phoenix	
1 long beep	Memory issues
1 long then 2 short	Video error
Continuous	Memory or video issue

Note that this information varies through time and model and that you need to refer to the manufacturer's website for accurate and up-to-date information.

▲ TABLE 4.2 *BIOS beep codes*

The beeping technique is used in case the display is not working.

If the BIOS is not working, you may have one of two possible faults:

- Nothing happens. The BIOS is dead and so is your motherboard. You will need to replace the BIOS or the motherboard.
- You will see an invalid CMOS error, and the system will load any detected defaults. This happens on older computers, especially those that have been in storage for over six months and have had no power.

Memory faults

Memory (RAM) faults are more common than most users appreciate. Often a computer will be operating on less memory for months, possibly years, before anyone identifies that there is a problem.

As a computer's motherboard can hold more than one memory stick, memory no longer needs to be paired. This means that a rack of three DIMM slots could hold three gigabytes of storage.

If a memory stick fails, one of the following may occur:

- Nothing will happen, that is you will not notice anything. However, the reported memory will be less than the memory expected in the system.
- The BIOS will display an error (or beep an error) after completing a comprehensive memory test.

▲ FIGURE 4.66 *Memory*

Hard disk faults

Hard disk failure and the resulting problems can have a considerable impact on the computer and the user.

- A fault with the IDE/SCSI controller can be fixed with the replacement of the motherboard.
- A fault with the IDE/SCSI cable can be fixed with the replacement of the cable.
- A head crash, or hard drive circuitry fault can be catastrophic, and cannot be reasonably repaired by yourself. If this occurs, you will need to send the hard drive to a specialist repair company.
- The hard drive not being detected by the BIOS may require a BIOS upgrade, or your checking the previous faults.
- The hard drive may be set to slave when it should be master.
- There may be disk surface issues that need repair by an application like scandisk.
- The hard drive may be too full and/or needs defragmenting.

CD or DVD-ROM misreads

This fault is often caused by the quality or type of the media, and seldom by the technology. CD/DVD-ROM readers are now so low cost that if a fault occurs you can easily replace them.

If a disk is 'faulty', ask yourself these questions:

- Does it need to be cleaned?
- Was it 'burnt' correctly?
- Is the media type compatible with the reader? This happens in the case of older readers being used, with the new denser, faster burn media.

CD/DVD technology (Figure 4.67) is recognised by the system the same way as a hard drive is and you can configure the BIOS to boot from the media, as well as configure the drive to be a master or slave.

▲ FIGURE 4.67 *CD-ROM*

The floppy disk (Figure 4.68) is a dying technology and only exists because of the large quantity of information still stored on them, as well as being an excellent backup device when the hard drive fails. Common errors include:

- floppy disk media corrupted by dirt, by being left on top of a CRT monitor, or being mistreated
- the 34-pin cable being damaged, or the wrong way around
- the floppy drive controller failing
- the disk being jammed inside the floppy drive bay.

▲ FIGURE 4.68 *Floppy disk and drive*

Keyboard faults or problems

Keyboard faults often occur, as the keyboard, apart from the mouse, is the most commonly used device:

- The incorrect region may be installed on the operating system, for example where £ is $.
- The keyboard may be dirty and the button stuck. (This will cause a BIOS beep code on boot.)
- The connection may be faulty; this could be the PS/2, USB or wireless connection. (Is the keyboard too far away?)
- You may be using the wrong keyboard, for example a German keyboard on UK settings.
- Keys are damaged.

These are simple solutions to such problems:

- change the settings
- clean the keyboard
- replace the keyboard.

Mouse problems

Like keyboard problems, these can result from heavy use. There are two types of mouse: optical and opto-mechanical (Figure 4.69). Some faults are common to both, others are unique to each:

- Dirt/fluff can collect around the ball or x/y wheels on an opto-mechanical mouse or in the eye of an optical mouse.
- There may be a faulty wireless, USB, PS/2 or serial connection.
- You may have the incorrect driver installed. (Most mice use a common driver, so this is now only an issue for specialist mice.)
- There may be a mechanical fault with the mouse buttons or scroll wheel.

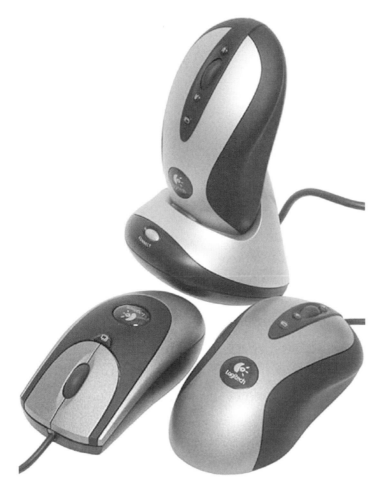

▲ FIGURE 4.69 *Mice*

Application crashes

Application installation and **application crashes** are covered on pages 260–2. Common causes of application crashes include:

- components of the application being removed, through deletion
- a new application, utility or driver being installed that conflicts with the application concerned
- new hardware having been added which causes a conflict
- a specific virus
- entries deleted from the registry
- essential files corrupted
- lack of memory or hard drive space.

With Windows XP, the program Files/Accessories/System Tools/System Information utility (Figure 4.70) can be used to find any faults as they occur.

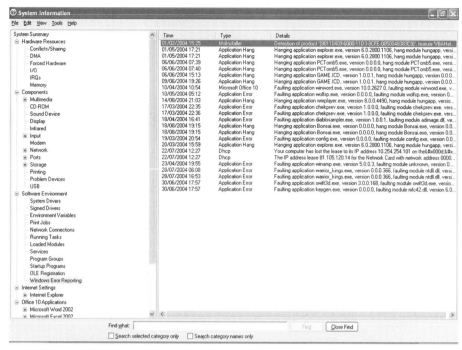

▲ FIGURE 4.70 *System information*

This can also be done with Dr Watson, which now exists as drwtsn32.

Operation system failure

As in applications, operating system failure can occur for many reasons. The likely faults are:

- a running application having a conflict with an operating system process
- a hardware component having a conflict with the operating system process
- a new application, utility or driver having been installed that conflicts with the operating system
- a specific virus, worm or trojan
- entries deleted from the registry
- essential files being corrupted or deleted
- lack of memory or hard drive space
- the operating system not being compatible with the hardware resources.

See pages 260–2 for a detailed exploration of these failures. As for an application, System Information and Dr Watson can be used to diagnose the problems as they occur.

Crashes after hardware or software upgrades

These are commonplace problems despite manufacturers' assurances that they seldom happen. To minimise problems, check the manufacturer's minimum specifications and ensure that your system has 50 per cent more processor and memory requirements. Also, you can access the manufacturer's website to see if they have 'patches' for the known problem or system incompatibility.

IRQ (interrupt request) conflicts

These occur when two hardware devices attempt to share the same processor resource. To check IRQ allocation, go to Control Panel/System Properties/Hardware/Device Manager (Figure 4.71).

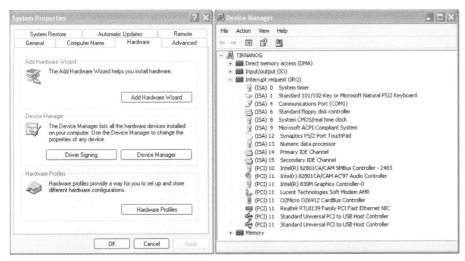

▲ FIGURE 4.71 *System properties and device manager*

Conflicts tend to be a feature of older hardware systems, where only one device could be allocated to an IRQ. Current technology allows multiple devices to share an IRQ.

Resolving an IRQ conflict may require:

- changing a jumper on the additional device
- changing the IRQ settings in Windows.

Printer consumable problems

You can have problems with:

- paper jams
- ink cartridges leaking
- ink running out
- running out of one of the inks on colour printers
- toner running out
- dot matrix ink ribbon jamming
- head jams, locks or drive-cable breaks.

The more advanced the printer, the easier it is to fault find. With smaller, lower cost printers, you have to take care during fault finding as they are often easy to damage in the fault-finding process. As each printer model is different, make sure you familiarise yourself with it. For paper jams never force paper through the system. It will rip and you will have a difficult job removing the pieces. Remember, a laser printer has a fusing system and the components may still be hot, so be careful not to burn yourself.

Ink can run out on combined cartridges for colour printers; it may be only one of the colour inks and you have plenty of the other colours. You can buy refill kits, but the cost and mess may make this prohibitive. Often, you have to replace the whole cartridge.

For toner, you can prolong the life of the cartridge by shaking this in the way advised by the manufacturer. This should prolong the life and quality of your output. Remember, you must only do this well clear of others and your own face, as toner is a known carcinogen.

Printer failure

Most printers (Figure 4.72) do not have serviceable parts, therefore mechanical **printer failure** has to be serviced by an experienced specialist. Most faults are caused by paper jams, where the paper has been mis-fed or you have elected to use card or acetate.

Acetate (clear plastic sheet) can be a serious problem, especially if you use the type that melts all over the internal components.

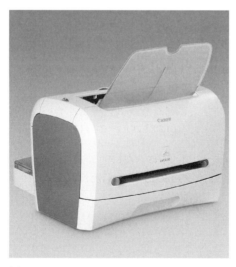
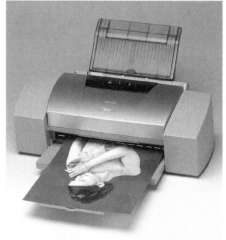

(a)   (b)

▲ FIGURE 4.72 *Printers: (a) Laser (b) Inkjet*

Other peripheral problems

Many other peripheral problems occur according to the device, and will depend on the technology and the interface. To summarise, these are the problems you may encounter:

- Interface issues, where there has been damage to the serial, parallel, wireless or USB ports
- Incorrect drivers installed
- There is damage or a physical fault on the device, which may be a scanner, digital camera, speakers, microphone, etc.

What are suitable tests?

Being able to recognise a suitable test for a specific problem is a skill that can only be developed through time, practice and experience. You have to be systematic in your approach to fault finding and carry out a variety of tests according to the problem at hand. Do not overlook the opportunity to carry out a test. It may be the one that gives you the answer.

The sort of tests to carry out may include those carried out with a variety of applications, checking that the application fault is general to the operating system or is only occurring on the one application that has been reported.

You need to ensure that the application will open and run successfully. If you are not an expert in the application, ask the user to try a 'common' task such as:

- entering data and saving work and reloading
- using features without application locking
- testing that components within the application load and work effectively
- ensuring you can close an application without any faults occurring
- running any self-test facilities within an application, if available.

You should also run anti-virus software and scan the system (see page 254), and check registry entries using your own skills or an appropriate tool (see pages 277–8).

Hardware problems and tests

Hardware tests tend to be more 'product' specific; that is, you have to develop knowledge of the product and the technology before you can decide if there is a fault. A common technique for testing hardware is to place it in a system where a duplicate is known to work.

As previously discussed, the BIOS produces **error reports on system booting**. This is an accurate report on where the problem may be, but not on the cause. The error report serves as a guide on where you will need to look to start the problem-solving process.

Operating system loads successfully is an excellent giveaway for 'all is working'. The only components that have a fault that may not be detected include:

- a serial mouse
- all printers or scanners
- any device on a wireless hub
- any USB device, as the technology is 'hot' swappable
- PCMCIA devices on a laptop, as the technology is also 'hot' swappable
- a monitor.

Disk defragmentation is required when the hard drive has been used for some time and the file space allocation has become disorganised. System performance can degrade and the size of the hard drive can be misreported. To resolve this, use the Windows disk defragmentation utility in Program Files/Accessories/System Tools/Disk Defragmenter.

It is considered good practice to defragment your hard drive at least once a month; you can configure the Windows scheduler to start the application for you.

The use of **system monitors** can help you to assess system performance and, hopefully, decide if there is a fault on the system based on too many applications, tasks or utilities for the processor.

While 'system information' is static, it gives an excellent snapshot of the state of the system as at the time of starting.

With Windows XP, you can check system performance with the Windows Task Manager (Figure 4.73), which opens when you press Ctrl-Alt-Del.

Disk scanning has moved on since the days of scandisk, which was first available with MS-DOS version 6.2. Windows XP uses a technology that has been around since MS-DOS version 1-CHKDSK (Figure 4.74).

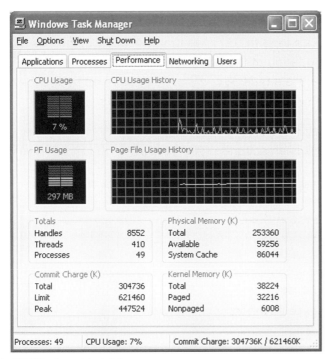

▲ FIGURE 4.73 *Windows Task Manager*

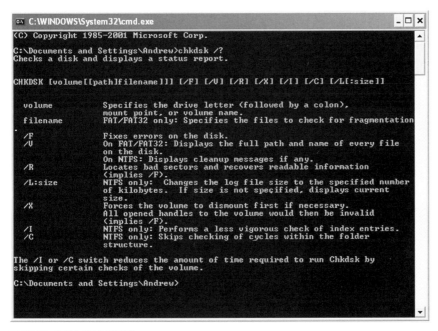

▲ FIGURE 4.74 *CHKDSK*

As you can see from Figure 4.75, if you use 'chkdsk/f', you can fix any possible errors on the hard drive. When started, the system will ask you if you wish to schedule this task for system startup.

Some **peripherals have self-tests**; this will depend on the complexity of the independent device. You may encounter the printer power on test, where the heads are aligned briefly as you switch the printer on (for a

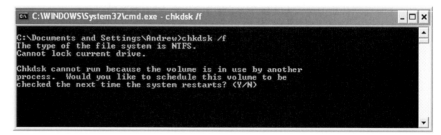

▲ FIGURE 4.75 *chkdsk*

laser a mysterious sound will issue from the printer, whilst the display declares 'please wait').

The **configuration of audio systems** on current Windows technology is very straightforward (Figure 4.76). There are many 'standard' sound systems that are included as part of your computer's motherboard. However, you may choose to install an advanced system for improved quality of the sound capture or if you are using the computer in a specialist music technology role.

▲ FIGURE 4.76 *Sound and audio device properties*

While you can configure what input/output settings you require, you can also ensure that the correct CODECs are used.

The later versions of Office and Windows now have text to speech software installed (Figure 4.77).

The use of **diagnostic software** allows you to benchmark a computer; you can do this once every six months and compare the results. If there

▲ FIGURE 4.77 *Speech properties*

is a decrease in performance, then you have the evidence required to carry out a wider range of tests on the computer.

Windows does not provide this feature, so you have to invest in the appropriate software. You can download for free FreshDiagnose from www.freshdevices.com (Figure 4.78).

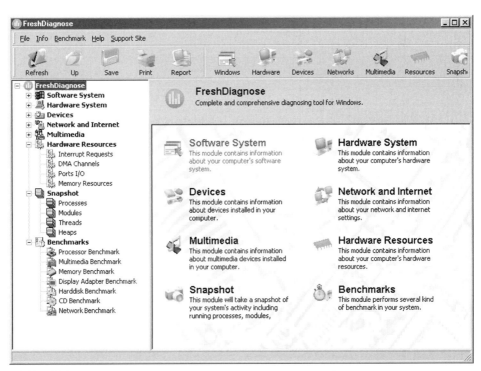

▲ FIGURE 4.78 *FreshDiagnose*

If you have installed FreshDiagnose, you can browse quickly to the benchmark resource. Here you can assess:

- processor performance
- multimedia, such as sound output, CODEC performance and microphone acceptance
- memory testing
- display adapter tests
- CD read speed
- network communication benchmark.

Figure 4.79 shows an example of a hard drive benchmark, completed on an older laptop. If this is a planned test, you may wish to save the benchmark results.

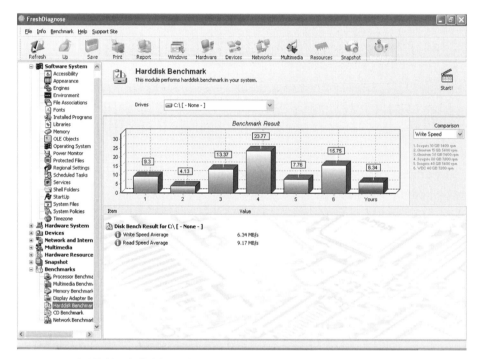

▲ FIGURE 4.79 *Hard disk benchmark*

Given the widespread access to the Internet, there is a need for firewall technology to protect computers from unwanted intruders. To test if a firewall on your computer is being attacked from outside is to commit 'ethical' hacking; to employ it on someone else's system is a criminal act.

Under the **Computer Misuse Act 1990**, it is a crime:

- to gain access to someone else's system or files, even if you take nothing, see nothing or change anything
- to prepare to access someone else's system.

It is not a criminal act to attempt to access a system that is your own. For example, burglary is a crime, that is entering someone else's property without consent to steal will lead to a criminal prosecution if caught. Whereas breaking into your own home is not a crime, even though it looks suspicious.

Practical task

An ideal application for checking a firewall is the 'Angry IP' scanner (Figure 4.80), which can be found on www.angryziber.com. It is very fast and has a very small file 'footprint'.

1 If you know the IP address of your computer, start the scan with the firewall switched off (remember 127.0.0.1 is the loopback). If you can scan your computer from another on a network, this test will be more valid as some firewalls do not treat 127.0.0.1 as a threat.

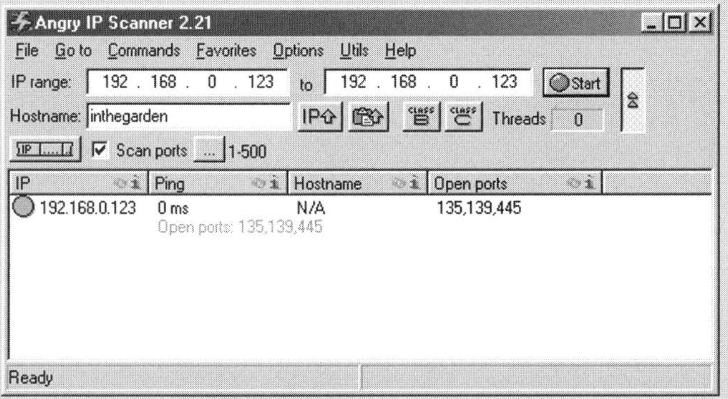

▲ FIGURE 4.80 *Angry IP scanner*

2 Before you start the scanner, set the ports it needs to check; there are a total of 65,535, so you will be waiting a while for this to complete for one connection. Instead try setting 1-500. In Figure 4.81, the computer had three ports open, therefore three vulnerable points.

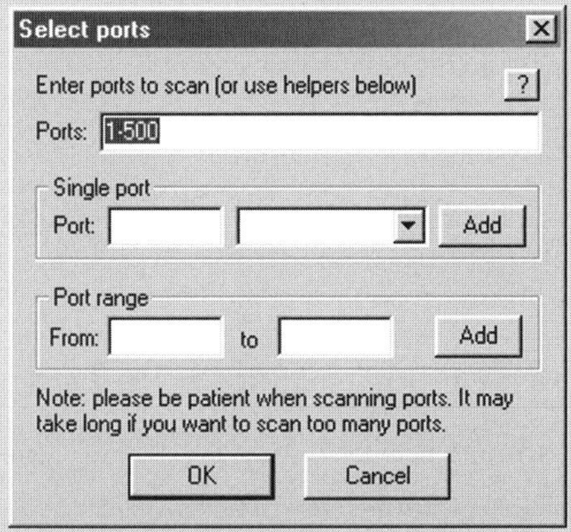

▲ FIGURE 4.81 *Port settings*

Restart the firewall on your computer and repeat the scan.

(Continued)

GLOSSARY

A **port** is a communication channel. In networking this could be:

- 21 File Transfer Protocol
- 25 Simple Mail Transport Protocol
- 80 Hyper Text Transfer Protocol
- 139 Windows networking.

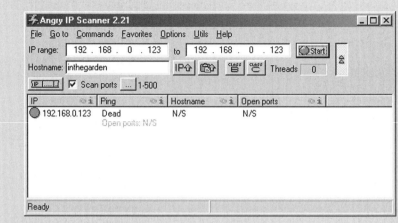

▲ FIGURE 4.82 *Angry IP scanner finds nothing*

In Figure 4.82, the IP scanner found nothing. This was scanning a computer with the Windows XP firewall, Service Pack 2. It may have thought that the computer was not there.

Identify and explain faults

The following are what you need to know when a fault occurs, in order to be an effective faultfinder in testing systems:

- The use of reference sources to identify fault(s) on booting BIOS
- The facility to disable a hardware device to isolate faults
- Error messages that can appear as the operating system loads and how to deal with them
- Locating the software or hardware manufacturer's website
- Use of software tools and the implications of working on the registry
- Reasons for operating factors affecting CPU usage, network traffic, motherboard monitoring and setting of alarm conditions
- Dialogue messages from peripherals through operating system or the application
- How the operating system recognises new hardware
- The need to sometimes manually add a driver
- Reasons why applications fail to produce audio output
- Cause of hardware faults, IRQ settings, ports, hard drives, memory, processor, interference and device temperatures

The use of **reference sources to identify fault(s) on booting BIOS** is of paramount important; the BIOS beep code guide on page 297 is only a guide. Most motherboards come with a manual, one you probably will not receive if you buy a pre-built computer. If you do not have access to the manual, look at the boot screen (Figure 4.83).

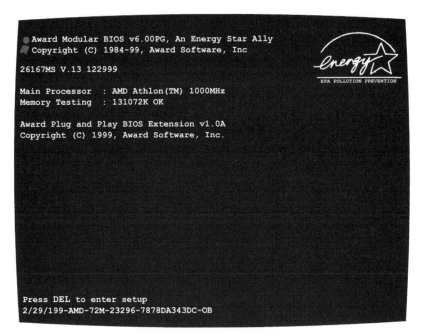

▲ FIGURE 4.83 *The boot screen*

In the bottom right, notice the BIOS code. This, together with the other details on the screen, identifies the manufacturer and serial number. You can then go to the manufacturer's website and, using the product code, 'discover' what you need to know about the product and its error codes (Figure 4.84).

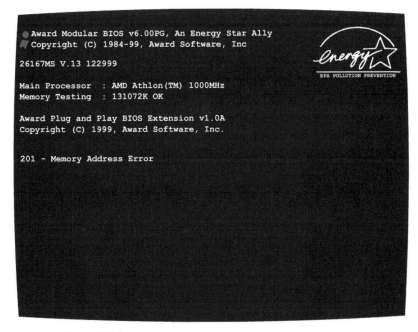

▲ FIGURE 4.84 *A BIOS error*

The facility to **disable a hardware device to isolate a fault** is available in all versions of Windows. If you go to Settings/Control Panel/System Properties/Hardware/Device Manager, you can right-click on any device and disable it (Figure 4.85). By disabling a device you can prove (or disprove) that it is the source of the problem.

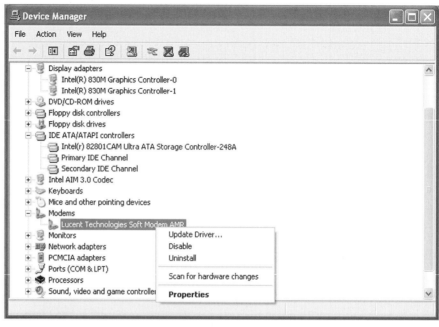

▲ FIGURE 4.85 *Disabling a device*

Sometimes **error messages appear as the operating system** loads, so you need to know how to deal with them. This is achieved in two stages:

● enter safe mode, if required
● check which programs run at startup.

To enter safe mode (Figure 4.86), restart your computer and press F8 prior to the operating system loading (you may need to press F8 more than once).

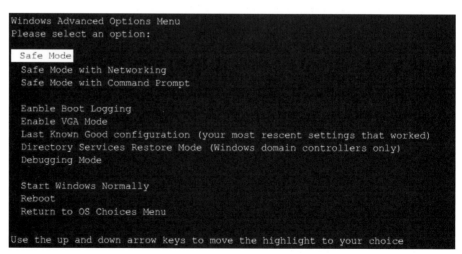

▲ FIGURE 4.86 *Safe mode selections*

You may choose safe mode (Figure 4.87), or safe mode with networking (unless networking is the issue). You will be asked which operating system to start if your hard drive has more than one operating system partition.

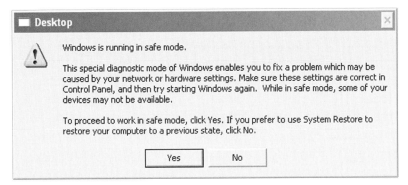

▲ FIGURE 4.87 *Operating system in safe mode*

Access the software or hardware manufacturer's website for information and help to identify and resolve problems. Most faults will be recognised by the manufacturer and they may offer:

● to provide a patch or a flash upgrade
● to replace the component if it is a known fault
● to provide a free upgrade
● to provide a workaround for the problem according to the system installed.

You need to take care with the **use of various software tools and the implications of working on the registry**, as you can do a great deal of damage; you should make a backup of the registry in case anything goes wrong.

In the case of **CPU usage**, the problems could include:

● overheating
● a faulty cooling fan
● the software or operating system being too high a specification
● your having too many windows open
● your having a trojan misusing your resources.

You could have problems with **network traffic**:

● suffering too much traffic
● under a denial of service attack
● the system being too slow due to a fault beyond your control
● the server being too busy.

Motherboards can cause a variety of faults due to the complex nature of the systems they contain. Apart from complete failure, other problems are:

- failure of the IDE or SCSI hard drive controller
- an issue with the PCI bridge
- a problem with the AGP system
- a fault with the onboard sound modem
- issues with the battery, clock or BIOS
- the reset button not working.

The monitoring and setting of alarm conditions can only be done if the system supports it and you have software that interfaces with that system. Some hardware manufacturers, such as Dell, will provide a 'system health' monitoring tool. This will report on the current status of the system and alert the user if a fault occurs. The most common 'alarm condition' is found on laptops with a battery. This can be found in Setting/Control Panel/Power Options (Figure 4.88), where you can elect to set the low battery and critical battery alarms.

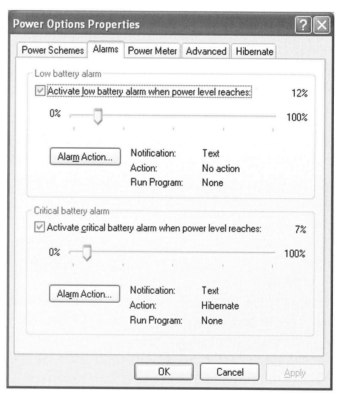

▲ FIGURE 4.88 *Low battery alarm settings*

Dialogue messages pass from the peripherals through the operating system or the application either because there is a fault or because there is some issue with the device. It is likely that you may see messages from:

- the printer when it is out of paper, jammed or has no ink

- the hard drive via the operating system, when there is a read/write violation
- a USB device, like a scanner, declaring that it is not ready.

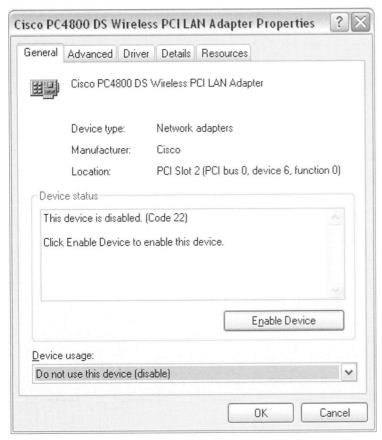

▲ FIGURE 4.89 *How a device reports a fault*

The **operating system recognises new hardware** in various ways:

- The hardware continuously sends an update to the operating system.
- The hardware uses plug and play technology, which means it will announce itself on boot up, and if this is the first time, Windows will install it.
- If the hardware is connected via USB, the USB hub will listen to the serial line, and if new devices are connected on it, the receiving power from the USB line will announce itself.
- If the device is part of the Windows device library, it will be automatically installed. Some devices contain the drivers, which will be passed to Windows, others require you to provide the driver disk supplied by the manufacturer.

There is sometimes a need to **manually add a driver**. This has to be done if the device is not plug and play or if the device driver provided is not compatible with the new operating system (or hardware platform). This can be achieved by using the Windows update driver facility as seen in Figure 4.91.

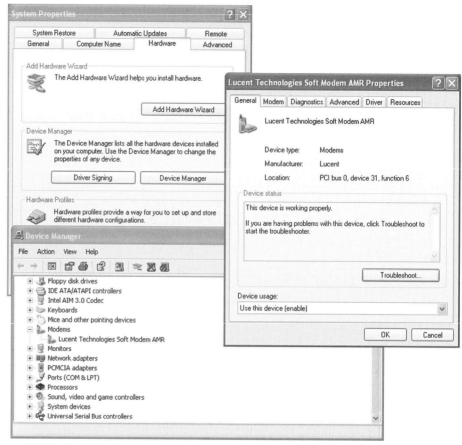

▲ FIGURE 4.90 *Update driver*

You can return Windows to a previous driver or completely uninstall the driver.

Some applications **fail to produce audio output** as they may have the incorrect CODEC loaded in the operating system. Some specialist formats for OGG, MP3, as well as many new video formats, require that you install the CODEC before you run the application. This may require a Windows restart and often some research on your part to ensure that your system has all the correct resources to run the application.

There are many **causes of hardware faults**, some too obscure to mention. It is likely that you may encounter faults with:

● **IRQ settings** being incorrectly set for the device in question
● **physical ports** not connected, not properly installed or having the incorrect IRQ or DMA (direct memory allocation) settings
● **hard drives** that fail, have the wrong master or slave setting, are not recognised by the BIOS, not formatted or partitioned correctly, or the driver is corrupted
● **memory** that fails and is not repairable (at least not by yourself – if it fails it needs to be replaced!)

Processor faults tend to be catastrophic and are usually caused by an inherent fault from poor design by the manufacturer (this is very rare). Often faults with a processor may be due to it overheating because the cooling fan is malfunctioning or not up to the task

Some device may cause **interference** to others inside the computer case. While uncommon, it has been known for sound or graphic cards to generate a suitable magnetic field that interferes with the operation of other cards. Modems are often susceptible to magnetic fields generated by other devices

Like the processor, **other devices may overheat**. If this is an issue, you may need to ensure that extractor fans are fitted to the computer case, or in some extreme cases you can acquire refrigeration systems.

Produce a log showing results of testing and analyse results

Keeping a log of all tests is essential. Through time, it allows you (or your supervisor) to develop a picture of the behaviour of the system. Testing may be routine, and you can build a picture of the system's normal behaviour over a long period of time. Or, the testing may be part of a fault-finding process, during which you ascertain the common faults or the actual root cause of the problems with the system.

A test log may contain:

- details of the hardware on the system in question
- its serial number
- any software installed
- user details
- date/time of test(s)
- the type of test
- the reason for testing
- results and explanation
- any action taken.

Check your understanding

1 List the main features of a plan for testing a computer system.

2 Say how would you prepare to carry out a test plan.

3 List some of the problems you can encounter with a hard disk.

4 What sort of tests are required for computer hardware?

5 What do you need to know about faults so that you can identify and explain them?

6 What information would a testing log contain?

Part 1

1 You are to install an application that is freely available to anyone. To do this you will:

- download and register for the software
- check the manual
- check the legal agreements
- virus check the media
- install the application in a unique location
- change settings to reflect user's needs
- configure the software
- check it is working.

2 You are also to install an application according to the guidance provided by your assessor. For this application provide a detailed account of the processes involved in pre-installation and installation. You may wish to use screen grabs where appropriate.

Part 2

Based on the installation you have completed on your computer system, produce a checklist which allows other technical experts to identify any problems that may be encountered and possible solutions.

Part 3

According to instructions given to you by your tutor, employer or supervisor, remove at least one **application** from your computer system.

To complete this stage you must:

- complete screen grabs
- create a restore point in case there are issues
- compile a log of an issue/fault encountered (or could be encountered) and what actions you undertook.

Part 4

Describe the reasons for uninstalling software, based on the work you have completed so far. Make sure that you have discussed your experiences from Part 3.

Part 5

1 Create a test plan that will test whether the system is working as required. This should include testing the application that has been installed and testing the system once an application has been uninstalled.

2 Carry out the tests detailed in the test plan and provide evidence that the tests have been run. For each test, explain why it was run and what the results signify.

3 Write a short report on what are the most common (or the most likely) faults that you have encountered while testing a system. Include any personal experiences.

Index

accelerated graphics port (AGP) 130

active listening 21

advanced technology attachment (ATA) 127, 224

adware 90

alarm conditions 316–17

angle of reflection 123

applet 245

application access log 40

application crashes 294, 301–2

architectural and engineering design 244

audio output failure 312, 318

audio system configuration 308

audit policy 38, 275

audit trails 37, 40, 47

automated procedures 47–63, 64–84
  complex 1, 2, 74–84
  routine 1, 2, 67–73

automatic backups 67

automatic scheduled task 48

autotext 72

AVG *see* viruses

backing up data 89, 252, 253, 255

backups 59–60, 67, 201, 224

basic input–output system 137, 173, 185, 192, 228,
  298, 300, 312–13, 318
  beep codes 297–8
  errors 294
  reports on system booting 306

batch files 7, 72, 74, 78–80
  commands 79–80

batteries 111

benchmarking 90, 113, 218, 219, 309, 310
  tasks 91

blue screen 88

body language 21

bookmarks 59

boot disks 93

booting up 138

bus 173, 219

cable faults 227–8

cabling and connector requirements 170, 181–2, 186,
  221, 253

call logging software 15, 23–4

carcinogens 98, 229, 304

Carriage of Dangerous Goods by Road Regulations
  1996: 233

Carriage of Dangerous Goods (etc.) Regulations
  1996: 232

cathode ray tube (CRT) 131, 132, 230, 233

CD/DVD technology 140–2, 185, 252
  misreads 294, 299

CD/DVD/ROM/RW, handling of 179
  installation 188–91

CD-ROMs as information sources 11

central processing unit (CPU) 312, 315
  handling 179, 180, 219

Centronic connector 182

chemical hazards 97, 100–1

chemical solvents 112

cleaning a computer system 102–10
  base unit 102, 107
  keyboard 102, 104–6
  monitor 102, 109
  mouse 102, 106–7
  printer 102, 107–8
  scanner 102, 103

closed questions 32, 35

coder decoder (CODEC) 243, 244, 308, 310, 318

common problems 263–73
  installation 252, 253, 260–2

coding data 18

common faults 87, 115–50, 293, 295–305,
  313–19
  BIOS 117, 137–8, 294
  cables 117, 143–4
  CD-ROM/DVD 117, 140–2, 294, 299
  CMOS 117, 137–8
  floppy drive 117, 124–5, 294
  hard drive 117, 126–8, 294, 298, 318
  keyboard 117, 144–6, 294, 300
  logical block addressing (LBA) 117, 127
  memory 117, 119–20, 294, 297–8, 318
  modem 117, 134–5
  monitor/video systems 117, 130–2
  motherboard 117, 133–4
  mouse 117, 121–4, 294, 300–1
  network interface card 117, 134
  operating system 117, 120, 294, 302

common faults (*continued*)
  parallel ports 117, 125–6
  peripherals/printers 117, 146–50, 294, 303–4, 305
  POST 117, 137–8
  power supply 117, 138–9, 294, 295–7
  processor 117–18, 319
  slot covers 117, 139–40
  sound card/audio system 117, 130
  universal serial bus (USB) 117, 142–3
communication methods 1
complementary metal oxide semiconductor (CMOS) 137
complex automated procedures 1, 2, 64–6, 73–84
components shopping list 174
compressed air canisters 112
compressed files 50
computer base unit 108
Computer Misuse Act 1990: 310–11
connectors 182–2
consumables 43, 89
  problems 294, 303–4
context sensitive 63
Control of Substances Hazardous to Health Regulations 2003: 98
copyright law 236, 237
Council of European Communities 233
customer/client, liaising with 151–2
customer satisfaction form 164–5
customer support 1–86
customer survey 164–5

data cable faults 143–4
data operators 4
data transfer 60
default 255, 263, 269, 283
default file locations 205
  bug fix 221, 222
demonstration 9–10
device driver 188, 201, 202
  disabling 313–14
  manual addition 317–18
diagnostic programs/software 89, 90, 93, 159
  see also fault
diagnostic routines 158
  see also systematic fault diagnosis
diagnostic tools 158

direct memory application (DMA) 318
directory deletion problems 284–8
Disk Cleanup 57, 68–9
Disk Defragmenter 68–9, 306
disk fragmentation 218–19, 224
disk operating system (DOS) 7, 226
disk scanning 306–7
display adapter/graphics card 130–2
disposal of hazardous resources 110–13, 113–14, 229–30
  batteries 110–11
  cathode ray tubes (CRT) 110–11
  chemical solvents 110, 112
  compressed air canisters 110, 112
  sharps 110, 112–13
  toner kits/cartridges 110, 112
disposal of ICT packaging 232–3
distribution group 52, 53
documentation about disposal 113–14
  about improvements 85–6
  automated routine 64
  see also logbooks; record keeping
dongles 241
Dr Watson debugger 40–1, 302
dust/dirt *see* cleaning
dynamic data 78
dynamic link library (DLL) 264, 278

earth 94
EC Landfill Directive 1999: 233
effective maintenance 87
  monitoring and reviewing 165–6
electric shock 96
electronic submission of forms 15, 16–19
electrostatic discharge (ESD) 93
  protective devices 94, 95
elimination method in fault-finding 294
email 50–5, 205
  registration via 238
End User License Agreement (EULA) 203, 206
end-user requirements 1, 3, 247, 252, 253, 257
  determining 3–15
  recording 15–25
Environment Agency 233
Environmental Protection Act 1990: 232
ergonomics 170, 171, 246, 247
error reporting 19–20

EU Directive on Waste Electrical and Electronic Equipment (WEEE) 233
European Waste Catalogue 233
existing provision of hardware/software 42–3
extreme conditions 181

fault identification/explanation 312–19
fault rectification 87, 102–9, 161
  see also parts by names
Federation Against Software Theft (FAST) 236
field 18
fire extinguishers 99–100
firewall 241
firmware 173
floppy disk
  drive 124–5, 139, 185
  errors 294, 299–300
Framework Directive on Waste (75/442/EEC) 233
freeware/shareware 238
frequently asked questions (FAQs) 3, 14, 26, 27

GNU public licence (GPL) 256
Google 12, 55, 56, 243
graphics adapter 250
guarantee 238, 253

handling precautions 170, 178–80
hard drive 126–7, 139, 185, 219, 224, 250
  failure 294, 298, 318
  handling 179
hardware and software resources 33–43
  potential improvements 44–6
hardware compatibility lists (HCLs) 27, 28
hardware improvement 87
  see also installing hardware
hardware tests 295–306
  suitable 305–11
hazards and risks 96–102, 113, 229–31
health and safety assessment 246
Health and Safety at Work Act 1974: 98, 246
Health and Safety Executive 229
health and safety guidelines 88, 96, 115
hints and tips available to user 3, 14
hit list 55, 56, 58
hot keys 70

hotlinks 58, 72
hyperlinks 67, 72–3
hypertext markup language (HTML) 55

icons 5
image manipulation 243
implosion 111, 48
improvements 2
  frequently used 47–63
  potential 1, 33–43, 44–6
  see also automated procedures; hardware and software resources
improving system performance 153–5
information gathering 1, 23–32, 46
  keystroke monitoring 46
  observation 46
  walkthrough 46
ink cartridges 107, 112, 303, 316
inkjet printer 107, 147, 316
inspection, periodic 90
installing a computer 183–98
  assembly 187
  CD/DVD installation 188–92
  components 183–6
  post-installation checks 198
  a pre-built system 186–8
  printer installation 192–7
installing applications 236–49
  health and safety assessment 246
  licensing 236–43
  registering software 238–40
  types 243–4
  user requirements confirmed 247
  wide range 243–5
installing hardware and ancillaries 170–234
  installation activities 183–217
  post-installation tests 198, 217–19
  pre-installation activities 170–83
  routine problems 221–9
installing software 250–62
  installation 253–9
  post-installation 259–62
  preparation and pre-installation 250–2
  testing 263, 268
integrated drive electronics (IDE) 127, 190, 191, 223, 298
interface compatibility 131, 173

interference 319
Internet 30, 55, 158, 250
    Explorer 203–4, 214, 271
Internet information sources 11–12
Internet/email access log 40
interrupt request (IRQ) conflicts 294, 303, 312, 318
interviews 34–5
Intranet 55

jumper 188

keyboards 104–6, 183, 186, 187, 188
    faults 144–6, 294, 300
keystroke monitoring 46, 47

laser printer 107, 147
laser products, hazards with 100–2
latency 130
learning styles 7–10
legal responsibilities 98–9, 246
licences 201, 210, 236–43, 274, 275
    conditions 242–3
    licence agreement 236–8, 253, 255
    see also EULA
line printer 147
local area network (LAN) 180
locating common faults 115–50, 154–6
logbooks 30, 319

macro recorder 75–6
macro wizards 74
macros 7, 61, 74–7
maintenance 87–166
    preventative 87, 88–96, 113, 165–6
    remedial 87, 88–113, 165–6
management software 158
managers 1, 4–5
manual handling/lifting hazard 97, 99–100, 229,
    230–1
manual logs 15
manuals 27, 253, 256, 312
manufacturer's advice 25
manufacturer's documentation/websites 25, 27,
    201, 252, 253, 312, 313, 315

manufacturer's instructions 115, 228
material safety data sheets (MSDS) 114
memory 185, 221, 224–5, 250, 262
    faults 119–20, 297–8, 312
menus 4, 62–3
methodology 292
Microsoft 8, 19, 25, 64, 65, 74, 88, 201, 261
    Installer (MSI) 266, 267
    Office 201–11
Microsoft disk operating system (MS-DOS) 278,
    306
modem/modulator demonstrator 134
monitor 186–7, 306
    cleaning 109
    display 130–2
motherboard 183, 185, 219, 241, 297, 312
    faults 133–4, 316
mouse 186, 187, 306
    cleaning 106–7
    faults 121–3
    problems 294, 301

navigation bar 62
negotiation 22
network access logs 40
network connection missing 221, 226–7
network traffic 312, 315
network/workstation log-in screens 74, 77–8
non-destructive testing 90
numerical and scientific modelling 243

observation 46, 47
office suite installation 210–11
    problems 212
online help 115–16, 253, 255
online information 25, 27
    sources 11
on-site/off-site training 8, 10
on-the-job training 9
open questions 35
operating system 250, 312
    faults 121
    new hardware recognition 317
operating system software 79, 93
    error messages 314
    safe mode selection 314–15

operating systems 220, 221, 243–4, 306
  cluster 199, 243
  dedicated 199
  disk 7, 199, 226
  multi-user 199, 243
  network 199
  real-time 199, 243
  server-based 243
  system failure 294
  workstation-based 243
optical mice 106, 123
opto-mechanical device/mouse 106–7, 121–2
overheating 319

packaging check 170, 172, 175–7, 185–6,
  252, 253
paper jam 147, 148, 303, 316
paper-based information sources 11
parallel data communication 181, 182, 192
parallel port 125–6, 193, 241
passwords 77, 257
payment to software manufacturer 236, 241–2
PCI slot/card 131, 173, 241
Pentium technology 121
performance monitor 214–15
peripherals 43, 219, 312
  problems 294
  self-checks 306–7
  see also printers
personal digital assistants (PDAs) 243
PING 226, 227
piracy 254
plug and play 142, 317
plug-in 202
pop-up menu 63
port 241, 311
  see also parallel; serial
portable appliance testing (PAT) 89
portable data format (PDF) 115, 262
post-installation testing 217–19
  disk performance 218
  registry integrity 218
  system performance 219
  viruses 218
power cables 186
power on self-test (POST) 138, 226, 228
power supply 138–9, 170, 172–3, 180, 185
  faults 294, 295–7

power surge 119
power users 4
  techniques 69
pre-installation activities/checks 170–82, 250–2
preventative maintenance 87, 88–96, 114
  products 93
  review 165
printed circuit boards, handling of 178
printers 107–8, 183, 306
  failure 294, 303–4, 305
  faults 146–50
procedure guides and notes 27
processor 185, 186, 201
  faults 117, 118–19, 319
Producer Responsibility Obligations (Packaging
  Waste) Regulations 1997: 233
PS/2 connector 182, 241, 301
publishing software 244
pull-down menu 62

quality assurance process 163
quality of service 164
questionnaires 16, 34–8, 47
questions, types of 32, 35

random access memory (RAM) 137, 201, 205
  faults 294, 297–8
range of applications 243–6
read only memory (ROM) 137
rebooting 263, 267–8
record (of data) 18
record keeping 64, 85–6, 113–14, 162, 198, 216–17,
  230, 319
recycle bin 285–6
recycling and metals recovery 232
registration of software 236, 238–40, 255
registry checking 159, 218, 261, 276–7, 301, 302,
  305, 312, 315
reinstallation 251, 263, 270
relevant information 22–3
remedial maintenance 87, 96–113
  cleaning and fault resolution 102–10
  disposal of hazardous resources 110–13
  hazards and risks 97–102
repair options 87, 160
repetitive strain injury (RSI) 170, 171
replacement components 93, 160

return into service 87, 162, 163–4

risk assessment 229

root 277

routine automated procedures 1, 2, 64–6, 67–73

routine problems 221–9

rules 53, 54

run-time errors 293

safe installation 170–1, 180

scanners 103, 306

scheduled utilities 68–9

screwdrivers 117–18

search engine 55

security log 37–9

serial data communication 181, 182

serial ports 241

servers 243, 245, 257

service 224, 256

sharps 112–13

shortcuts 4, 67, 69–72

site survey 170, 171–2

slot covers 139–40

small computer system interface (SCSI) 127, 298

software/driver installation from media/Internet 200–16

software registration card 220–1

software updates 89, 222
  see also installing software; software/driver installation

sound cables/speakers 186

sound card/audio system 130
  see also audio

source file replacement 263, 264

spam 50, 51, 53
  filter 53

Special Waste Regulations 1996: 233

sponsored links 55

static electricity 93–6

static menu 62

step-by-step instructions 9

storage, quality of 89

storage, quantity of 89, 201, 221, 223–4, 252, 297, 301, 302

sub-menus 62, 63

suitable hardware 170, 172–3, 180

support team 6

surfing the net 56–8

SVGA plug and socket 131

system monitors 306

system software loading/configuring 199–216, 258–9

systematic fault diagnosing 157, 294–5

task scheduler 66

technical information for customer/end-user 1, 2

technical information sources 11–13, 25–32

technical staff 3, 5–7

technical support for customer/end-user 1, 2

telephone help lines 25, 31

templates 74, 82–4

testing 85, 263, 268, 293–311, 312–19
  analysis of results 319
  hardware 295–305
  test plans 293–4
  test procedures 294–5
  suitable tests 305–11

thin film transistor (TFT) 131, 132

toner 107, 108, 112, 229, 230, 232, 233, 303

toolbars 74, 76–7

trade press 29

training requirements 3, 7–10

transmission control protocol/integer protocol (TCP/IP) 135, 136, 226, 227

transport/storing equipment 229–31

triboelectrification 93, 94

trojans 48, 89, 90, 201, 215, 251, 302

troubleshooting 115, 135, 217, 250, 260
  systematic approach 154–9

uniform resource location (URL) 11, 55, 58, 59

uninstalling 211, 216–17, 223
  data backup 274, 276–7
  deleting of directories 274, 284–8
  implications of registration 274, 275
  justifying decision 274–5
  removal of application 274, 278–84
  restoration of utility 274, 288–92
  why uninstall? 274

unique driver 149

universal serial bus (USB) 142–3, 173, 181, 183, 192, 193, 241, 301, 306, 317

upgrading performance 87, 153–9, 160

user acceptance 219

user, contact with 89, 151–2
  see also end-user

utilities 48–50, 68–9, 201, 243, 245
  restoring 288–92
utilities disks 93

verbal communication 15, 20–2, 25, 31–2
virtual memory 225
virtual network computing (VNC) 255, 256, 257, 258,
  259
viruses 89, 93, 216, 251, 254, 301, 302
  anti-virus software (e.g. AVG) 48–9, 218, 256,
  264, 305
  checks 201, 252, 253
Visual Basic 7, 74, 75, 77, 245
visual display unit (VDU) *see* monitor display
visualisation 5

walkthrough 46, 47
warranty 96, 126, 221
Waste Directive (91/156/EEC) 233

waste disposal 186, 230
  see also disposal of hazardous substances; ICT
  packaging
web browsers 12, 203–4
web installable applications 201, 202–4
websites 25
wide area network (WAN) 180
Windows 26, 37, 67, 88, 142–8, 192, 193, 196, 199,
  218, 222, 225, 226, 243, 261, 262, 268, 276–7,
  278–83, 301, 306–7, 317
  errors 153
  Task Manager 212–16, 224, 270–2
wizards 18, 48, 54, 64, 74, 282, 290
  printer wizard 192–7
Word 8, 72, 73, 77, 81, 83, 103
World Wide Web 55
worms 48, 89, 251, 302
written information 25, 27–30

zipped files 14, 50, 51

Let the web do the work!

Why not visit our website and see what it can do for you?

Free online support materials

You can download free support materials for many of our IT products. We even offer a special e-alert service to notify you when new content is posted.

Lists of useful weblinks

Our site includes lists of other websites, which can save you hours of research time.

Online ordering – 24 hours a day

It's quick and simple to order your resources online, and you can do it anytime – day or night!

Find your consultant

The website helps you find your nearest Heinemann consultant, who will be able to discuss your needs and help you find the most cost-effective way to buy.

It's time to save time – visit our website now!

www.heinemann.co.uk/vocational

And what's more, you can register now to receive our FREE information packed eNewsletter. Register today at www.heinemann.co.uk/vocnews.

 01865 888068  01865 314029  orders@heinemann.co.uk  www.heinemann.co.uk

Heinemann
Inspiring generations